HIDDEN
KITCHENS

HIDDEN KITCHENS

STORIES, RECIPES, AND **MORE** FROM **NPR**'s **THE KITCHEN SISTERS**
NIKKI SILVA & DAVIA NELSON

Image credits and permissions appear on page 269.

Library of Congress Cataloging-in-Publication Data

Nelson, Davia Lee.
    Hidden kitchens : stories, recipes, and more from NPR's The Kitchen Sisters / Nikki Silva and
Davia Nelson.
        p.   cm.
    Includes index.
    ISBN-13 978–1–59486–313–4 hardcover
    ISBN-10 1–59486–313–X hardcover
    1. Cookery, American.   2. Food habits—United States.   3. Kitchen Sisters.   I. Silva, Nikki.
II. Kitchen Sisters.   III. Title.
TX715.N4267   2005
641.5973—dc22   2005022658

Distributed to the trade by Holtzbrinck Publishers

2   4   6   8   10   9   7   5   3   1   hardcover

We inspire and enable people to improve their lives and the world around them
For more of our products visit **rodalestore.com** or call 800-848-4735

Dedicated to Studs Terkel

Contents

Foreword
BY ALICE WATERS

To a superficial observer it might appear that Americans mostly nourish themselves in just two ways: quickly, predictably, and cheaply, with mass-franchised, mass-produced processed food; or impractically, elaborately, and expensively, by following the examples of high-profile Food Channel celebrity chefs.

Of course, the reality is vastly different, and it's neither fast nor fancy. All over America (and not just on the coasts) there are extraordinary eating traditions hidden in plain view for the farsighted and sharp-eared to discover. One American meal out of every five may be prepared by strangers and eaten in an automobile by a lone driver, but there are still plenty of American meals that are small, quiet, out-of-the-way celebrations of friends and fellowship. There are still traditions that bring communities and families together instead of propelling them apart. And there are people out there pumping new life into old traditions and inventing new ones, people for whom food is an all-American reason to slow down and pursue some happiness.

This pursuit of happiness is one hundred percent democratic. Everyone eats. And everyone tells stories, too. The genius of The Kitchen Sisters has been to discover a nation of stories filled with humor, imagination, and passion. The stories the Sisters have gathered are exhilarating, accessible, and real, and they give me a lot of hope. They capture the authentic connections between people and food and the culture that's created around it. They remind us that we have a real food culture, and not just a fast-food culture. They remind us that we are a people who really *do* care about food and about each other. And most of all, they remind us of what I think of as the transformative power of food.

These wonderful stories are literally all over the map. They take us to people in their own small kitchen universes and demonstrate to us how cooking creates communities and communities can change the world. The Kitchen Sisters take us right into the thick of things, to places we otherwise might never go to, into worlds we think we could never relate to. I never thought I would have a connection to George Foreman, for example, but it turns out we're both worried about kids going to school hungry.

Just as we can't live without food, we can't live without stories. The curious and wonderful thing about the stories in this book is how much they resemble good things to eat: They can be surprising and they can be reassuringly familiar; they can be comforting and they can be outrageous. **To me, stories *are* food**, especially when they're in people's own voices, told in their own way. These are stories that can reconnect us to disappearing ways of eating and inspire us not only to uphold old traditions but also to make a big changes in the way we eat.

The Sisters are like excellent cooks themselves: They know how to forage for their raw materials, and they are masters at orchestration. They know how to extract the maximum flavor from their subjects, by layering and editing, and by building atmosphere from the deployment of a few subtle clues. They make us feel the multivarious texture of reality. The Sisters also know how to make themselves disappear into the background. Their documentaries are little repasts, and when they're over, you feel the way you do after a memorable meal: satisfied and full of spirit.

The decisions we make about food should nourish our children, strengthen all kinds of families, and build lasting communities. And so they will, too, if we choose to conserve local resources and value local resourcefulness and if we choose to keep revitalizing our own stories and telling them to each other.

All these stories are connected and they connect us.

The Kitchen Sisters are onto something big.

Alice Waters

FREE THE KITCHEN SISTERS

KUSP 89 FM   TUESDAYS 4-6PM   SANTA CRUZ

Introduction

Although we call ourselves The Kitchen Sisters, until now food has never really been our beat. We've been telling stories together for some twenty years on National Public Radio—*Lost & Found Sound, The Sonic Memorial Project, Waiting for Joe DiMaggio, WHER: The First All-Girl Radio Station in the Nation*. Stories that chronicle the hidden parts of history, the traditions and rituals that people carry with them from one country to another, across one generation to the next, the vibrant, changing, and fading sounds of America. Stories told by people in their own voices, layered with the music and sound of their time and place.

THE KITCHEN SISTERS

It was 1979. Foggy. We were both living in Santa Cruz but hadn't met. Each of us was wandering around the region gathering stories, on the same path but in different mediums. Nikki was creating museum exhibits about local history, and Davia was recording oral histories with the old-timers for KUSP, the tiny community radio station in town. People kept telling us about each other—seems we were drawn to the same storytellers and offbeat characters. One day we finally met. Next thing we knew we were caught up in each other's lives, doing a live weekly radio show together, driving throughout California interviewing farmers, railroad workers, Italian midwives, politicians, poets, the 1946 world champion cowboy, becoming best friends.

We took our name from two eccentric brothers, Kenneth and Raymond Kitchen, who were stonemasons in Santa Cruz in the 1940s. You can still see traces of their work all over town: fireplaces, chimneys, porches, not to mention the yogi temple and goat milk bar they built by the light of the moon, the mysterious Byzantine bungalow with brick turrets that looks like it fell off the back of a pack of Camels, and the abalone towers they built to intercept messages from enemy submarines they believed were lurking in Monterey Bay.

We were reading about The Kitchen Brothers in a book about Santa Cruz architecture, preparing for an interview with the author on our show. At the same time we were cooking dinner for twelve in the funky kitchen on the commune Nikki had just bought. We were so caught up in the thrall of these legends of local masonry that we didn't notice our dinner was a disaster. As the salmon lay in ruins, we started calling ourselves The Kitchen Sisters. The next day on the radio, when the author told the tale of The Kitchen Brothers, we told the story of The Kitchen Sisters. Somehow, the name stuck.

As it turns out, the name is us, but it's bigger than us. "The Kitchen." It conjures up conversation and comfort. It's the room in the house that counts the most, that smells the best, where families gather, where all good parties begin and end. The room where the best stories are told.

Sometimes we find the stories, sometimes the stories find us. A headline in the newspaper calls out "Pool Shark in Town," and we head to the pool hall to chronicle the world champion one-handed pool player. Route 66, the legendary Mother Road is closing, and we take to the highway to document its last traces. An invitation comes to a Tupperware party, and two weeks and two pounds of Tupperware later we're recording in the midst of the California delegation to the Tupperware annual convention. We hear a 1920s recording, and it leads us into the world of the *lectores*, the men who read aloud to the cigar rollers in the old Florida cigar factories. We are lured by stories of people possessed by a vision, a highway, a plastic bowl, a dream.

Like we said, food has never really been our beat, but it has managed to find its way into every interview we've ever done. **"What did you have for breakfast?"** It's the opening question we've asked everyone for two decades while we fiddle with the levels on the tape recorder and make sure people feel comfortable. It's an easy place to start. Everyone has an answer. But the answers often lead to surprising places. Food, or the lack of it, breeds stories, sparks memories. It's our common ground, the universal language.

THE CAB-YARD KITCHEN

A lot of Kitchen Sisters stories are born in taxicabs. *Hidden Kitchens* was conceived in the back of a Yellow. Davia lives in San Francisco and hates to drive. She started noticing that every time she got into a Yellow cab, the driver was from Brazil, and not just from Brazil, but from the same town in Brazil: Goiâna. Inevitably, these cab-ride conversations turned to music and food. That's when the story of Janete emerged, a woman from their same hometown who comes every day after dark to the abandoned industrial street outside the cab company and sets up a makeshift, rolling night kitchen—hot salgadinhos, bollinhos, pão de quejo—she cooks the food of home. Then by dawn Janete and her blue tent are packed up and gone.

Certain stories have Kitchen Sisters written all over them. This sounded like one of them. One night around midnight, we decided to go in search of this secret cab-yard kitchen. A driver had given us a sketchy map and told us to park in the cab lot and walk to Janete's outpost from there. "Just look like you know where you're going," he said, assuring us no one would notice we didn't work for the company. It seemed pretty obvious to us—neither of us is from Goiâna, and no other cabbies in sight were wearing headphones and packing ten pounds of recording equipment. We walked through the fleet of parked cabs, past the graveyard-shift mechanic working on a taxi up on the racks, past the checkout point, and out onto a street in the middle of nowhere.

Janete's cab-yard kitchen

There, under a streetlight and a small blue tarp, four drivers were laughing, huddled over big plates of food, eating and talking in Portuguese. Brazilian music spilled out of a parked cab. Janete, shy and smiling, presided—a hidden kitchen vision.

CLANDESTINE COOKING

If Janete was making rice and beans on this street at midnight, gathering her community like a campfire, who else was out there, cooking on some other corner? What other tiny kitchen economies, clandestine cooking, and secret kitchen rituals were waiting to be discovered?

We began noticing things—a woman surreptitiously selling tamales out of a baby carriage in downtown Santa Cruz, an after-hours restaurant tucked away in a car wash in L.A., Vietnamese manicurists gathered for a Christmas Eve feast of *pho* and fish and spring rolls in a neighborhood nail salon in San Francisco. Once we started looking, we found unexpected, improvised, tiny kitchen cultures in places and at times of day we never thought to look before. Our journey began.

Jay Allison and The Kitchen Sisters
in Memphis

We like to collaborate with each other and with just about everyone we know. We try to build community through storytelling. As we began to think about hidden kitchens, we called radio visionary Jay Allison, our longtime friend and collaborator, our kitchen brother. He and his radio team in Cape Cod began uncovering the hidden kitchen rituals of the Eastern Seaboard—the clambakes, the blueberry breakfasts, the *samos* and goat dinners of Somali refugees in Lewiston, Maine.

Hidden kitchens. They were everywhere. We told Ellen McDonnell, head of NPR's *Morning Edition,* about all these little kitchen discoveries and the stories emanating from them, and she was as intrigued as we were, and a new series began to emerge.

We started as we always do, asking everyone we've ever met if they know anything about what we're looking for. It's a tried-and-true Kitchen Sisters method. When we were searching for lost one-of-a-kind recordings during our NPR *Lost & Found Sound* collaboration, we asked the archivist at the Lincoln

Lost & Found Sound, a nationwide collaboration spearheaded by The Kitchen Sisters and Jay Allison, on NPR's *All Things Considered.*

Center Sound Collection if he knew of any hidden recordings squirreled away in his vault. He said, "Well there are those eight cardboard discs that Tennessee Williams recorded in a penny arcade in New Orleans in 1947 that no one has ever heard before." All we had to do was ask. The same held true for *Hidden Kitchens.*

OLD STOVES

If you're looking for a hidden kitchen, Peggy Knickerbocker, food writer and home cook, is a good place to start. Peggy grew up in San Francisco and has been combing the neighborhoods for years chronicling kitchen elders and pioneers. **"In North Beach they're called 'old stoves,'" Peggy tells us, "the people who have put in some serious time in the kitchen cooking for their community for decades on end.** They could be restaurant cooks or home cooks or men who learned to cook from their mothers, but they're people who love to cook, and not just for themselves. And the life on their block centers around them because of it."

Within hours, Peggy leads us to Lou the Glue, a neighborhood kitchen legend, an old stove if ever there was one. Lou "The Glue" Marcelli is the seventy-seven-year-old caretaker of the Dolphin Club, a swimming and rowing club that's been around since 1897, tucked away in a little cove near Ghirardelli Square.

"There are all kinds of people in this club, but it's mostly men," Peggy says. "A lot of old Italian, Spanish, and Portuguese men. Most are retired, some work—firemen, policemen, painters, chefs, waiters. They exercise a little, swim a little, and they have wine, cook, sit around, and talk about the old days. And they talk about sex, about what's going to happen to somebody if he has testicular cancer. And they cook and eat together, and I think it really keeps them going. One of the things about getting old is so many people don't have a place to cook anymore, and when they lose that, I think they lose a part of themselves. Most older people are relegated to smaller and smaller spaces, usually without a kitchen, and then they're given terrible food. No wonder they die."

When we spot Lou, he is far from his deathbed. Dressed in a Speedo, red bathing cap, and goggles, he's walking determinedly toward the icy bay. "The temperature of the water will get your attention. It's between fifty-one and fifty-two," he tells us as he takes the plunge. Lou swims in San Francisco Bay four days a week, no wet suit, rain or shine. "The number one thing about swimming in this water is not to think about it. **Just look it in the eye and go.** You don't have to swim to Alcatraz. Just go."

Lou's been the "commodore" of the Dolphin Club for thirty-five years. After his swim he shows us around the 130-year-old boathouse, a large, white

Lou the Glue

wooden lodge with cavernous dark-paneled rooms full of handcrafted wooden boats and a galley kitchen, which is Lou's domain. **"They call me 'Lou the Glue' 'cause I have a tendency to hang out in one spot.** Here's my headquarters. This is where I cook right here." He starts tinkering with some tomatoes.

About once or twice a week he cooks for the old-timers at the Dolphin Club. He hits the wholesale fish markets, where everyone knows him, and picks up bags of calamari or the special fish of the day. "I'm not a gourmet cook by any means. I just can put a little pasta together. My cooking is for survival. I have been a bachelor for seventy-six years. If I didn't learn how to cook, I would have starved to death."

Swimmers stop by to greet Lou as he rattles around the galley. "The family people, you know, they come and swim and row, and then they leave. It's the bachelors and people that live alone, they don't want to go home. They just want company, the camaraderie. When I cook, I always cook enough for a few more people, and there is always somebody around. They kind of smell it."

THE PASTRAMI HIGHWAY

Our search for stories always seems to expand to our in-laws, the people we sit next to at holiday dinners. "So what are you girls working on now?" asks Nikki's mother-in-law, Marian Watt, who worked as a county home advisor for the agricultural extension service in California in the 1950s. She tells us about the Radio Homemakers, who went on air each week across the nation helping housewives decipher the newest vegetable to hit the market—the avocado, for example—or giving tips on how to eat pizza, when the pie was first introduced in America.

Davia's brother-in-law, filmmaker Bryan Gordon, digs deep and recalls a hidden kitchen in his childhood driveway in Dover, Delaware. Mr. Bronson. "Mr. Bronson came to us on Thursdays," recounts Bryan. "He would load his old pickup with delicatessen, and he'd have a scale on the back of the truck and a big pickle barrel, and he'd drive through the various small towns of Delaware, Maryland, and Virginia, delivering deli to Jews all along the route. He had these huge, hairy arms, with big muscles from cutting so much kosher meat. Mr. Bronson would tell us stories about other Jewish families some ten miles up the road—who was sick and who was dying and who was making money. **He would spread pastrami and the gossip."**

Mr. Bronson, gluing his community together through food, carving meat and a living.

SIGNS BY THE SIDE OF THE ROAD

Along with pumping friends and relatives, we start rooting around for experts—archivists, librarians, writers, historians, pack rats—people who have been thinking

about what we're now thinking about for a lot longer than we have, people like Phyllis Richman, food critic for the *Washington Post* for about a quarter of a century and mother of our radio friend, Joe Richman. Phyllis opened our eyes to the side of the road.

"When you are traveling, there are ways of finding unexpected food, food that's outside of the mainstream," says Phyllis. "I always look through the Yellow Pages for restaurants that sound very local. Restaurants named after somebody or that talk about home cooking. I look in the classified ads for pancake breakfasts or fund-raisers, firehouse dinners, political picnics. **I keep my eyes open for hand-lettered signs on the road. You know, look around for signs on schools, church marquees, and you ask people.** I am always asking. And if you go to local events, sales or church bazaars, you'll find foods that people make only for special occasions where they expect them to be appreciated. All their friends and neighbors are going to be there. Like St. Mary's flannel-wrapped ham—it's a fascinating dish you only find in one county in the entire world, St. Mary's County, Maryland."

THE MIGHTY POWER OF THE TELEPHONE

We had queried the usual suspects, and then we put the question to the nation on air. We opened up the NPR phone line and invited listeners to tell us about their hidden kitchens. The project took on a life of its own. Over the years we've come to understand the mighty power of the telephone and a voice mail hotline as a way of bringing the public into the storytelling process. People feel comfortable on the phone. **It's a natural microphone—intimate, personal, immediate.** A good place to tell each other secrets and revelations, where to go and what to do. These phone messages have become a major part of our story-gathering process—a sort of street anthropology, involving citizen storytellers, and a way of discovering material we never could have imagined.

Like our other NPR series, *Hidden Kitchens* has become a big, sprawling nationwide collaboration. Over one thousand people have had a hand in shaping and suggesting these surprising stories of food and culture in America—radio producers, home cooks, street vendors, grandmothers, butchers, writers, anthropologists, artists, culinary historians, pit masters, submarine captains, veterinarians, fishermen . . . small kitchen stories, mysterious and revealing, first heard on NPR's *Morning Edition,* now unfolding further in these pages.

Dolphin Club members call 77-year-old Lou Marcelli The Commodore. He's been swimming in the bay at Aquatic Park since 1973.

"Hey, Lou, you goin' around the horn?!"

STUCK IN THE MUD

It turns out that Lou Marcelli's galley at the Dolphin Club isn't the only hidden kitchen in his life. "I grew up in a tiny fishing village north of San Francisco and started to commercially fish when I was twelve years old. When you go out commercial fishing, the first thing you put in your boat is the pasta. In Alaska there are these huge twenty-five-foot tides, and when the tide's out, your boat is stuck high and dry. We'd be six to eight small boats just tied together out there. And there is nothing else to do but cook a nice plate of pasta. You can't put a huge pot for twenty people on one little stove, so everybody cooked in their own individual pasta pot on their little stoves. There was always one guy that could make a nice sauce. He'd have all the ingredients, and everyone else would go out and dig for clams for a nice clam sauce. When everybody's pasta was ready, we'd go to the sauce guy's boat and put the sauce on it, and then we'd sit around and eat together. You're all stuck in the mud, and it's nice and calm, and everybody's having a good time.

"All of a sudden, the tide starts coming in, and your boat's rocking, and it's every man for himself. The party is over. You gotta quickly put the pots away, put the fire out, tie everything down, and go out and bounce around, fishing. But in the meantime you got your belly full of nice pasta. Leave it to the old Sicilian fishermen. The pasta pot'll be around forever. That's just the way it is. A way of life."

Lou the Glue's Pasta Calamari

After a short swim to a long pier, San Francisco's Lou the Glue jumps out of the bay and into the sauna to warm up. On Wednesdays, when the calamari looks good on Fisherman's Wharf, Lou cooks pasta calamari for his fellow swimmers in the galley kitchen tucked back with the rowboats in the Dolphin Club:

"Okay, first you get your calamari and then you have to clean it, which is a very simple thing. Calamari is nice and white when it's fresh. After a couple of days it starts getting a little red and pinkish. That's how you know it's not fresh. If I want to keep it a couple days or a week or so, I freeze it—but I freeze it in milk. That's a new trick I learned. Soaking the calamari in milk takes all that kind of fishy, slimy stuff out. And when it thaws out, it's perfect. I take 1½ pounds of squid and chop it into ½" rings. If the tentacles are large, I cut them in half.

"Then I get ½ cup chopped parsley, 2 cloves chopped garlic, 2 tablespoons or so olive oil, a shallot or an onion or whatever, and a cup of good white wine. Lately, I've been putting in vodka . . . try that.

"You sauté your garlic, your parsley, and your onion or shallot in this hot olive oil and add a can of tomato sauce. Then you pour in the vodka—good stuff—and you get this huge flame that comes up, and it looks very dramatic. Keep the sauce on high heat for 5 minutes, then lower the heat and let it simmer.

"In the meantime, you got your water boiling. You're cooking your pasta, and you've got your sauce all ready, and you add your calamari to the sauce, which takes 3 to 5 minutes to cook. When the pasta is done, pour the sauce over the pasta, and you've got a gourmet meal in 20 minutes. Don't overcook it—that's the secret of calamari. But just like pasta, you can undercook it, too. Undercooked calamari tastes like a rubber band. Just pick one up and taste it as you cook, and you'll be fine. It doesn't take a rocket scientist to do what I do. But when it comes to making pasta, I am the one."

WRAPPED IN A FLANNEL SHIRT

"Sometimes you find local specialties that people don't make anyplace else," Washington, D.C., food writer Phyllis Richman tells us. "In southern Maryland there is St. Mary's County stuffed ham. It's ham that is stuffed with kale and garlic and hot pepper and a myriad of things and wrapped in a flannel shirt and boiled and sliced and served cold. You find it at church suppers, and there are a couple of small restaurants that serve it, but it's hard to find. You have to keep your eyes open for it."

Some say this recipe dates back to slave days when cooks wrapped the ham in quilts and flannel shirts to keep the stuffing in while boiling. This recipe is from Henry Bonner's book, *350 Years of Cooking in St. Mary's County, Maryland.*

Although the shirt might have added a bit of extra flavor, the following recipe uses cheesecloth. If you can't find corned ham at your local supermarket, ask your butcher to special order it.

St. Mary's County Stuffed Ham

2 large cabbages, finely chopped

4 pounds fresh kale, finely chopped (see note)

3 large onions or 6 bunches green onions (either spring or scallions), finely chopped

1 bunch celery, finely chopped

2 pounds other hardy greens such as turnip tops, spinach, or field cress, finely chopped (see note)

2 tablespoons celery seed

3 tablespoons mustard seed

3 tablespoons ground red pepper

1 tablespoon black pepper

1 tablespoon salt

1 corned ham (14 to 20 pounds)

Put the cabbage, kale, onions, celery, and other hardy greens into a large bowl and mix in the spices.

Trim the ham, leaving a thin layer of fat. With a sharp boning knife, cut 1 to 2 deep slits perpendicular to the ham bone, making staggered rows of slits 2" apart. Stuff the greens into the slits, packing each one firmly. When there is no room left in the ham, pack the rest of the greens mixture on top. Wrap the whole ham, with extra stuffing, in several layers of cheesecloth (or muslin sheeting or a pillowcase or even a clean T-shirt) and then truss it with several lengths of butcher's string.

Put the ham in a big stockpot, cover with water, and bring to a boil. Lower the heat and simmer for 20 minutes per pound. Take the pot off the heat and let cool, about 2 hours. Remove the ham and let it drain thoroughly.

Carefully unwrap the ham and place it on a platter, making sure to remove all the stuffing and put it back on top of the ham. Cover the platter with foil or a damp cloth and refrigerate. When ready to serve, bring the ham to room temperature.

MAKES ABOUT 14 SERVINGS

NOTE: Some cooks like to wilt the greens before chopping them.

Gỏi Cuốn—Fresh Vietnamese Pork and Shrimp Rolls

We eat the consequences of war. After the United States left Vietnam and many refugees made their way to the States, Vietnamese food made its way to American tables. These pork and shrimp rolls are part of that journey.

One of our favorite Kitchen Sisters stories is "French Manicure: Tales from Vietnamese Nail Shops in America." We spent months chronicling life in the salons. One Christmas Eve we were in a neighborhood shop and noticed that as the last customer left, manicurists from throughout San Francisco were arriving with trays of food and homemade dishes. Some thirty-six manicurists from six salons and their families gathered. The nail stations transformed into family tables. The small kitchen in the back bulged with food. The salon is the largest communal space they all share, the place all can come together.

Diane Dinh, manager of Cole Valley Nails, says you can make these pork and shrimp rolls by yourself, but they taste better and it's more fun when you make them with family and friends. Diane recommends that you buy these ingredients at an Asian market.

PORK AND SHRIMP ROLLS

 1 pork butt (2 to 3 pounds)

30 large shrimp (size 31 or 35)

 1 large package vermicelli rice stick noodles

30 large rice paper rounds (10" or 12" diameter, Diane's favorite is K Brand)

 2 heads iceberg lettuce

1½ pounds fresh mung bean sprouts

 1 bunch mint

 1 bunch cilantro

To make the pork and shrimp rolls, preheat the broiler. Cut the pork butt into 2 or 3 equal pieces and broil each piece approximately ½ hour, turning occasionally, until each piece is cooked through and is no longer pink inside. Remove the meat from the broiler and let it rest for about 15 minutes. When the meat is cool, cut into very thin slices. Set aside.

Steam the shrimp in a big pot for about 5 minutes, until they turn red. Take off the shells, remove the veins, and cut them in half. Set aside.

Boil the noodles until soft, approximately 10 minutes. Put them in a colander and rinse in cold water. Drain and dry. Set aside.

Lightly moisten the rice paper with warm water until soft, about 1 to 2 minutes. Handle them gently as the rice papers

HOISIN DIPPING SAUCE

2   jars hoisin sauce (Diane's favorite brand is Koon Chun)

½ cup water

3   soupspoons sugar

Chopped roasted peanuts (see note)

are brittle. Place them on a linen towel to absorb excess water. Place a wrapper on a plate or cutting board and layer with a leaf of lettuce, a sprinkling of bean sprouts, a thin layer of noodles, 3 or 4 mint leaves, 3 or 4 cilantro leaves. Do not overload. Fold in the 2 opposite sides of the circle about an inch and add 2 or 3 slices of pork in the middle on top of the greens and noodles. Roll the rice paper tightly but gently so as not to break it. Before the last roll, add 2 or 3 pieces of shrimp, then finish rolling. (Diane says you add the shrimp close to the last roll to show it off.) Cut the rolls in half and serve with hoisin dipping sauce.

To make the sauce, pour the hoisin sauce into a bowl. Heat the water in a saucepan and add the sugar to dissolve. Add the warm sugar water to the hoisin and stir until blended.

Divide the sauce among small dipping bowls and sprinkle each with 1 to 2 tablespoons peanuts. Serve the sauce cold.

The rolls can be made up to 4 hours ahead. Cover each roll with a damp, clean kitchen towel, wrap tightly in plastic wrap, and refrigerate.

MAKES 30 APPETIZERS

NOTE: If you don't have chopped peanuts, stir 2 soupspoons peanut butter into the main bowl of hoisin sauce.

Kitchen Sisters
Hidden Kitchens
Hidden Kitchens
23
Hidden Kitchens
Kitchen Sisters #13
Hidden Ki
30
The Kitchen Sisters
Kitchen 11
Phone li
Hidden Kit
32
33
Kitchen Sisters
Set 2
HK Calls cd 2
Hidden Kitchens
Phone line
npr
Copyright 2004
National Public Rad
Hidden

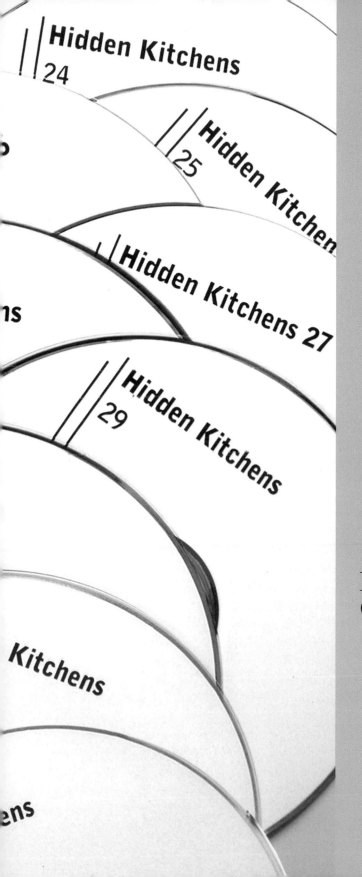

Hidden Kitchens
24

Hidden Kitchen
25

Hidden Kitchens 27

Hidden Kitchens
29

Kitchens

Kitchens

STORY #1

Hidden Kitchens
Calling

Jay Allison, curator of the
Hidden Kitchens hotline

Thanks for calling the Hidden Kitchens project. I'm Jay Allison. The Kitchen Sisters and I are gathering stories for a new radio series about street-corner cooking, kitchen traditions, and visionaries—how communities come together through food. Tell us, who glues your community together through food and where do they cook? Who are the local pioneers and kitchen visionaries? What food tradition is disappearing from your life, from your neighborhood, from the planet? What should be captured and documented before it disappears or changes beyond recognition? You tell us."

On Fourth of July weekend, 2004, Jay Allison, curator of our quest for hidden kitchens, went on the air inviting listeners to collaborate with us on our nationwide search. The NPR hotline flooded with calls, an astonishing array of voices telling stories from nearly every region of the country. We listened to tales of underground kitchens at nuclear test sites in Nevada, a shipyard in Michigan where the night shift roasts chicken in the welding-rod ovens, about clambakes, church suppers, test kitchens, kitchens on movie sets . . . the response was overwhelming.

Even more amazing to us than the stories was the sense of urgency and the intensity of the messages. People were demanding that we come chronicle their kitchens immediately because their tradition was just too good to miss, or the peaches would only be ripe for another week, or the senior center's hot lunch program was being closed for lack of funds, or the last keeper of the clams was about to die. These weren't just invitations to interview, these were demands for a house call.

"Hi, this is Mary Logan calling. **You need to go to Prospect, Tennessee,** *which is four miles north of the Alabama border. It's where my grandpa grew up. It's near Pulaski, Tennessee, which is on the map. There's a lady who has lived there her whole life and who's known as the best cook around, and she has won a lot of prizes at state fair and local events. She has a great recipe for souse meat.*

"You take the head of the hog. You cut it off and cut it into four pieces. Put it in a pot of cold water and soak it for three hours.

"Then you boil it for three more hours, strain it, and pour the liquid into a nine-by-thirteen-inch pan. When it gels up, you cut it into slices and you eat. Anyway, you need to go talk to this lady now."

We put up a big map in our dinky San Francisco office, sticking pins in the places with stories we wanted to track down: the Puckerbrush Potluck in Iowa, an immigrant's pickle barrel in Manhattan, the road crew lunch in Traverse City, Michigan.

"Hi, this is Linda Fedewa. I'm calling from East Lansing, Michigan. Our son works up in Traverse City on a road-building crew. These fellows are grimy, hardworking physical laborers, and when they take their asphalt trucks out, they use some of the asphalt as an oven. They bring in food in the morning raw, and then they lay several folds of asphalt over the food so it works as an oven. And at lunchtime, they go back to that spot on the road, dig up their hot lunch, and they've got the community food ready."

The calls began arranging themselves into themes—endangered kitchens, immigrant kitchens, workplace kitchens, seasonal kitchens, war and food, kitchen music, political kitchens.

Message #65 was received Wednesday at 4:15 PM
"Hello, my name is Keith McHenry. My story is about one of America's largest hidden kitchens, serving thousands of people every week on street corners in cities all around America and the world. It's called 'Food Not Bombs.' We cook meals in somebody's apartment or at a church, and we hand them out to the homeless and hungry in approximately three hundred U.S. cities and in about five hundred cities worldwide. Yet, we've been arrested over a thousand times in many parts of the United States for serving free food . . ."

Food Not Bombs, August 15, 1988

People were passionate about the traditions of their home states, determined to spread the word about their community's kitchens, insistent about the accomplishments of their local kitchen pioneers and visionaries.

Message #54 was received Friday at 9:34 AM
"My name is Carie Rives McIntyre, and I'm from Louisiana. You could do your entire series in the state of Louisiana and never run out of kitchen stories. But my story is actually about my father, who lives in the small town of Mansfield and is essentially the town cook. **He has his 'big butt bundt,'** *which is a combination of pound cake and pecan pie, and which actually sold at a charity auction for four hundred dollars. He has worked for the sheriff's department for over twenty years, and I think his story would be something worth diving into."*

Or Message #26.

"My name is Susan MacIntosh. I'm calling about a Friday night fish fry in my local community in Lake Waccamaw, North Carolina. Every Friday night, Frank Gault, a local cook, gets his big fryer and fries up fish for the community on the most gorgeous pier in the state, owned by John McNeill. These two neighbors put this thing on every week. Everybody in the county is invited, and people bring a side dish. You go out on the pier on the lake—it's just loaded with flowers. It is just a sight to behold. They have a treasure chest, and people are asked to make a donation every week, and all the money they've collected goes to the local library and museum. Frank's fish. It's the glue food that holds our community together."

Although we didn't ask for recipes, people just couldn't help themselves. They told us about mysterious and evocative dishes like Herman cake, ladylocks, burgoo, finnan haddie. Somewhere locked into these recipes and ritual meals was something essential to maintaining family life—a sense of belonging.

We asked people *not* to tell us about their grandmothers. (We knew if we opened up the grandmother option, we'd be in over our heads, and we didn't have the staff for it.) But people insisted.

Message #77 was received Friday at 9:22 AM
"My name is Cornelia Lambert. I'm calling about my grandmother's kitchen. She is an eighty-four-year-old woman living in Mt. Airy, North Carolina, and she builds community through food. About two years ago she started inviting people to dinner and charging them ten dollars a plate, and all of the money she would give to Habitat for Humanity. People turned their pockets inside out for some of Ruby's food."

We heard about kitchens reviving traditions, about bringing back old recipes for saguaro cactus on a reservation in Arizona, about men cooking in the dark over fire pits in the far north and the Deep South. People spoke about the private shared cooking rituals that happen when babies are born and when people die.

Message #222 was received today at 2:30 PM
"This is Emma Clark. I grew up in Gainesville, Florida. When my father died, I was eighteen and **my family got a pounding**. *A pounding happens when someone dies or a new minister moves into town or someone gets married or has a baby. And people from the community come by and give a pound of sugar, a pound of flour, a pound of butter, whatever they have. The pounding gave us a sense of being at home."*

It's hard to describe why or how certain messages filtered to the top. It was definitely not a scientific process. We listened, logged, numbered, transcribed, categorized, and described them to each other—and some messages just stayed with us. They were the ones we retold over the dinner table to friends and family. Sometimes it was because they provided a window into hidden, taboo worlds, like the one described by Moira who called us but didn't leave her last name: "I wanted to share with you how my community has come together through food. I'm a compulsive overeater and a member of Overeaters Anonymous."

Other calls became emblematic of dozens that flowed in about keeping communities alive and healthy through local food traditions and epic cooking extravaganzas—*sopas* for two thousand at the Portuguese Holy Ghost Festa in Hanford, California; the annual 4-H cooking contest at the Southwest Washington County Fair; the ramp suppers in Green Mountain, North Carolina.

Message #37 was received Tuesday at 4:24 PM

"This is Eloise Kaeck, calling about an old, old tradition. It's called a ramp supper, and it's a fund-raiser for the volunteer fire department. People have been digging ramps around here for a hundred years or more. Ramps are wild leeks that grow in the woods. The whole community gets together in mid-April and goes digging up on the heights of the mountains. The ramps are fried with eggs and potatoes. Everybody comes, hundreds of people."

Selling ramps by the side of the road

Many of the messages were just plain funny and eccentric.

Message #342 was received Tuesday at 11:55 PM

"Hi. My name is Tony Paul. I was a member of the U.S.S. Dixon's Dive Locker, a submarine tender. We were about fifteen Navy deep-sea divers and spent most every day

underwater doing a ship's husbandry on nuclear-powered fast-attack submarines. We would bring up a lot of very tasty seafood, lobsters, scallops so big they were the size of a coffee cup saucer. It was something that we all shared. A bunch of gnarly, shark-riding, barracuda-killing, seaweed-eating, **green scaly, hairy-chested Navy divers** *picking scallop scraps out of a coffee can on a coffee burner with our fingers. I don't think you can get more community than that while we were serving our country."*

Food triggers memory. Our callers spoke about food as personal inheritance, a connection to vanished generations, as the secret defining ingredient of a particular fam-

ily. Cynthia Ebbert told us about her grandfather, who had been a jeep driver during World War II. She said he used to heat up cans of beans right on the engine of his jeep, a road cooking tradition he carried back home to his family and maintained throughout his life.

Many of the calls we've received are laments, not simply for what we have left behind but for what we will leave behind if we're not careful. People seem nostalgic even for the present.

Message #293 was received Monday at 4:25 PM

"My name is Rachel Hull. I moved from a small town in Louisiana to Eagle Rock, a suburb of Los Angeles, primarily Hispanic, a lot of families, small homeowners. In the late afternoon I'd be in my front yard, and I would hear this sad, haunting music. It took me forever to figure out that it was an old man walking around with a pushcart selling roasted corn. You know, you're used to the ice cream man with his carousel jingle. This sweet, sweet old man was walking around selling boiled corn and playing this sad song. I could sing it in my sleep—it just became part of my psyche. That was one of my favorite things about living in Eagle Rock."

Some of the stories we received were not of kitchens today but of strange and hidden kitchens gone by.

"Hi. My name is Sandra Sherman, and I'd like to talk to you at some length about turtle feasts in the eighteenth century and how they were used as a way for men who were otherwise very civilized to come together to celebrate blood sports in a Beowulfian manner . . ."

One short, simple call stood out in particular, from a man who told us a lost kitchen story about something he was hoping to find again. John Miller had been a soldier in Vietnam when he received a pineapple upside-down cake in the mail, a cake that was intended for another soldier. If he had forwarded it on, it would have spoiled, so he kept it, and he and his friends ate it, and it was delicious. Then he wrote a letter to the parents of the soldier it was intended for.

"Anyhow," Miller told us, "I wrote and thanked them and told them I'd never gotten anything like that before in the mail. About two weeks later they sent me a tin of homemade chocolate chip cookies, and they were delicious. I kept their address for a long time, and then I lost it. They were from Connecticut. If I knew how to get in touch with them, I would."

As the *Hidden Kitchens* series aired on NPR, dozens more calls swamped our hotline. Some 2,879 minutes of messages so far—a kind of accidental archive of how people live, adapt, and cook in twenty-first-century America. These messages have led us around the country to secret, underground, off-the-grid, almost-forgotten kitchens and traditions and introduced us to some of the visionaries and cooks who tend and feed our communities. The stories are powerful, poignant, wild, and funny—full of hope and imagination—a map of possibilities for coming together through food and story.

PUCKERBRUSH POTLUCK

Roxann Ryan, an assistant attorney general in Iowa, called to tell us about the Puckerbrush Potluck held at the Iowa State Fair each year in honor of Bess Osenbaugh, an Iowa solicitor general who died of cancer in 1999. The event is named for the rural area in southern Iowa where Bess grew up. Throughout her life, Bess Osenbaugh rallied her world through potlucks. She'd regularly bring together lawyers in the attorney general's office over chili-cheese casserole, macaroni salad, and other potluck perennials to talk about their cases and get to know each other personally.

When she moved to Washington, D.C., to work for the Clinton Administration, she continued her potluck politics in the U.S. Department of Justice. Janet Reno said she thought it was one of the best ways for people to get together and talk informally.

"The potlucks helped create bonds and closer working relationships; everyone loved them," says Roxann Ryan. "So when Bess died, two women attorney groups in Iowa decided that a statewide potluck was the way to perpetuate her legacy. People from all backgrounds and walks of life are invited to bring food to the potluck competition at the fair and share stories about how the dish has created community in their lives and what it means to them. "We really want to encourage this kind of community conversation through the Puckerbrush Potluck."

Heck Bars

Puckerbrush Potluck Entry #2138 was a recipe for Heck Bars, created by staff attorneys for the U.S. District Court, Renae Angeroth and Patty Trom-Bird, as part of their line of "Procedural Bar Treats." The bars are named after *Heck v. Humphrey*, a complicated case known more commonly as The Heck Bar. This recipe was submitted by Kay Bartolo.

8 ounces unsalted butter

4¾ ounces unsweetened chocolate

4 extra-large eggs

2⅛ cups granulated sugar

½ teaspoon vanilla extract

½ teaspoon salt

1⅛ cups all-purpose flour

1½ cups walnuts (optional)

8 ounces semisweet chocolate chips

Preheat the oven to 300°F. Line a 12" × 8½" × 1" baking pan with parchment paper.

Gently melt the butter and unsweetened chocolate in a double boiler. When the chocolate is completely melted, set aside.

In a large mixing bowl, use a wooden spoon to combine the eggs, sugar, vanilla, and salt, just until blended. Fold the melted chocolate–butter mixture into the egg mixture.

In a medium mixing bowl, mix together the flour, walnuts (if using), and chocolate chips. Fold into the chocolate-egg mixture. Do not overmix. Fold only enough to incorporate the dry ingredients, or the bars will be too tough and too cakelike. The consistency should be like a thick chocolate sauce.

Pour the batter into the pan (the batter does not rise much, so it is okay if the batter rims the pan).

Place the pan in the center of the oven and bake for 40 to 50 minutes. Thirty minutes into baking, check the surface; a thin crust should form. It is done when it's very moist inside, with a thin, crispy, sugary surface (like a thin crust of ice forming on a pool of water). To achieve a fudgelike consistency, you must underbake the bars.

MAKES 12 TO 15 BARS

Ruby Blackburn Lambert's Persimmon Pudding

Cornelia Lambert called the *Hidden Kitchens* hotline to tell us how her grandmother Ruby turned her legendary cooking into a local fund-raiser for Habitat for Humanity. During the Depression Ruby's family moved to Mt. Airy, North Carolina, the inspiration for the town of Mayberry in *The Andy Griffith Show*. Ruby later married Fred Lambert, who was, in fact, a very distant cousin of Andy Griffith.

1   **cup butter or shortening or butter-flavored Crisco**

2   **scant cups sugar**

4   **eggs**

1   **quart ripe persimmons, hulled and put through a food mill or ricer to remove seeds to make approximately 2 cups puree**

1   **cup whole milk**

2   **cups self-rising flour**

1   **teaspoon salt**

2   **cups fine bread crumbs**

3   **teaspoons ground cinnamon**

Chopped pecans, whipped cream, ice cream, and/or other toppings

Preheat the oven to 325°F. Grease 3 rectangular pans or pie pans.

In a large bowl or food processor, cream the butter or shortening and the sugar. If using a food processor, transfer the mixture to a bowl. Stir in the eggs, persimmons, and milk. Add the flour, salt, bread crumbs, and cinnamon.

Pour the mixture into prepared pans and bake for 45 minutes, or until the pudding has pulled away from the sides of the pan.

Serve hot from the oven and top with chopped pecans, whipped cream—or better yet—butter pecan ice cream.

MAKES 10 TO 12 SERVINGS

Kitchen Music

"Hey, this is Don Rosler. I am sending you guys a song about a refrigerator, which, I guess, is a fairly essential appliance in just about every kitchen. The refrigerator is not only the center of activity in a lot of kitchens. For a lot of people, it's the emotional center, and I don't mean just in terms of emotional comfort from food. It's where the pictures and drawings, stuck-up memos, Little League schedules, and recipes are hung. It's probably where everyone you know or people you've hung out with in the kitchen at various times of life are represented. It also, in a weird way, represents the pictures we've taken down off the fridge. That is ultimately what the song is about. I guess it is actually about family and what that is to you. A kitchen is where the family gathers and changes over the years. The people who end up at our dinner tables and are at the center of our lives. So here are a couple of verses from a bittersweet song called 'Christine's Refrigerator.'

"I want my picture to stay up on
   Christine's refrigerator
Though I'm no longer with her
I want to stay there taped between
Her sister with her birthday cake
Her little brother standing on his head . . .

"I've had many a dinner beside
Christine's refrigerator
All those faces smiling at me
And I was thrilled to be above
Her parents by the Christmas tree
Her girlfriend with the tinfoil in her hair
But nights over there towards the end
When I'd somehow aggravate her
I could swear I'd see those smiles turn
To disapproving stares . . ."

An Unexpected Kitchen

The George Foreman Grill

Message #23 was received today at 1:22 PM

"Hello, I'm Margaret Engel from Baltimore, Maryland. A friend of mine who works for Legal Aid was talking to me about what a struggle it is for many of her clients to get food on the table. These are people who don't have an official kitchen and who are using the George Foreman Grill to get a hot meal. Everybody knows the George Foreman Grill has been an amazing success story as a kitchen appliance. But what I think many people don't realize is what the grill has meant to immigrants and low-income people, people without a real place to cook. That, to me, is the epitome of a hidden kitchen."

This story snuck up on us. We'd been thinking about hidden kitchens for months, from every vantage point we could imagine—test kitchens, harvest kitchens, cattle roundup kitchens, soup kitchens—then Message #23 came in on the *Hidden Kitchens* hotline. The Lean Mean Grilling Machine as a clandestine kitchen? We had never considered that an appliance might be part of this world of below-the-radar, not-so-legal cooking.

Where do you find a homeless man who cooks on the street with a George Foreman Grill? Lots of places, apparently, if you go looking. When we asked the people at the Chicago Coalition for the Homeless, they told us about Jeffry Newton. Sometimes life without a kitchen leads to the most unexpected hidden kitchen of all.

T esting, testing, one-two-three," says Jeffry Newton into the microphone as we adjust the recording levels and ask him our standard warmup question. "What did I have for breakfast? I didn't have breakfast," he answers. "I don't have a kitchen."

Dressed in dark jeans and a warm hooded jacket, Jeffry shifts his weight from one leg to the other. He's got arthritis in both knees. All the homeless in Chicago have arthritis, he tells us. It comes from living on the cold pavement.

"The George Foreman Grill, yeah," he says. "That's the grill I had for a while under Wacker Drive. Me and a fellow named Smokey."

Jeffry Newton is fifty-seven years old. Until recently, he lived in a refrigerator box, part of a makeshift cardboard community tucked in around trash cans and restaurant loading docks hidden under Chicago's Wacker Drive. "You know, where the expressway goes through downtown, there's about thirty or forty refrigerator boxes down there. You take your box, mark it up, and put in blankets and pillows. That's going to be your home."

During the Great Depression, this lower stretch of Wacker, nicknamed the Catacombs, was home to thousands who sought out its rain-sheltered corners. "You don't get as much snow down there as on top," Jeffry says, "except that wind blowing in from the lake. But the refrigerator box is pretty sturdy. Once you close and lock it up and get in there and cover up, you're all right."

Under Wacker Drive

"The George Foreman Grill? That's the grill that I had for a while under Wacker Drive . . . you just get you a long extension cord and hook up."

—JEFFRY NEWTON, CHICAGO

"Me and Smokey found the George Foreman Grill at the shelter," Jeffry remembers. Someone had donated it, broken, without a plug, so the two guys jury-rigged it. "Then you just get you a long extension cord and hook up. There's a lot of electrical plugs on the poles down there. You'd come home in the evening, and you'd fire up your Foreman. Some of us had jobs. Some of us had food stamp Link cards. You could put anything in that thing: bologna, hamburgers, grilled cheese sandwiches. We used to take an iron and do that too, press down, hot on the bread and cheese. You'd be inventive like that."

THE BOTTOMS, HOUSTON

George Foreman, two-time heavyweight champion of the world, Olympic gold medalist, former street preacher, and King of the Grills, is in a radio studio in Houston, Texas. His son, George—they call him "Three"—is with him. Each of George Foreman's five sons is named George. Foreman never knew who his father was, and he wants there to be no mystery about who theirs is. As "Three" settles things in the studio, we tell George what we've been hearing about his grill. The story hits a nerve.

"Whoa . . . what a story! I've never considered it at all," he says, "how homeless people and low-income people, wanting to cook but not being able to, how that little grill afforded them a kitchen. I'm just happy that it's helped so many people. It helped me, of course.

"Growing up in Houston, my whole life was spent trying to get enough to eat. Having seven kids, and my mother raising all of us by herself, there just was never enough food for me. **I always dreamed not about a car, not about a beautiful home, but about having enough to eat.**"

The Bottoms, that's what they called the Fifth Ward area of Houston, where George Foreman grew up, poorer than poor. Sometimes George's mother would come home with a cheeseburger and try to divide it among her seven kids. "I remember the taste of the mustard. It was the most supreme thing in our family when she'd come home with a burger."

During lunchtime at Atherton Elementary School, you could buy greens, vegetables, and meat for twenty-six cents. But even twenty-six cents was beyond George's wildest dreams. "I didn't even know what that looked like. I'd sit at the table, and it was so embarrassing. **So what I would do is I'd get a greasy bag, blow it up on the way to school to make it look like there was a sandwich in it.** Then I would get

George Foreman,
age eight

to my classroom and say, 'Boy, I ate my lunch,' so that they wouldn't look at me, and I wouldn't be embarrassed during the lunch hour. I learned to disguise my not having any food."

During the summer days, it was worse. Mothers would call their kids in for lunch and tell George to go on home to eat. "These people knew I had no food at home. I'd hide and peek through the window at the kids eating, and the parents would peel the crust off the bread, and I would just sit there hoping that they would throw it out the window for me."

George was always big and tough for his age, and when the school kept him back more than once, it made it harder and harder for him to fit in. "I think if you ever go to school hungry, it puts a chip on your shoulder," he tells us. "To go to school without breakfast, then without a lunch, it makes for a bad boy.

"I tried to conceal my lack of things by fighting all the time. Pretty soon I became an expert at fighting. But I never did get good at schoolwork."

George became a dropout and a mugger. "I actually mugged people. Took their money and ran away with it. I think hunger makes you angry.

"One night after mugging a guy, the police chased me. I crawled under a house to hide. I thought they were going to send out the hound dogs to find me. I covered myself with sewage from a busted pipe so the dogs wouldn't sniff me. And as I was laying there, a criminal hiding from dogs, I heard in my head what my cousin Rita had told me, 'George Foreman, you're not going to be anything. No one from this family has ever become anything."

THE TENDERLOIN, SAN FRANCISCO

Poverty and danger lived side by side in the Bottoms, where George Foreman grew up, and they are neighbors to this day in San Francisco's Tenderloin district, a borderline neighborhood of tourist hotels, soup kitchens, street people, junkies, and the homeless. Legend has it that the area got its name because the police who worked that beat in the 1920s got paid overtime in beef tenderloin for the risk they took patrolling some of the toughest streets of the city. Glide Memorial Church sits in the middle of all this, trying to deal.

We've come to talk to Pat Sherman, program coordinator for Glide's Walk-In services. When we arrive, Pat is leaning over her printer, ear pressed against it, listening to it lurch and gasp. It's on its last legs, and Pat is trying to coax one more job out of it before it gives up the ghost. The Walk-In program is a shoestring outfit—no fat, no margin. The sign outside Pat's office announces, "World Famous Glide Fried Chicken," today's offering for the lunch program that will serve some eight hundred free meals to the addicted, the hungry, and the homeless.

Not much fazes Pat, a calm, solid woman, with red dreads and dimples. Not the man darting in and out of the office as if he were being chased by something only he can see, not the phone that never stops ringing, not the steady stream of people she sees every day who need something to eat, somewhere to sleep, somewhere to work. She knows who they are because she used to be one of them.

"When I was in an SRO," says Pat, "I couldn't cook in my room. I mean, legally I couldn't. A lot of places don't have kitchens. **So you have a Crock-Pot disguised as a plant holder,** and you have a fry skillet that you know you're not supposed to have hidden in the closet. A toaster oven tucked under the bed. I'd get me a big bowl, put me some ice in it, and—voilà—that became my refrigerator."

SRO—single-room occupancy, no kitchen, some government-assisted, some one step away from a shelter. It is a life defined by eating out every day, which costs too much, or standing in food lines, where fights break out and where sometimes the food runs out altogether before you reach the head of the line. "Hunger pervades your whole life," says Pat, "and it's surprising what people come up with to fight it.

"I did the Crock-Pot thing for a while. I made it look like a flowerpot. I would take my flowerpot out, put my rice and beans in, go to work, come home, and have dinner. You need to use dry beans, because you can soak them and it doesn't look like anything. The water's dark, so if someone comes in to check out the apartment, they don't want to mess with that.

"The George Foreman Grill, that's the newest thing," says Pat when we ask her about the grill. "Doesn't set off the smoke detectors. And since they come in colors, it just looks like you're getting real fancy in your room and decorating. It works well for people who have to live like this, because it doesn't take up much space. I've seen where people put a covering or cloth over it to disguise it so it looks like you have a nice tabletop in your room. It's your own kitchen. You make a kitchen for yourself so that you can survive."

TRAILBLAZING

Jeffry made a kitchen for himself on the street before he even got close to having a room. "Hey, I'm a great cook. Something I learned from my grandmother," Jeffry tells us. "I can cook and I can bake, but I just haven't had a kitchen. I've been homeless most all my life."

When Jeffry was a boy, his parents left him with his grandmother in Colorado. For most of his teenage years, he was in and out of reformatories and boys' homes. By age seventeen he was in prison. When he got out, at age twenty-one, he headed to Chicago, "land of opportunity," selling magazines on the road along the way. Just out of prison, newly arrived in Chicago, Jeffry got married. When that didn't work out, he turned to drugs and found himself scrounging on the streets.

"When you're homeless and living on the streets, you've got to look around. You've got to keep your eyes open in order to survive. It's called trailblazing. You've got to blaze the trail, you know." Trailblazing has taught Jeffry where he can get a free cup of coffee. He knows who will give him a doughnut and who won't and where they're giving free haircuts in the parks. On Sundays he knows which churches are serving and what the Salvation Army is offering for supper.

The winter pavement is blue cold in Chicago. Some nights Jeffry would slip into Cook County Hospital. "You go in coughing, you know, and they give you one of those little plastic bracelets. And when they call your name, you don't answer. And you got a band around your wrist, so now you can sit there half the night and go to sleep or **look for a hospital microwave to cook your Cup o' Noodles in.**"

Or your popcorn. Jeffry would go into office buildings downtown, sometimes looking for a job, sometimes not. "They'd say, 'Have a cup of coffee,' and I'd see there was a microwave in the lunchroom. I would never steal or anything like that. Mostly I just wanted a place to pop my popcorn. Sometimes I survived for days on popcorn."

THREE MEALS A DAY

In 1965, at age sixteen, George Foreman was headed for a life of crime, when he happened to be in the right place at the right time, watching TV. One of his heroes appeared in a commercial for President Lyndon Johnson's Job Corps program, part of the country's war on poverty.

"I heard about the Job Corps," remembers Foreman. "The great football player Jim Brown did a commercial. He said, 'If you're looking for a second chance to get an education, join the Job Corps!'" George Foreman decided to take him up on it—signed up and shipped out to Grants Pass, Oregon.

"It was the first time I'd been treated right. These people I had never met, they didn't look anything like me. I couldn't believe it. I had three meals a day for the first time in my life. It took me about two months before I realized, 'Hey, they're gonna have breakfast every day.' It changed my whole life. I started reading books, started doing my assignments."

In the Job Corps, George met an older boy named Richard Kibble, from Tacoma, Washington. "Sort of a hippie fellow. He listened to Bob Dylan. When I boasted about how I was going to fight somebody, he was not impressed. He said to listen to the music, 'Just listen to the words.' He explained every song. Bob Dylan, oh boy, I had never heard anyone sing songs that actually had meaning. I'd sit on the side of his bed and listen: 'They'll stone you when you're at the breakfast table, they'll stone you when you are young and able . . . But I would not feel so all alone, everybody must get stoned . . . ' And he explained that song. In other words, everything that I was doing was physical and brutal and, to him, out of style. And I started to admire something about him."

But fighting was still in George's blood. One day the boys were all sitting in the dayroom, listening to the radio broadcast of the championship fight between Cassius Clay and Floyd Patterson, when one of them challenged Foreman. "If you think you're so tough, why don't you become a boxer?"

"I really didn't want to be a boxer," George remembers, "but I took that challenge that day in the dayroom, and here we are today."

IT WASN'T LEGAL AT ALL

When the city of Chicago put up fences under Wacker Drive and evicted the residents of the refrigerator city, Jeffry managed to get a room at the YMCA.

"For a while there, I was selling plates of food to the other homeless people. At the YMCA I had a microwave and a little stove—whatcha call it? You know, you hook it up, and it just warms up—a hot plate, there you go! A hot plate. I started cooking for everybody even though we weren't supposed to be cooking. I could take commodity food and do wonders with it—canned chicken, canned pork. Once you add some garlic and some bell pepper and some onion and tomatoes and get it all stirred up, you would be surprised with what you got."

Every Sunday Jeffry was cooking—fried chicken mashed potatoes, string beans. "I had my door wide open. I'd turn the music on. **They'd know once they hear the music on, Jeff's cooking.** It wasn't legal at all."

But shelters have limits to how long a homeless man can stay, and low-income housing has waiting lists, so Jeffry's kitchen comes and goes with opportunity. At the shelter, there's no privacy, no place to store anything. Commodity canned food and boxes of Hamburger Helper sit stacked like small shrines by the beds. His day jobs vary. Sometimes he works for the Chicago Coalition for the Homeless, a job he got after sitting in their lobby every day for five years until they finally made him a member of their speakers' bureau. On occasion he also gets day work on setups and breakdowns at the Convention Center when a big convention hits town. But for the most part, he is unemployed.

On the rooftop of the Chicago Coalition building for the homeless, Jeffry has created a garden—eggplant, squash, and a few turnip greens and tomatoes. "I grow cherry tomatoes, peach tomatoes, purple tomatoes, green tomatoes. I got these tubs upstairs that are all filled with dirt and such, and every day I'm out watering. That's my little joy. I never knew I was a farmer, you know. I just like doing it. It eases my mind. Takes my mind away from the cares."

KING OF THE GRILL

"When I left boxing," remembers George Foreman, "I realized I didn't have any friends. People weren't pouring into my home anymore, but I noticed that if I barbecued something, they would come over. Even the guys, we'd go fishing, I wanted them to stay and come back so much, I would always clean the fish, do all the cooking. I found that more satisfying than even winning boxing matches, when people would lick their fingers and say my food was good.

"When I made a comeback in 1987, I was over 315 pounds and everybody made a joke of it. 'How can George Foreman, if he wants to be the prodigal son of boxing, do it when he's looking like the fatted calf?' And I'd gotten advertising sponsorships from all these companies—McDonald's, Doritos, Oscar Mayer weiners. A fellow I knew asked, 'Why don't you get your own product to promote?' And he told me about this little grill sitting up there, and no one wanted it. So I thought I'd just take a few grills and never see any revenues. You know, get the grills in my training camps because it really helped me with dieting. If I tell you I knew it was coming, I'd be lying. I had no idea this grill would be successful. There's over sixty million sold. It's the most successful electrical appliance in the history of England."

The Grill lets Americans grill indoors on a rainy day or in a college dorm, and it gives the homeless a way to have a hot bologna and cheese. It gave George and his brother Roy the means to open the George Foreman Youth Center. Foreman has never forgotten the central lesson of the Job Corps: All that most kids need is a chance. He still imagines what his life might have become, and so he holds out the same chance he got to kids who are hungry, and angry.

"I have these summer camps, put athletic equipment there, and these kids they can have three meals a day!" says George. "I've learned that any kid, any kid, if you give him a second or third chance, can make it. Never give up on anyone. Doesn't matter if you spend years in prison, or whatever. You never lose your citizenship as a human being because you're in trouble.

"I never forget peeping through that lady's window when she was serving lunch to her kids after she told me to go home. We've got to be there for those kids, no matter what. I'm pushed, I'm compelled, I'm motivated because of that. If there's a food bank, all they gotta do is ask George Foreman. If I can find a dime, I'm going to make sure you get it. I try to keep those little visions alive for myself. Feed them."

George Foreman's Grilled Salmon or "Sir Loin"

When we asked George Foreman for his favorite recipe, the former heavyweight champion of the world said, "Oh, just give me a grill and plate. And salmon steak. That's my favorite. I can have it for breakfast, lunch, and there's nothing like a salmon dinner. When I do go for meat, there's nothing like 'Sir Loin' himself.

"Then you get out your garlic. I think that's the most exotic thing that you can have, is some garlic. You can't mess up; the room will smell nice, and you can smell it out the window. Then you get some lemon pepper, a wonderful invention.

"I cook both salmon and sirloin in the same fashion. Not too many exotic spices. I make a marinade with garlic, lemon pepper, black pepper, and balsamic vinegar. I use that with a little oil. I marinate the salmon or meat in the refrigerator, but not too long.

"Take that salmon steak or sirloin and put it on the grill so that the smell is there. Everybody loves smells. If you want to add other spices or ingredients, I just say go ahead. When you got ten kids like I do—five boys and five daughters—you can't go too far to the left or to the right with spices."

Pat Sherman's "Hidden Beans and Rice"

When Pat Sherman lived in an SRO with no kitchen and no cooking allowed, she came up with some ingenious clandestine Crock-Pot solutions.

"Beans and rice would probably be the best hidden kitchen recipe, because you can put your beans on in the morning, go to school or to work, and come home to a hot meal without anyone knowing. You soak 'em overnight and put them in your Crock-Pot in the morning before you leave (my personal favorite is pinto beans). Midday, you come back, throw your rice and

spices in. (Now they've got these great 99 Cents stores. You can get a sixteen-ounce container of chile peppers, chili powder, onion powder and just spice it up!) Put your onions and your bell peppers in, if you want. Turn your cooker down—you start it off on high, then you turn it down. And then you come back—say, four or five-ish—and you have your beans and rice all ready for you. You don't have to do anything else but grab a bowl."

The Sound of Home Cooking

"Hi. My name is Chelsea Merz. I'm a radio producer. The hidden kitchen story I have is about Matthew, a homeless man. Occasionally he gets to house-sit for an old friend. The last time he was indoors, I gave him a tape recorder so that he could make an audio diary documenting what he likes most about living inside, what he misses most when he's back on the streets.

"After being indoors for ten days, he gave me the tape. In ten days he made only one entry: the sound of him frying eggs. He said as a homeless man, he misses nothing more than the sound of home cooking."

To: morningedition@npr.org
Subject: George Foreman Grill

"Hi. I heard a segment about the George Foreman Grill and how important it is for people with no kitchens. My mom, Edith, has been in a nursing home for a few years now. She's pretty much inca- pacitated, and the only thing she can still enjoy (besides her family) is food. I bring her all of the

Edith and her George Foreman Grill

things she likes, but I had a problem when the deli near her place closed and I couldn't bring her favorite food, a kosher hot dog. After hearing this story, I saw a small George Foreman Grill in Target for, like, twelve dollars and thought hmmmm. I bought it, put it on her nightstand, cranked it up, and she had a perfect dog in five minutes. The whole floor enjoys the aroma. I thank you, George, and my mother thanks you."

—Sara Blumenstein

STORY #3

The Chili Queens
of San Antonio

Some kitchens are in hidden locations; others are obscured by time, lost because their era has come and gone—like the saga of the Chili Queens. We first heard about the chili queens while interviewing Jeffrey Pilcher, a professor of history at The Citadel in Charleston, South Carolina, about his intriguing research on the "globalization of the taco." In the middle of the conversation, Professor Pilcher, an expert in the field of Mexican cooking and its historical meaning and significance, veered off the taco and onto another of his essays, "Who Chased Out the Chili Queens? Ethnicity and Urban Reform in San Antonio, Texas, 1880–1943." Forget the taco. We wanted to know more about the chili queens. Within a week, seven pounds of chili queen research lay on our doorstep in San Francisco.

Jeffrey had never actually spoken with a chili queen, so we decided to go to the source. All roads led to Jorge Cortez, whose family has owned the restaurant Mi Tierra since the 1940s, located on the old Haymarket Plaza in San Antonio, where the chili queens were last seen cooking. It took us ten calls to get this busy *patrón* on the phone, and when we at last finally did, the news was not good. "You're too late," he told us. "She died two weeks ago."

"She" turned out to be Trinidad Garcia, one of the last of the chili queens, a woman who had worked for the Cortez family as a waitress since the chili stands closed on the plaza in the 1940s.

Time was wasting, and the trail was growing cold. We headed for San Antonio looking for chili and ghosts, trying to find traces of a story that stretches back across Texas more than one hundred years.

I was a little boy in the 1930s, just before the chili queens were banished," begins Felix Almaraz, professor of history and a lifelong San Antonian. "On Saturdays my family would bring my brother and me to the marketplace. The plaza was buzzing with life, with people yelling greetings to each other. The chili queens would bring their pots and their fires and set up shop for the night. Their makeshift tables were decorated with ribbons, papier-mâché, and red-and-white oilcloths. There were handcrafted lanterns on the tables, little *farolitos*. For a dime, you could get chili con carne, tamales, beans, coffee. The chili queens were entrepreneurs. They were business ladies. And they made enough money to take care of their families."

Professor Felix Almaraz, a proud, stately seventy-two-year-old, sits in his small office at the University of Texas in downtown San Antonio, very near the plaza he remembers from his childhood. He is a historian, an expert on the Alamo, and the deep, booming voice of San Antonio's Fiesta Week. He's also one of the keepers of the chili queen story—an eyewitness. He's eaten the chili queen's food, heard their conversations, and smelled the black coffee, hot chili, and enchiladas that once perfumed the night air.

Celebrated in all the tourist brochures, the chili queens are deeply embedded in the legend and lore of old San Antonio. At the Conservation Society's annual Night in Old San Antonio, young, beautiful girls dress up in white peasant blouses, twirling skirts, ribbons, and flowers, and play at being chili queens. So popular are the queens that at festivals and special events businesses sometimes hire women to dress up like them and sell chili to the tourists. But the last real chili queens have been gone from the plazas of San Antonio for more than sixty years, and their stories, their cooking traditions, and even their identities remain shrouded in myth and memory.

Everyone seems to have a theory about the chili queens. Some people told us that the older mothers and grandmothers cooked the chili at home and then sent the prettiest girls of the family to sell it in the plaza. Others speculate that many of the chili queens may have been washerwomen by day, because the lamps that they used to illuminate their long serving tables were the same as those found in the laundries of old San Antonio. Some people hint at a darker secret, believing that the chili queens were temptresses, young women of the night, who lured customers to their tables with their charm and beauty.

Chili Stand

Haymarket Plaza, circa 1904

"The chili queens were romanticized in the press as being exotic Spanish women with sable hair and fiery tempers," Professor Pilcher tells us. "They became the stuff of tourist legend. This meant that no trip to the Southwest was complete without a visit to the chili queens. And these women were often people's first introduction to that spicy, dangerous Mexican food."

FIRE-BRICKS FROM HADES

Chili con carne, said by many to be a San Antonio invention, was very different back then from the chili we know today—more fiery sauce, less meat, and no beans. A newspaper account from 1874 described the curious new dish as "various savory compounds swimming in fiery pepper, which biteth like a serpent . . . a compound of chopped meat and pulverized red pepper stewed until the meat has been thoroughly saturated with the pepper."

Another 1870s account tells of a man from out of town who ordered a bowl of chili, took one bite and immediately screamed, jumped up, and ran over to the saloon on the edge of the plaza to douse the fire in his mouth. The renowned author Stephen Crane, traveling the West a few years after writing his *Red Badge of Courage,* described tasting his first bowl of San Antonio chili in 1899, likening it to a "pounded fire-brick from Hades."

"Burning your tongue on chili became a rite of passage for tourists," says Jeffrey Pilcher. "In the 1880s, the newly built railroad brought waves of visitors to the area for the first time. When these tourists returned home, all they could talk about was the Alamo and the chili queens."

WE'VE ALWAYS RELIED ON THE KINDNESS OF ARCHIVISTS

Archivists tend the quiet corners of history. Tom Shelton has been the archivist at the Institute of Texan Cultures since 1978, spending many hours scouring the records for even the tiniest mention of the chili queens. Many people have written about the queens, and Tom knows them all. Or at least he knows where their stories are filed. Part detective, part archivist, he sits surrounded by newspaper clippings, maps, and photographs of the chili queens, as well as those of the street musicians and other vendors who have filled San Antonio's plazas throughout its history. Normally a gentle, quiet man, Tom ignites when talking about the chili queens.

San Antonio Daily Express, 1894

"Look at this," he says, pulling out a brittle newspaper clipping from a folder. The 1894 article shows an artist's sketch of a chili queen wearing a rebozo and smoking a cigarette. Tom squints and runs his finger along the lines of tiny newspaper type as he reads to us from the fading story: **"The ever-attentive, always jolly 'chile queen.'** They are 'good fellows,' these 'chile queens,' and are able and willing to talk on any subject that may be named from love to law. As a general rule they are bright, bewitching creatures and put themselves to much trouble to please their too often rowdy customers. Every class of people who come to this city visit the places and partake of their piquant edibles."

"The earliest chili stands were set up on Main Plaza before the Civil War," Tom tells us. "That ended in 1865, when they closed the stands because of inadequate police protection in the plazas in the evening. But by the 1870s they'd opened back up again on Military Plaza."

He brings out a copy of "The Enchanted Kiss," an O. Henry story written in 1904 in which the writer described plaza life at that time as "a carnival, a saturnalia that was renowned throughout the land. Then the caterers numbered hundreds; the patrons thousands. Drawn by the coquettish señoritas, the music of the weird Spanish minstrels, and the strange piquant Mexican dishes served at a hundred competing tables, crowds thronged the Alamo Plaza all night. Travellers, rancheros, family parties, gay gasconading rounders,

MAIN PLAZA

MILITARY PLAZA

sightseers and prowlers of polyglot, owlish San Antone mingled there at the centre of the city's fun and frolic. The popping of corks, pistols, and questions; the glitter of eyes, jewels and daggers; the ring of laughter and coin."

As the afternoon wears on, Tom acts as our tour guide through time, poring through the archival history, coaxing the chili queens to life. He tells us that for more than one hundred years, the chili queens migrated from one San Antonio plaza to the next—Plaza de las Islas (Main Plaza), Plaza de Armas (Military Plaza), Alamo Plaza, Milam Plaza, Plaza del Zacate (Haymarket Plaza). The reasons they moved were many, from redevelopment to what some called racism. But regardless of how many times they were displaced, the chili queens always seemed to come back.

PLAZAS FOR THE USE AND ENTERTAINMENT OF ALL

From San Antonio's earliest days as a Spanish military encampment, life in the town revolved around the plazas. When the town was first mapped out by the Spaniards in 1730, the viceroy mandated plazas "for the use and entertainment of the colonists."

Mary Ann Guerra, the grand dame of San Antonio history, has written an essay about the chili queens especially for our visit. A warm, gracious woman in her eighties with white hair swept back and large, dark glasses protecting her failing eyes, Mary Ann holds court in the sitting room of her large 1920s hacienda and reads to us from her writings.

"San Antonio's chili queens reigned over the town's plazas for almost one hundred years and brought to the Old Town and this city, almost as much fame as its

Military Plaza, 1880s

The chili queens were not the only ones selling food on the streets and plazas of San Antonio. Candy vendors sold *envueltos* (candy rolls filled with pecans), *calabasate* (candied pumpkin), and *cubierta de viznaga* (cactus dipped in melted sugar).

River and the Alamo." She reads on from her hand-typed document bearing witness to the history of the town that she loves. "San Antonio was an isolated outpost, a refueling place for the military, a rest-stop for travelers and tourists, a haven for political refugees, and a gold mine for rustlers and thieves. From its founding days, San Antonio had a foreignness about it, and it was on the plazas that its lifestyle and character were shaped."

Mary Ann lives and breathes the history and rich traditions of old San Antonio. The walls of her home, painted daring deep Mexican reds and blues, display historic santos, paintings, and photographs of the town's missions and plazas. "The plazas were once the center of life," she tells us. **"They were the marketplace, the midway, the front porches of government and the church**—the places where treaties were signed with the Comanches, where buffalo meat and skins were sold, where weddings, funerals, festivals, and hangings took place."

At dusk, as the public market closed down, came the arrival of the chili queens, pulling their carts loaded with sawhorses, plank tables, pots, and baskets of food. As darkness fell, the townspeople and tourists would crowd around the chili queens' tables to eat chili using tortillas rolled up like funnels to scoop the hot food. The plaza was a place to exchange news and compare notes on one's children and to share food and conversation. People could argue politics with a neighbor or listen to the guitars and sad songs of the troubadours walking amid the crowd.

But later in 1890, when the town council chose to construct the City Hall building right in the center of Military Plaza, the chili queens and the bustling life of the market and plaza were forced to relocate. Some of the queens migrated to Alamo Plaza. Others moved to Milam Plaza, where they remained for a few years until they were forced to move again when the city decided to landscape the plaza. San Antonio was growing quickly—at the end of the nineteenth century, it was the fastest growing city in Texas. Newcomers were arriving, the town was developing, and the queens were feeling the push and pull of progress.

TEXAS CHILI HITS CHICAGO

In 1893 the chili queens became widely known when Texas featured them in a chili booth at Chicago's Columbian Exposition World's Fair. There, on display somewhere near the twenty-two-thousand-pound "monster" cheese from Canada, and the thirty-thousand-pound temple crafted of chocolate, was a large sign for "Texas Chili." This irony is not lost on Professor Pilcher. "At the time they were selling chili at the World's Fair," he says, "the city had just banned the chili queens from setting up in Alamo Plaza! **So you could get a bowl of chili in Chicago, but not outside the Alamo.**"

"Around the turn of the century, Alamo Plaza was becoming more for Caucasians and businesspeople," Professor Almaraz tells us. "Every parade in town had to pass in front of the Alamo. It was the place where politicians came to

A night at Haymarket Plaza, 1933

announce for office. It was a cultural center. The chili queens with their little setups were now considered an eyesore."

By 1900, plaza life as San Antonians had known it for generations had moved west to Haymarket Plaza, in the more Mexican part of town.

GOOGLING THE CHILI QUEENS

Combing the Web, the words "chili queen" pop up in a speech given by Graciela Sánchez, director of the Esperanza Peace and Justice Center in San Antonio. Graciela had given a talk about her family roots and her great-grandmother—Teresa Cantu, one of the chili queens. The Esperanza Center, where Graciela works, serves the primarily Mexicano population on the west side of San Antonio—legal aid, health and housing resources, honoring the elders and gathering and holding together the history of the community.

When we arrive, Graciela and her seventy-five-year-old mother, Isabel—the great-granddaughter and **granddaughter of a chili queen**—sit on folding chairs in the large, boomy community room.

As we talk, Isabel digs back through the years. "My grandmother's name was Teresa Cantu Rocha. She was a chili queen. I would hear from my mother that they had tables outside around the *mercado*, around the cathedral."

Isabel strays and struggles to remember. Memories, along with the chili queens, have slipped away. Her daughter, Graciela, picks up the thread. "Plaza del Zacate, Haymarket Plaza, was the place where the Mexicano community in San Antonio used to congregate, a true farmers' market. And in the afternoon people would come to listen to the newspaper being read aloud. You had a lot of people

Interviewing Isabel Sánchez, granddaughter of a chili queen

who couldn't read. They'd post the newspaper, and one or two people would read the paper to the community. There were people in San Antonio who were fleeing the Mexican Revolution—both pro-revolution and anti-revolution—so there was a lot of the political dialogue occurring right there in the plaza. As it got dark, the chili queens would arrive, and the walking troubadours, musicians like Lydia Mendoza and her family, would begin to set up and play. They were all trying to make some money to survive."

PROGRESS THREATENS HAYMARKET PLAZA

"These are the last days of the chili queens," explains Tom Shelton, showing us a newspaper clipping from 1933. "Progress Threatens Haymarket Plaza," reads the headline.

"Some of the picturesqueness of San Antonio's Haymarket Plaza may go with the installation of flood lights to replace old-fashioned lanterns in use for years at the chili stands."

—*SAN ANTONIO LIGHT,* 1933

All along there had been issues with the night crowds, rowdiness, lack of police patrol, the noise, the open fires, and the unregulated, unlicensed cooking. "Over the years, the chili queens went back and forth, moving from plaza to plaza, and the struggle continued all the way up until the 1930s," says Jeffrey Pilcher. "That's when the official perception of the presence of the chili queens changed from being somewhat of a public nuisance to being a health hazard."

Chili stands in screened tents, following a city health department order in 1936.

"Juanita and Esperanza Garcia making tortillas. Action of city health department ordered removal from Haymarket Plaza of chili queens and their stands, brought an end to a two-hundred-year-old tradition."

—SAN ANTONIO LIGHT, 1937

The health department eventually lowered the boom. By 1936, the chili stands stood shrouded in screened tents, in response to complaints that open-air stalls endangered people's health.

The archivist looks at one last newspaper article from 1942. An old woman holding a big iron chili pot on her lap stares straight into the camera. The caption below her reads: "Chili con Hitler. Into the scrap metal piles, which San Antonians are gathering to defeat the Axis Saturday, went a 125-year-old chili pot, contributed by Mrs. Luce Treviño." The chili queens were officially relegated to history.

The mayor of San Antonio, Maury Maverick, tried in the last days of the chili queens in the early 1940s to revive the tradition, but those days were gone. Some of the queens moved indoors and started their own restaurants or worked for others. By then, chili and tacos and enchiladas—once the street food of San Antonio—had become mainstream San Antonio fare. What had once been a lively, thriving night scene was moving into more licensed, sanctioned places.

Health regulations and the war ended the chili queens' reign in San Antonio's

Mrs. Luce M. Trevino holds 125-year-old chili pot that she is donating to scrap metal drive picture. -- published in: San Antonio Light (October 10, 1942.

Picture caption: "Chili Con Hitler / Into the scrap metal piles which San Antonians are gathering to defeat the Axis Saturday went a 125-year-old chili pot contributed by Mrs. Luce M. Trevino, 89, 4222 West Houston street. The pot was used by Mrs. Trevino's mother for chili cooking in the first Mexican food restaurant in the city. Later the pot was used in an outdoor restaurant in the plaza in front of the Menger hotel."

plazas, and the postwar boom changed plaza life forever. The thriving culture of Haymarket Plaza disappeared in 1956, when the newly constructed Interstate 35 cut off the western third of the plaza. The queens' home was gone, and the life of the street cook altered forever.

"To this day, the street vendors who sell their tacos and other dishes are really carrying on an old Hispanic tradition," Jeffrey Pilcher tells us. "The problem arises in the United States because we have different ideas about urban life, you know. Streets should be places that are efficient, where people go places and don't loiter around eating and drinking and making merry. There's always that tension between the way corporate America wants to establish their food traditions and the way people from immigrant cultures want to carry on their own traditions."

TWENTY-FOUR/SEVEN

Today, a part of what was once Haymarket Plaza is called Market Square, a tourist area consisting of indoor souvenir shops, margarita bars, and a new branch of the Smithsonian focusing on Hispanic art and culture. The lynch pin of this revitalization effort is Mi Tierra—a colorful, multiroomed Mexican restaurant, born

"For sanitation purposes all chili queens have their health cards on display on the wall of their central kitchen in the Market House."

—*SAN ANTONIO LIGHT*, 1939

in 1941 just as Haymarket Plaza was dying. The restaurant never closes. It is open seven days a week, twenty-four hours a day. Its walls are full of old photos of the queens and the troubadours that used to play in the plaza. Long ago, Pete Cortez, founder of Mi Tierra, delivered meat to the chili queens. Now Pete's son Jorge still encourages the old guitar players to stroll through the restaurant singing to customers.

Felix Almaraz's office at University of Texas, San Antonio, is not far from Market Square. In fact it's just on the other side of Interstate 35, the highway that cut through and put an end to Haymarket Plaza. Felix often goes to Mi Tierra for lunch.

"The atmosphere at the Market Plaza today is very touristy, especially at night," Felix laments. "But in the daytime, at noon, it is different. This is when I like to go. I run into people I know. It still has something of the *mercado*. It has layers. People are making contact."

Professor Almaraz, handsome and proud in his traditional Mexican guayabera shirt, is getting ready to leave his office. Night is falling. The queens would have been out on the plazas by now, with the first smells of chili and smoke wafting up into the night sky. "When they were here, we didn't protect them," says Felix. "I miss it—the chili queens, the music, the aromas. The plaza was where you met your friends and you exchanged news. That was life. It was just a coming together."

THE LARK OF THE BORDER

When Lydia Mendoza was a little girl in the 1930s, just ten years old, she sang and played her twelve-string guitar in Haymarket Plaza with her mother, two sisters, and brother. The family's music began as a way to earn a meal and tips, but Lydia quickly became the most popular of the Tejano singers.

The legendary Queen of Tejano is eighty-nine now, a beautiful, pale bird of a woman with piercing dark eyes. She broke her hip recently and is now stranded in bed in a care center on the west side of San Antonio. Her long hands with polished bright red nails dominate the conversation just as they used to command her guitar. Her daughter Yolanda translates her stories into English.

"Down at the Plaza del Zacate, there used to be the chili queens—they sold spicy *menudo* soup and chili," Lydia remembers. "And at night, whole bunches of people would be down there, going from table to table. So we would bring our old chairs and sit right there and start singing, too. The others were strictly male trios or duets with their guitars, making their living like us. We were the only family. Everybody was chasing after the centavos in those days. And near the chili was the place to get them.

"Some people would throw in pennies, a nickel . . . we would put together fifteen, twenty-five cents a day," says Lydia. That was the Mendoza family's daily income, for their rent and food. And they played every night, even in the dead of winter.

"The people would form a circle around us, so we didn't feel the cold as much," Lydia remembers. "And Mama had this little can with a nickel's worth of charcoal. And before we left the house, we would light it and get the coals burning nicely. Then we would go down to the plaza and put it next to us on the ground so our fingers didn't get too numb to play our instruments."

One day a man drove up and asked if she would play on the radio. Lydia's life moved out of the plaza, away from the chili queens, and into record studios and dance halls throughout south Texas. She became known as *La Alondra de la Frontera*—the Lark of the Border.

The music that filled the plaza and surrounded the chili queens had its roots deep in Mexico, but it also had elements of American country music, German polkas, and accordion. It was a mix of south Texas and border music—a mix like chili itself, of the old world and the new.

Lydia Mendoza (far left) and her family played nightly near the chili stands in the plazas during the early 1930s.

Original San Antonio Chili

Although the campfires and little decorated booths of the chili queens are gone from the plazas of San Antonio, some of the earliest recipes for chili have been collected and preserved in the archives of the Institute of Texan Cultures Library. You won't find beans in this chili, but you will find "various savory compounds swimming in fiery pepper, which biteth like a serpent."

Flour

2 **pounds beef shoulder, cut into ½" cubes**

1 **pound pork shoulder, cut into ½" cubes**

¼ **cup suet or raw beef fat**

¼ **cup pork fat**

3 **medium-size onions, chopped**

6 **garlic cloves, minced**

1 **quart water**

4 **ancho chiles**

1 **serrano chile**

6 **dried red chiles**

1 **tablespoon cumin seeds, freshly ground**

2 **tablespoons Mexican oregano**

Salt to taste

Lightly flour the beef and pork shoulder cubes. In a heavy chili pot, add the lightly floured cubes with the suet (or beef fat) and pork fat and cook quickly, stirring often. Add the onions and garlic and cook until they are tender and limp. Add the water to the mixture and simmer slowly while preparing the chiles.

Remove the stems and seeds from the chiles and chop very finely. Grind the chiles into a paste in a *molcajete* (mortar and pestle) and add the cumin, oregano, and salt to the chile mixture.

Add the chile mixture to the meat. Simmer for another 2 hours. Remove suet casing and skim off some fat. Never cook frijoles (beans) with chiles and meat. Serve as a separate dish.

MAKES 8 TO 10 SERVINGS

Mexican *Fideo*

When we were talking about the chili queens with longtime San Antonian Annie Madrid Salas, she didn't want to talk about chili. She wanted to talk about *fideo,* a Mexican comfort food made with Italian-style vermicelli (angel hair pasta). For many Texans, it is considered home food. Nikki lives on a commune, and every time we come back from a *Hidden Kitchens* expedition, she tries to cook the food of the trip. Every man, woman, and child on her commune swears by this Mexican noodle dish. It can be eaten at any time of the day as an *antijito* (a little snack) and is often found cooking on stoves in many Mexican border towns.

1 **bag (8 ounces) vermicelli**

2 **tablespoons vegetable oil**

¼ **cup diced onions**

1 **clove garlic, chopped**

1 **can (8 ounces) tomato sauce**

2 **cups water**

  Salt to taste

  Black pepper to taste

  Cumin to taste

While the vermicelli is still in the bag, use your hands to break it into small pieces. In a frying pan over medium-high heat, add the oil.

Add the noodles to the pan, stirring constantly so as not to burn, and cook for 2 to 3 minutes to brown. Add the onions, garlic, and tomato sauce along with the water and cook for approximately 4 minutes, until the onions are clear. Add the salt, pepper, and cumin. Reduce the heat to low. Cover and simmer for 5 minutes, or until the noodles are soft.

MAKES 4 TO 6 SERVINGS

JOSEPH AGUILAR'S *MERCADO*—
A STREET KITCHEN VISION

If you walk a block or so over from the Alamo to Commerce Street and head west, you'll hit most of the spots the chili queens once haunted.

We were walking in that direction, hoping to find some remnant of what had once been San Antonio's vital commercial hub full of butcher shops, bakers, drugstores, plazas, and chili queens. But there's not much commerce on West Commerce anymore. It's one way with no parking on the street, blocks of mostly empty buildings with no shop windows to look in, and no people, except the homeless and those standing at a bus stop waiting to go someplace else.

Then, amid the endless gray, a beacon of bananas glows in a doorway. A tiny storefront with a scale hanging out front surrounded by baskets of ripe mangoes, nopales cactus, deep green chiles, brilliant red tomatoes. We pick up our pace, pulled in by the life force.

As we approach, a horn honks. A middle-aged man darts out of the store, runs up to a car idling out front, hands off a plastic bag, grabs a bill, and runs back inside as the car pulls out into the fast-moving traffic. The man is Joseph Aguilar, owner of West Commerce Mercado.

"Everything we do here is illegal," he tells us. "But it's not bad illegal. I don't sell beer. I don't sell cigarettes—just produce. A little produce stand. A family thing.

"I just delivered a snack bag. That's what we call them. A bag with a banana, apple, orange, and a pear for a dollar. Cars come up and just honk. They don't even get out of their seats. We already know who they are and what they want. It's illegal because this is a bus line in front of our store. It's kind of exciting."

A handsome man with salt-and-pepper hair and a thick mustache, fifty-seven-year-old Joseph Aguilar proudly takes us through his tiny market. It has everything "from salsa to sweet peaches." Old-fashioned wooden shelves display hot sauce with lemon and dry pepper that he's selling for a friend who lives in Mexico; crisp tortillas wrapped the old traditional way in paper, imported from a family in Chicago; beautifully packaged spices and herbs; *molcajetes*—grinding bowls and pestles made of volcanic rock—"we call them Mexican blenders," Joseph says.

"My customers are downtown working people, senior citizens, and 'the criminal element' who come in for food. The courthouse and probation office are nearby. A lot of them are pretty good people; it's just that they had bad luck and got caught."

The walls of the market are papered with old photographs of the Aguilar family and old San Antonio. "My grandfather had a produce stall right here at Haymarket Plaza, where the chili queens would gather and make tacos and tamales. In the 1920s and 1930s everyone congregated there. One o'clock in the morning, it was booming—thousands of people. There were trucks and trucks and trucks of produce. People would go from stall to stall, and they would buy. I got to see it before we lost it, before they started tearing down the old buildings. Look at this picture. This was our

"Everything we do here is illegal. But it's not bad illegal. I don't sell beer. I don't sell cigarettes—just produce. A little produce stand. A family thing."

—JOSEPH AGUILAR, OWNER OF WEST COMMERCE MERCADO, SAN ANTONIO

KITCHEN VISIONARY

farmers' market. Can you believe they knocked that building down?"

Joseph fell in love with the business when he was six years old, cleaning tomatoes for his grandfather. "My grandfather used to yell from his produce stand, *'Esta la casa forte.'* Everybody knew that sound; they loved that old man.

"But eventually the laws started changing. People here had a different vision for downtown—there were tourists and this was a landmark area—and the produce brought flies and bees. We eventually lost it and lost it and then just lost everything. I think it has been twenty-five years now. There is no produce at all. The last farmers' market eventually just died out."

When things began changing for produce sellers, Joseph became a renegade of sorts, continuing on, cowboy fashion. "It was against the city ordinance, but I used to come downtown in my truck, sell, get caught, and they'd run me out. I'd come back the next day and do it again. I used to love coming downtown. Downtown was always where the produce was when I was raised.

"You know, a few years back I had an aneurysm. They opened the side of my head. I had three surgeries in less than twenty-four hours, and I was gone for five days. When I opened my eyes, I said as I was recuperating and thinking about my life, I said, 'I am going to get back to what I really love since I was kid.' It's this. I love being around people. I love dealing with ripe fruit, fruit that's sweet.

"Now we are trying to see if we can get the laws changed so we can have things like this *mercado* in the downtown area. We need an open-air market, a meat market, tortillas, tamales, a few mama-papa concessions. And we need to cater to the people of San Antonio. Don't worry about the tourists. We are going to treat the tourists just as good. When the tourists come, invite them! It doesn't have to be an arm and a leg, just because they are tourists. If I sell tomatoes in this place for three pounds for a dollar, when tourists come in it's going to cost them three pounds for a dollar."

When Joseph started up his little business, he spent two thousand dollars to have the windows in his market set back off the sidewalk so he could display his produce outside "so people could see the beauty of how produce looks outside your little store." His market is right across the street from the health department office.

"The city is coming along, but they are not used to this type thing. And they're not used to having the doors open to the street. They close them every time they come over here, you know. They get tired of me, and they get mad at me and make me close the doors. But they just have to be open. A wide-open store."

Look around you. Little hidden kitchens lurk in our parking lots, our baseball diamonds and soccer fields, our street corners. Food that can't be suppressed. When the restaurant rent is too high to make, permits too hard to get, staff more than you can afford, the language too big a leap, there's always a cart, a cooler, or a tailgate to open and sell from.

Most everyone who comes to this country comes from a culture of street food, of cooking porchetta sandwiches in the plazas of Italy, of hawker food from the stalls of Singapore, of the *chicharrones* vendor selling with his street cries from the zocalo in Mexico.

America, for all its noise and commotion, is quiet when it comes to its public spaces. We cluster our food indoors in food courts, in repeating chains in repeating shopping centers and mini malls. But just below the surface there is another kitchen strata made up of people, tenaciously holding on, grabbing the first economic toehold they can when they get here. Maybe it's a sack of oranges being

sold by a Mexican in L.A. from a median strip in rush-hour traffic, maybe it's a *raspa* vendor in San Antonio with his barely legal snow cones for sale from a cart outside the Alamo, or the *chimichurri* truck outside the hospital on the Upper West Side of New York City with the Indian food for the West Indian immigrants who all work the graveyard shift. Or the Mud Truck that circles Manhattan with some of the best rolling coffee on the island.

We can't be everywhere. So many of you citizen storytellers have taken it upon yourselves to call our attention to some street-corner cooking we need to chronicle and eat.

Message #412 was received today at 8:52 PM

"This is Jim Rochester. In the city of Lancaster, Pennsylvania, at the intersection of Chesapeake Street and South Duke Street, every Friday and Saturday a Puerto Rican family sets up shop and grills chickens over an open fire. It seems to be quite the cultural gathering place for folks in the southeast portion of the city who are of Puerto Rican descent. I cannot tell you their names, I've never had the nerve to talk to them, but they might be a very interesting family to talk with."

Mr. Pig

"My name is Kristifer Dillehay. My wife and I lived in a place in the middle of Cincinnati called Over-the-Rhine, an area like every large city has that is fairly depressed, maybe sometimes a little bit dangerous if you're not careful. Findlay Market there has probably been around for a century or more. When I first visited, I was in architecture school, and I kept smelling this smoke. It smelled so good that I just sort of followed my nose. There was a gentleman on the corner with this big barrel smoking some meat. He went by the name of Mr. Pig. I tasted his beef brisket—my mouth exploded—it was the best meat I ever tried. All they sold was meat. The store was a place where people came together, white and black. We still talk about Mr. Pig's brisket and chicken. Mr. Pig, if you get to hear this, man, we love you."

NASCAR Kitchens

Feed the Speed

Message #216 was received
Saturday at 4:20 PM

*"Hi, this is Jon Wheeler. I'm the chef for the
Chip Ganassi Racing Team on the Indy,
NASCAR, and Grand Am circuit. I travel around
the country cooking for the car racing team in a
small kitchen hidden in a trailer. I'm calling from
Kansas City right now, and I'm in the middle of
the speedway. I hope you can hear me.*

*"I land in a town and go right to the grocery store. The highlight, to me, after all
these years of cooking on the NASCAR circuit is meeting the local people in these
stores. I try to use regional foods and do a little exploring and investigative work
ahead of time just to find out what local foods might be in an area or what's on
special at the butcher counter that day.*

*"Right now, I'm thinking about what I am going to do with steamed crab legs
tomorrow for lunch for the team. . . . They just restarted the race. You can probably
hear the race cars in the background. Sorry, got to go."*

Jon Wheeler's kitchen kept moving with the racing circuit. When we finally hooked
up, he got us in behind the scenes at the Richmond International Raceway and the
hidden kitchens of NASCAR, crammed in the corners of garages, tucked into crew
pits, jammed between haulers, squeezed into trailers, and spread out on tailgates in
the parking lot.

Nobody expects to hear "NASCAR" and "great food" in the same sentence. North American Stock Car Auto Racing is primarily about the other senses: the smell of fuel, the glare of blinding sun on a stock car's hood, the feel of sweat collecting under the bill of a baseball cap, the numbing sound of engines revving and tools clanging in the crew pit.

But the NASCAR tribe is on the move for some forty weeks of the year, from Lincoln's Birthday to Thanksgiving, traveling from the Budweiser Shootout at Daytona International Speedway to the Food City 500 in Bristol, Tennessee, to the Coca-Cola 600 in Charlotte, North Carolina, to the Subway Fresh 500 in Phoenix, Arizona, and on and on. One race really takes up an entire weekend, between settling in and the qualifying heats followed by the actual race and then breaking down the setup to travel to the next speedway. Nobody actually wants to eat hot dogs for three days straight, not the drivers, not the pit crew, not the scorers, not the mechanics—not when racing has become big business and drivers train like athletes.

This is a loud, noisy workplace on wheels, a migrant industry, and the hundreds of people who populate it are almost always hungry. In fact, NASCAR is all about meals. It is the home of the ham ball and the polka-dot salad, of a smoked quarter of a cow and a dessert table that won't quit, of high-carb, low-carb, and trucks full of

produce. Kitchens sprout in between the haulers that carry the cars or inside a tagalong trailer. They hook up to a power source, and then they move on.

"We're always in one of the corners in the NASCAR garage," shouts chef Ken Enck over the deafening roar of the track. "**If you look for the hardest place to find, you'll find us.** We're down here in the corner, right on turn three, up against the fence. You've got to know, to know where to find this kitchen."

Ken Enck's cooking crew feeds twenty-four racing teams three squares a day for the Nextel Cup drivers, owners, and crew—about two thousand people on any given weekend. He pays no attention to the chaos of cars and people around him as he rolls ham balls the size of lug nuts in preparation for the crew lunch.

"Today we have pork loin, roast turkey, chicken, ham, beef, and also steaks," says Ken. "Also pastas, 'cause some of the guys are pretty fond of their pastas. We have fresh fruit and assorted salads. Then we get to the dessert table. We have a lot of homemade desserts that we do, and we also buy some that are favorites of the different guys. We're looking at cheesecake, carrot cake, chocolate mousse, blueberry supreme, a chocolate supreme, a strawberry delight. A chocolate cake and some brownies and what we call 'pickup' cookies."

Ken, wearing a shirt displaying the names of his sponsors, surveys his kitchen kingdom. "Our sponsors furnish the products. Weber furnishes all our grills. Swift gives us our meats. We've got Jennie-O turkey, Papetti eggs, Peter Piper pickles, Coca-Cola, and Bush's baked beans. And our chicken sponsor is Pilgrim's Pride."

A WALKING MEAL

"I think people would be shocked to know how many grills, how many different meals, and how many people are eating in this racetrack," says Scott Riggs, who drives the number 10 Valvoline Chevy. "They're cooking outside the racetrack where everyone is in the parking lot doing tailgates; they're cooking in the pits. There's a lot of food getting cooked around here."

Riggs is no likelier to live on junk food than a star forward for an NBA team would be. "I'm thirty-three and I've been racing since I was thirteen. I eat approximately six meals a day. I eat about every three hours, which is what my trainer has me on. It takes a pretty good toll on us, anywhere between four and five hours in the race car under intense heat. You usually lose four to nine pounds in the cars."

A man who spends half a steamy workday wedged inside a race car had better be in shape, and that means good food and plenty of it. That's why there's stroganoff and baked ziti, smoked tenderloin and fresh fruit. That's why every team chef knows the special dishes his drivers and crew members like, which he's sure to have around at all times.

It wasn't always like this. Frank "Rebel" Mundy drove with the Jimmy Lynch Death Dodgers at the New York World's Fair in 1939 and 1940. He won the first night race in NASCAR history in its first year of operation, 1947, and he lays claim to cofounder status, alongside Big Bill French. Mundy, whose real name is Francisco Eduardo Menendez, raced all over the country, back when a sponsor was somebody who poured you a free cup of coffee. In the old days, he was as close to a NASCAR kitchen as the drivers and the crew members got.

"In those days you'd buy the food and make it in the motel room," says Mundy. "I used to get up in the morning and make about sixty or seventy sandwiches for the Roger Penske Team. Mainly tuna fish with a little curry. The curry does put a little tang to it. It was a hobby with me. I enjoyed it—and the boys ate better, because they didn't have time to go to a restaurant during the qualifying and pre-race. The only thing you could get at the concession was the hot dogs and stuff they handled—and that wasn't my desire. We made sandwiches and took them with us."

Once he got to the track, Frank set up an umbrella in the dusty pit to keep the tuna from spoiling in the sun. "I had to worry at each racetrack because of the heat. I was worried I'd make the whole crew sick. The boys'd come up, and I'd have the sandwiches on the table, and I'd put a piece of paper underneath each one to tell what was in that particular sandwich. It was strictly a walking meal."

A driver got to stand in the broiling sun eating a sandwich that, with luck, was on the safe side of healthy. In Rebel Mundy's day, that was about as fancy as a NASCAR meal got.

RACETRACK KITCHEN TRADITIONS

Buz McKim's office is just up and running again after two tornadoes hit Daytona and nearly tore up his archives. Buz is NASCAR's historic database coordinator. In his own words, he's the "resident history guy," and he carries the NASCAR stories around with him in his head.

Take Buck Baker, voted one of NASCAR's fifty greatest drivers, a three-time NASCAR champion. Buck cared about what he ate before there were grills and chefs and three different meats for dinner—and it nearly killed him, sort of.

"Back in the late '50s, he was one of the first ones to rig up a thermos system for racing, especially on the hot southern summer days," says McKim. "Buck had hooked up this thermos behind the seat, with a tube running to his mouth, and he would suck on the contents of the jug, which this day was iced tomato juice. Well, he was involved in a real bad accident, and he hit the rail, tore the car up, and the thermos split open. And one of the rescue workers ran up there to see how Buck was, and he ran back and said, 'Poor ol' Buck. He's a goner.' But it turned out to be just the tomato juice. Buck was fine. Wasn't hurt at all."

As the circuit grew, two things were clear: Racing was a dangerous sport, and not everyone was as lucky as Buck. The teams needed more than tuna sandwiches and trackside hot dogs to keep body and soul together. The racing wives formed an auxiliary in 1964, a fund-raising group created to raise money for injured drivers and their families, and they figured one good moneymaking project was a cookbook of racing wives' recipes. They put out a tenth anniversary cookbook in 1974 and a twenty-fifth anniversary book in 1989.

Racing got bigger, and so did the auxiliary's ambition. Now they raise money for major charities, as well as for their own individual communities, and they draw in their own corporate sponsors.

Buz McKim talks of the legendary breakfast feasts hosted by NASCAR great Junior Johnson and his wife, Flossie, whenever the circuit came to their hometown of North Wilkesboro, North Carolina.

Johnson won 310 Winston Cup events between 1959 and 1966, but he couldn't leave the track behind when he stopped competing.

Champion race car driver Junior Johnson was legendary for feeding the entire racing car community whenever they came through North Wilkesboro, North Carolina.

"Junior and Flossie, they didn't miss too many meals. They loved to eat, and she loved to cook. They would open up their house to the entire racing community. She would just cook hundreds of eggs—and grits, bacon, and sausage. It was one of the highlights of the season and a racetrack kitchen tradition." Junior's life is country ham now. He owns the largest country ham operation in North America. And Junior is still cooking, but now it's every morning for his farmhands instead of for his racetrack crew.

Now that NASCAR has gotten to be big business, the food comes to the track instead of the other way around. NASCAR is number two behind pro football, in terms of attendance and popularity, and closing fast—just the kind of place a sponsor wants to be.

A COMFORT FOOD POSITION

Jon Wheeler speaks not just of food but of "food and hospitality" when he describes his job for the Target/Chip Ganassi two-car Indy racing team. After working in restaurants and attending a culinary school in San Francisco, he catered for film crews on location. When he ended up on a shoot with actor/racing fan Paul Newman, he saw a new future for himself. Jon had loved the racetrack when he was a little boy, and he nursed a lingering affection for fast cars.

Jon's job involved not just cooking but talking to the film's stars about what they liked to eat, and he went to his first meeting with Paul Newman wearing a souvenir racetrack T-shirt. "I asked him about the different foods he wanted to eat, and he pointed at my shirt and said, 'I see you are a racing fan, huh?' I talked to him about having seen him at a race when I was a child . . . that started our initial conversation off. He mentioned that anytime I wanted to come by the trailer and talk about racing or food, 'There's the door,' and pointed at the door of his trailer." A few days later he told Wheeler that Chip Ganassi was looking for a chef for his team.

"It's kind of a comfort food position" is the way Wheeler describes it, "where you provide a break for these folks when they are traveling, doing their type of work." Wheeler's command central started as a large luxury bus, then morphed into a large bus with a trailer housing a kitchen and storage space, and now lately a fifty-three-foot semitrailer that has an office, restrooms, and a kitchen. With tents set up on both sides and temporary flooring, he can seat 120 to 130 people at a time. He can turn on the air-conditioning in the tents. He can get specialty items sent by FedEx or Air Freight. And he makes friends with local suppliers in every town NASCAR visits.

"I'll travel to an event on, say, Tuesday night, set up the trailer, the tents, and then pretty much do my gathering on Wednesday. In Milwaukee, there's a gentleman that I get my bratwurst from that makes them himself and drives down and delivers to just about every chef on the teams. He usually brings me some elk sausages and salamis that he makes. There are interesting food things in Wisconsin. **I keep a little black book**, and it's filled with my secret contacts for stone crabs in Florida, abalone in San Luis Obispo. I could look back and tell you what meal I made, what race, what year, where I bought the fish, how much I bought, and so on."

CHICKEN BOATS

Not too far from Jon's mobile kitchen, Leslie Britton has set up in her tiny kitchen between one of the truck cabs and trailers that hauls the Richard Childress Racing Team cars. Leslie coordinates all the travel for five race teams, scores and keeps the laps during the race, and cooks for the team. "I cook for the guys in a kitchen squeezed between the haulers," Leslie shouts over a wangy electric guitar blaring out of the speedway loudspeakers. "In between where the truck hooks to the trailer, there's a little section, about three feet. And we use that as our kitchen space. You're hidden. We like hiding back here."

Leslie steps inside the hauler and shuts out the noise of the track. "I go to the grocery store," she says. "It takes about five or six carts, about one thousand dollars, and I try to buy everything I possibly can for the whole weekend." Running out to the grocery store for the one item she forgot is not an option once the races have begun—with one hundred thousand people in the stands and their cars in the parking lots, there's just no way to navigate a quick dash to the market. So she buys big in advance, puts everything in freezer bags, and packs it with ice in the coolers. She gets her basics from the sponsors, but the perishables and the spices vary from town to town. Leslie's cuisine is a map of America.

"The different places where we go, like South Carolina, in the grocery store they have a local barbecue sauce. It's great. **The food tastes like the region.** Then we go up north, and the vegetables are so fresh, so you get that. Fresh corn. I always try and add a little flair." All Leslie needs is a grill, and she can turn out meat loaf, pork tenderloin, a casserole of macaroni and cheese, and anything else the team desires.

Leslie's signature dish is the chicken boat, so named because the filling sits in a scooped-out piece of bread that looks like a little boat. "The guys nicknamed it a chicken boat. I take a hard roll, cut out the

inside. It fits in the palm of your hand. I marinate chicken in fat-free Italian dressing, then I cook it on the grill; season it with some Lawry's; put it in my food processor with celery, onion, Duke's mayonnaise; cover it with hickory-smoked provolone cheese; and let it melt over the top. I serve it to them on their toolboxes—you know, they eat on those like tables."

NO PEANUTS AT THE TRACK

Race-car cooks have to build their menus around more than the drivers' likes and dislikes. "Everybody has their own superstitions and rituals," confides Ken Enck. "Some guys say you don't eat green. So we have to make them chili with red peppers instead of green peppers." Another superstition: no peanuts at the track.

"Peanuts for years were a major taboo around the racetrack, especially around the pit area," confirms NASCAR historian Buz McKim. "The story goes back to 1937 in Nashville. Somebody, as a joke, had sprinkled peanut shells over the hoods of the first five cars, and those five cars were involved in a horrible accident. And one of the drivers didn't make it. From then on, it was 'Boy, you don't want to be around peanuts.'"

Cynthia Lewis is with the Penske Racing South/Kodak Racing Team, working the same hot and dusty landscape as Ken and Leslie, and she bills herself as "co-truck driver and the mom and the cook for the team." She figures it's her job to keep the drivers and crew members healthy and happy, so she devises her menu with an eye toward the stress of the job. "You figure out a menu that you can fit into the day. Like, a qualifying day is a busy day. Race day, you want to give them something that's easy on their stomachs. A lot of them like to eat pasta because that way, when they are out there jumping over the walls, burning the calories, it makes for a better day. Sometimes you can make them a plain peanut butter and jelly sandwich, and that makes them happy.

Cotton Owens, toolbox dining.

"And you always keep the coffeepot going."

Leslie Britton loves the Sunday meal. "Sometimes the racetrack is the only place these guys get a good home-cooked meal. Actually, they spend more time on the racetrack and on the road than they do at home. A lot of the guys are single, and most of them don't cook. I've been cooking probably for ten years, and we're all just like a big family."

"Food brings the community of NASCAR together," says Ken, "because all the guys, the different teams mingle and socialize together. As far as I'm concerned, we're one big happy family. When they're out on the racetrack, they're fierce competitors, but when they're in our kitchen, they're friends dining with each other and talking racing."

Jon Wheeler remembers back to his first year cooking for the team. "Michael Andretti drove for us, and I got to know his father, Mario Andretti. He always had his pasta pomodoro with some fresh tomatoes and fresh basil. That was his standard dish. He coined the name Mama Jon for me because I prepared the food for the team and took care of everybody kind of like a mom. Being able to make something for Mario Andretti to eat was a highlight. And traveling around the country, feeding the entire racing team, from VIP types all the way to mechanics that have to work the long hours, it's kind of a dream come true and more."

Pasta Pomodoro Di Zanardi

Jon Wheeler, chef for the Target/Chip Ganassi Racing Team, says this recipe is a favorite of Mario Andretti, star racer of the 1970s. Jon uses spaghetti, but any pasta will do.

60	ripe Roma tomatoes
¾	cup olive oil
4	medium yellow onions, peeled and finely diced
3–4	heads garlic, peeled and minced
2	tablespoons dried oregano
2	tablespoons dried thyme
8	pounds dried Italian pasta
2	cups chopped fresh basil
	Kosher salt to taste
	Black pepper to taste
3–4	cups shredded Parmesan cheese

Cut the tomatoes in half and scoop out and discard the seeds. Dice the tomatoes and set aside.

In a large skillet, heat the oil over medium heat and sweat the onions. Add the garlic and cook for another minute, stirring constantly. Add the tomatoes, oregano, and thyme and cook for 4 to 5 minutes, stirring occasionally. Remove from the heat and set aside.

Bring a large pot of salted water to a boil. Add the pasta and cook until it is al dente. Drain the pasta and add to the tomatoes with the basil, salt, and pepper. Toss and serve.

Top with the Parmesan cheese.

MAKES 16 TO 20 SERVINGS (½ POUND PER SERVING)

HAM BALLS

3 **pounds freshly ground smoked ham**

¾–1 **pound fresh ground pork**

4 **eggs**

1½ **cups milk**

2 **cups bread crumbs**

SYRUP

½ **cup vinegar**

¾ **cup brown sugar**

1–2 **tablespoons mustard**

Ham Balls

Ken Enck and his crew were cooking for twenty-four teams at the Bristol racetrack in Virginia when he gave us this recipe for ham balls, the pride of his kitchen.

Preheat the oven to 350°F.

To make the ham balls, in a medium bowl, mix together the ham, pork, eggs, milk, and bread crumbs. Use your hands to roll into individual balls the size of golf balls or lug nuts (or you can shape into a loaf) and place on a straight-sided baking sheet. Place the baking sheet on the center rack of the oven and bake for 55 minutes.

To make the syrup, combine the vinegar, brown sugar, and mustard in a small saucepan. Cook over medium heat for 6 to 8 minutes, until the mixture has reduced to a thick syrup.

Remove the baking sheet from the oven and drizzle some syrup on the ham balls (that's what gives them their special flavor). Continue cooking for another 15 minutes or until done. Serve the remaining syrup with the finished dish.

MAKES 48 HAM BALLS

Racing Wives' Auxiliary Cookbooks

The Grand National Racing Wives' Auxiliary cookbooks include recipes for favorite race day and racing family dishes. The cookbooks are sold to raise money to aid families who are faced with the injury or death of a driver. Many of these original recipes reflect the cooking of the golden age of racing, from race day rump roast and busy day casserole to polka-dot salad.

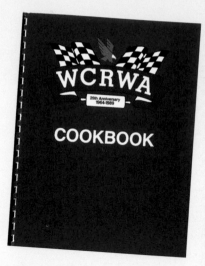

Clam Balls

From Mrs. Juda Rainer (Harry), Lexington, Kentucky

6   hard-cooked eggs, chopped

1   tablespoon minced chives

1   can (8 ounces) minced clams, drained

½   teaspoon salt

     Dash of black pepper

¼   cup mayonnaise

⅔   cup finely chopped peanuts

Combine eggs, chives, clams, salt, pepper, and mayonnaise. Shape into balls and roll them in the peanuts. Chill.

MAKES 36 BALLS

NOTE: You'll need to keep these balls cool on ice, especially if it's a hot day at the track.

Speed Balls

From Faye (Mrs. Ed) Negre, Car #8

1   pound hamburger

½   cup bread crumbs

½   cup milk

     Margarine

1   package onion soup mix

1   cup water

Mix together the hamburger, bread crumbs, and milk. Shape them into small balls.

In a large skillet over medium heat, melt some margarine and then add the meatballs and brown them. Stir in the onion soup mix and water. Mix gently so the meatballs don't break. Simmer 15 to 20 minutes, until cooked. Serve over brown rice.

MAKES 12 BALLS

SLAP IT ON THE THIGHS BUTTER BAR

Mrs. Stephanie Brooks (Dick)

1   box yellow cake mix
1   egg
1/2   cup margarine - melted

Mix all ingredients well until stiff. Press into greased and floured 13x9 inch pan. Push part way up the sides.

1   box powdered sugar
1   8 ounce package cream cheese
1   egg

Beat all ingredients well with mixer. Pour mixture into center of cake mix. Spread evenly. Bake at 350 degrees for 45 minutes. Cut into squares. *This is guaranteed to make you shop for a larger size!*

Woodruff, South Carolina

Dick received the 1969 Rookie of the Year honors. He is the last Winston Cup driver to win driving a Plymouth - Talladega 500 (1973)

The *Hidden Kitchens* hotline bulged with messages about cars and kitchens.

Assembly Line Kitchen

"Hi, my name is Marty Kapanowski, and I'm from Michigan. I'm calling about a hidden kitchen that I experienced about fifteen years ago. I used to work in a luxury car assembly plant for one of the American automakers. One time I missed lunch, and the cafeteria was closed. This one guy sort of grabbed me by the arm and pulled me aside and quietly led me down the assembly line. When we got to his toolbox, he opened it up, and inside was a heater, and there were brats cooking and steamed buns right there. **He pulled out a brat and put it on a bun**, and I bought it from him. And that was my lunch, just hidden right there in the middle, right in front of everyone's eyes, but you couldn't tell it was."

Last Night's Impromptu Truck Stop Buffet

"My name is Bob Stanton. I'd like to tell of a hidden 'nomadic' kitchen that forms among the itinerant professionals that make their living over the road—long-haul truck drivers. Usually, this kitchen begins in the back corner of a truck stop parking lot when a driver pulls out a grill that he keeps hidden in his toolbox. This is a special grill as most carriers do not allow drivers to carry charcoal grills, which they perceive as a fire hazard.

"He starts grilling the pork chops he purchased that morning, halfway across the country. As the smell begins spreading across the lot, other drivers gather to see what's cooking that night. One driver goes back to his truck and brings out barbecue sauce. Another driver says, 'Well, I've got eighty pounds of raisins.' Another one brings in his Tabasco and Cajun pepper. Quickly, an improvised mashed raisin, Tabasco, Cajun pepper glaze is tried on the pork chops, which turns out to be amazingly good. Potatoes, onions—**a make-do potluck dinner** begins. But the poor flatbed steel hauler, not having much food in his truck, laments he can't offer any food to this buffet. It is suggested, 'Well, build the table.' Pallets, load jacks, and other improvised lumber are found, and a buffet table springs up.

"Now, problems arise. First, the livestock truck with the pigs parks across the street upwind from the improvised buffet. A quick bribe gets the truck moved to the other side of the parking lot. Next, the truck stop manager appears. Trucking is a business, and the manager recognizes that the drivers eating in his parking lot for free are not coming into his restaurant to eat. He talks to the drivers, but it's apparent that they are not in the mood to move their potluck. Offers to fuel trucks for two or three thousand dollars before leaving appease the manager, and he leaves the impromptu buffet to go on unabated. The truckers gather around the grill, swapping stories of missed families, the storms they've weathered, the nomadic lifestyle of an over-the-road trucker.

"So, the next time you're merging onto the interstate, planning to cut off that eighteen-wheeler, think of last night's improvised truck stop buffet and go cook with the people in your life."

Work and food—you can't have one without the other. It's where most of us spend most of our lives. Some individuals and organizations are finding ways to bring their workforce together via the kitchen.

A Dirty, Grimy, Filthy Job

"Hello, Jay. Hello, Kitchen Sisters. My name is Heather Arney. My husband has been working for several years at a metal technology foundry in Three Rivers, Michigan. It is a dirty, grimy, filthy job. Miserable work, quite actually. But every Friday night, they bring food, recipes that wives have made or grandmothers have handed down, things that they have come up with themselves. It has become a tradition, something that makes it a little more bearable to work. It is a third-shift job, so it usually takes place between one and three o'clock in the morning, all these men coming together eating homemade food."

"Dear Sisters,

"The *Wired* Kitchen started in the early 1990s. *Wired* magazine was conceived as part of a media empire (remember those days?), and everyone was working long, late hours. There were very few places to eat in South Park, and so someone was brought in to make dinner. It eventually grew to three meals a day.

"Conceptually I think of this as a very high-style soup kitchen, although breakfast is two dollars and lunch is four dollars, and we feed about forty people a day.

"And everyone eats here—from the editor-in-chief to the newest intern—although not always on a daily basis (sometimes you just have to leave the building).

"The *Wired* Kitchen is here to let people feel taken care of on some small level."

—Philip Ferrato, Chef, *Wired* Magazine

"Dear Kitchen Sisters,

"Dan Moulthrop here. You've got me noticing things. Two days ago I was flying back to California from Ohio, and the crew on this America West flight were strikingly older in their appearance. It was like AARP airlines, with silver-haired flight attendants. I found myself chatting with the two coach-class attendants, Elizabeth and Kathleen, both in their late fifties, both from Phoenix, both former successful small-business owners, both in their third career here with America West, and both totally charming.

"Well, they told me, 'We buddy-bid for all our assignments, so we always work together. But we love this, and when we work, they give us a per diem, and we just save most of it because we almost never eat out. We pack these little frying pans—you know the ones with the little legs and you just plug them into the wall—and we just cook in our rooms, and we'll have dinner together, and oh, it's just great.' They met each other in training five years ago and have worked and dined on the road together ever since."

CALVIN STATHAM—
A FLOATING KITCHEN VISION

"They say that the heart of a ship is the kitchen. If you ain't got good food on a freighter, you got trouble."

Calvin Statham Sr. has been a steward on the Great Lakes going on thirty-three years. Right now, he's the head chef on the motor vessel Wolverine. "Lake freighters—they call them iron-ore carriers and stone carriers. They're over one thousand feet long, the length of three football fields. As far as you look, all you can see is ship."

Calvin meets the ship in Cleveland, in Sault Ste. Marie, or Milwaukee. And when he gets on, there's no turning back. "You work seven days a week, twelve hours a day. Sixty days on, thirty days off. When you're out on the water away from home for days and days, you look forward to a good meal.

"Freighter food, you just learn and learn from so many different people. In the cook business out here on the lakes, I have to wear about five different hats. Some days I got my Italian hat on; sometimes I got my Chinese hat on. You cook all different varieties for all different kinds of people."

Calvin Statham Sr. was born and raised in the small town of Fort Valley, Georgia. Now there are eight thousand people there. When he was coming up in the 1950s, it was half that number. In 1974 he joined the Merchant Marines. "I had two friends. They used to come home in the wintertime, and I asked them, 'What're you doing?' They said, 'We're cooking on the Great Lakes.' I said, 'Could you get me on?' About six months later I got on.

"When I went out on my first vessel, I got so seasick, I told the captain, 'The first piece of land you see, I'm going back to Georgia.' One of the guys said, 'Calvin you're so sick, you're turning white!' About six days later the captain came around and said, 'Calvin, here's your check.' And I said, 'No, you're making a mistake. This is too much money. I've only been here less than a week!' He said, 'Oh, yeah, this is all yours.' Well, guess what? After that first paycheck, I didn't get sick anymore, and I been out here ever since."

Freighters are like floating cities, and the galleys of the Great Lakes are the kitchens that feed the muscle that moves America. "We're moving seventy thousand tons of iron, twenty thousand tons of ore. Your car is made out of what we're hauling. The highway you're driving on is what the guy I'm cooking for loaded on board. We carry the first thing steel is made out of.

"Driving a ship is almost like driving a car," says Calvin. "You got stop signs, you got speeds. You go from Detroit River to Lake Huron, from St. Mary's River to Lake Superior. It gets rough sometimes, and I just put my seat belt on, and you'll see me standing at the stove trying to cook food, holding it from sliding from side to side. When storms come up, we got places we can run and hide. Devil's Island, Mackinaw Island, the straits, and the coves. You know, it gets very cold up here, and the Great Lakes freeze over in November and early December. That's when the lakes start really talking and getting very rough and ships have gone down and accidents have happened.

"Right now it's choppy from here to the end of the year. A lot of times you'll run into an unexpected storm and go to rolling. You try to keep about five thousand dollars' worth of food in stock in case you run and get caught in a storm or ice. When you're feeding twenty-some guys, it don't take long for ten thousand dollars' worth of food to go away. I got stuck in the ice for a whole week one time. Our food got so low I had to have a helicopter do a drop for us on the deck.

"They always call Lake Superior 'Gitche Gumee,' because it never gives up the dead. It's over thirteen hundred feet in some place, and we never recovered a ship out of Lake Superior, as far as I know. Back in 1975, I was behind the Edmund Fitzgerald when it sank. Twenty-nine of my friends was on it. I was only six hours behind that ship.

"Cooking just come easy in my family," says Calvin. "My father was a good cook, and my grandmother ran a barbecue café out of Byron, Georgia, for years. **You cannot be a calendar cook on the lakes**. That's the reason I think I got a pretty good reputation being a variety cook. A calendar cook, they know what you're gonna have Monday through Friday. You got to mix it up, whatever different ethnic background. I talk and mingle with the guys. I let them put their input. Sometimes guys say, 'But, Cal, my mama don't make it that way.' I say, 'Give me your grand-mama's recipe.' So next day I surprise him and take his favorite grandma's or mama's recipe out there to him, and that brings the biggest smile of joy on me."

Freighter recipes are legendary in the Cleveland area, and you see them printed in the *Plains Dealer* and other local and union newspapers. Incredible goulash and strudel, pierogi, chicken paprikash. This hearty working man's food made its way from Eastern Europe with the immigrants who came to work in the steel mills and on these freighters. Back then, the galley served five meals a day, and diets were heavy on meats. Old-time chefs can remember guys taking a line and tying it around a quarter of a beef and half a pig and hauling it aboard for the duration. All meals were prepared from scratch, and it wasn't unusual to see a big fireman eat six eggs and a half a pound of bacon for breakfast.

"A lot of them now like chicken stir-fry, and some of them are on the Atkins. But

we still serve a lot of things like spaghetti, beef stroganoff. For breakfast, hot cereal, eggs any style, pancakes (plain, blueberry, or buckwheat), bacon, sausage, ham, fried Spam, fried bologna. Fried bologna is a big seller. And I got this beef Wellington I make. Every ship I go on they say, 'Cal, when you gonna make that beef Wellington?' Beef Wellington is expensive, but sometimes I can slip it in, with that puff pastry crust around it, and they love when I put the butterfly flower roses between the crust and the meat. Thanksgiving and Christmas are our great meals. When I first started, Thanksgiving lasted almost a week on the ship. A lot of these folks aren't married; this is family. And the ones that been married for years still feel like newlyweds; they see their families so little."

As long as freighters have plied the Great Lakes, the mess hall and galley were the places where young seamen could listen and learn from their elders. Each and every one depends on his shipmate to stay alive out there, and the older ones show the young ones the ropes. Television has had a big impact on that time spent in conversation over the table. "It got to the point in the last few years," says a veteran seaman, "where I've seen workers kind of slow down so they could watch *The Young and the Restless.*"

When Calvin first started cooking on freighters, he served thirty-five men three meals every day. "Now I'm down to twenty-four. That's a big cut in the crew. When I started, we had five people in the galley; there's only two of us now. You got one guy working doing three guys' jobs. They're replacing people with machines. Automation have took something from me that I used to have pride in and I loved to do. Everywhere in America this is going on. We're getting away from what got us here. I'm an old country Georgia boy. I got to stay with what my father embedded in me. Everything I make now, there's a question behind it. Why? I want to make a scratch cake. They say no. Make a box cake, that's easy. **I'm home cooked, scratch cooking.**

"I always admired Donald Trump," says Calvin. "I always said I was going to be the first black Donald Trump of Georgia, come home and do for my neighborhood." Calvin has been brewing this plan for years now. He's had a lot of time to think about it on the lakes. "Real estate, beautifying, build nicer homes, places to stay, just inspire, you know." When Calvin is off the ship and home in Georgia, he takes out his truck, goes driving through the streets, and when he sees a can or some trash, he picks it up. "When I retire, I want to come back. I just want to rebuild it, make it beautiful again. Get the respect of the older people with the kids. I know what it used to be, and I just believe it can come back to that. It don't take that much. It's keeping it clean, taking pride. It's like cooking. I have been on inspection thirty-three years, and I've never hardly come in under one hundred percent when they came aboard my ship to inspect for cleanliness. That is my dream."

Last week out on the lake, up on Superior, Calvin and the crew were enjoying the northern lights, the aurora borealis, marveling at how beautiful it was, big sheets of greens, blues, and reds. The peace was refreshing; the quiet and the beauty and the water calm.

"When I have trouble sleeping," says Calvin, "I like to hear water. It's dangerous, it'll take your life, but it can make peace in your life. Freighter cooking has made me the man I am. For all these years I have been the only black on my ship. I give respect as strong as I receive it. It's just my life. If you be good to it, it'll be good to you."

Cranberry-Glazed Cornish Hens with Wild Rice

This recipe comes from Calvin Statham Sr. We found it in Paula McKenna's *Ships of the Great Lakes Cookbook*, a collection of stories, recipes, and photos—the bible of freighter food.

1   box Uncle Ben's long grain and wild rice, fast-cooking recipe

½   cup sliced celery

⅓   cup slivered almonds (optional)

1   can (8 ounces) jellied cranberry sauce, divided

4   Cornish game hens

2   tablespoons olive oil

Preheat the oven to 425°F.

Prepare the rice according to package directions. Stir in the celery, almonds (if using), and ½ of the cranberry sauce and let cool.

Spoon approximately ¾ cup rice mixture into the cavity of each hen. Tie the drumsticks together with string and place on a rack in a roasting pan. Brush each hen with oil. Roast for 35 to 45 minutes, or until the juices run clear, basting with oil occasionally.

Meanwhile, heat the remaining cranberry sauce in a small saucepan until melted.

Remove the hens from the oven. Remove and discard the string. Spoon the warm cranberry sauce over the hens.

MAKES 4 SERVINGS

Harvest on
Big Rice Lake

Nanabozhoo and Nokomiss harvest
the first wild rice in the New World,
Rabbet Strickland

Some hidden kitchens are seasonal. They show up when they are ready, and we have to be ready for them. On the White Earth reservation in northern Minnesota, the wild rice harvest begins when the rice is ripe. All that we can do is wait. As

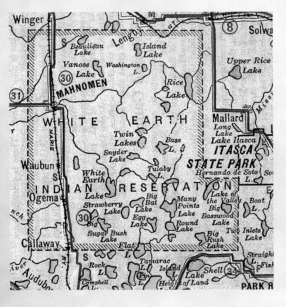

September approached, we'd been calling the White Earth Land Recovery Project for weeks, trying to zero in on when we should come to record the harvest. No one on the Ojibwe reservation would commit. It all depended on the rice.

When we finally got the word, we got on a plane to Fargo, North Dakota, and drove two hours northeast to the reservation in Minnesota in time for the harvest on Big Rice Lake.

The ricing season is short in northern Minnesota. It lasts maybe a month if the rain and cold weather hold off. Toward the end of August, the guys on the White Earth reservation start cruising by Big Rice Lake, Cash Lake, Lost Lake, Mitchell Dam, studying the stands of green rice growing in the shallows, plants so thick that it's hard to see the water. Everyone is waiting.

"The ricing moon, *Monomekaygeses*. That's what they call it here in the fall, in harvest season." Winona LaDuke looks out her kitchen window across Round Lake. "We've got a lot of rice on this reservation. It grows out there on the lakes like tall grass. We've got forty-seven lakes on this land, and who lives up here? Ojibwes and ducks!"

Winona's cabin is on the reservation, thirty miles from the nearest town. It's wet, green, boggy, and beautiful country, the headwaters of the Mississippi, with forests of pine and maple and not many people. A small patch of wild rice grows in the lake in front of Winona's place. It hasn't always been there. Some of her neighbors say it followed her when she came back. She just laughs and blames it on the ducks.

Winona LaDuke is a force to be reckoned with. A poster on the wall of her study shows her on horseback as part of her campaign for vice president on the Green Party ticket with Ralph Nader during his first bid for the presidency. Striking, with dark hair and pale eyes, she's confident, brilliant, funny, and busy—director of the White Earth Land Recovery Project, the mother of three, and raising her niece and nephew as well. Born in Los Angeles and raised in Oregon, she moved to White Earth, her father's reservation, after she graduated from Harvard in 1982. When she first arrived, she worked as the principal of the reservation's high school and immersed herself in local issues. Seven years later, she started the nonprofit White Earth Land Recovery Project (WELRP), an organization dedicated to restoring the local economy and food systems and preserving wild rice.

Winona LaDuke

There have been Ojibwes on this land since it was reserved under a treaty in 1867, one of nineteen Ojibwe reservations in the United States and about one hundred in Canada. Almost all of the tribes have wild rice growing on their lakes, and **wild rice laces through their history** and creation stories.

"Early prophets instructed Ojibwe to move west from the Eastern Seaboard to where the food grows on the lake," says Winona. "We found *Menomen* here—that's the Indian word for wild rice. And in a lot of ways, it defines what it is to be an Ojibwe people, because we're the ones who have that rice. All other native peoples elsewhere, they all know that we're the people with that rice.

"Wild rice is not actually rice," she explains. "It's a grass, and this is the only place in the whole world that grass grows. There used to be more of it all over the continent. Now it doesn't exist anywhere else. And this is really the center of biological diversity of wild rice. We have different strains of the grass growing on our lakes, each with slight variations, which helps ensure that if one strain fails in a season, the grass will not be completely wiped out. So this is the last place, right here. That is why we have to protect it. It's the native grain of North America."

"This is one of the biggest times in our community," says Winona. "As soon as the rice starts coming up in the spring and summer, there's bantering about which lakes look good and where they're going to go ricing. These guys are excited, really, to get rice for their family. And they're going to get to sell that rice. They'll make a couple grand, a lot of them. When you've got maybe sixty percent unemployment, that's a lot of money."

Ron Chilton, Winona's right-hand man on the White Earth Land Recovery Project, has seen a lot of rice in his time. "I ain't sayin' ricing is easy money, because it's not easy money. It's fast money. I put a lot of school clothes on my kids with rice money because it's that time of the year."

Ron's job title is sustainable project coordinator, but actually he's in charge of everything. Truly, everything: rice in the fall, strawberries in spring, the sugar bush in March, building solar greenhouses, constructing wind generators, planting gardens, delivering healthy food to the elders of the tribe. Ron is in his late forties and has five kids, three grandchildren, and another on the way. He's hardworking, with that droll Minnesota sense of humor, and he's been ricing every fall since he was a boy.

Ron steers his pickup down a back road and pulls in near the lake. The weather is cool; the skies are huge and moody. All around, the maple leaves and underbrush are ablaze with fall. "There you go," Ron says, pulling the canoe off the homemade wooden rack on his beat-up truck. "This is our ricing canoe. There are bigger ones, and there are better ones, but she's hauled a lot of rice in her day."

"You usually try to tie your canoe on the night before," Winona explains, describing the rituals of ricing for us. "The canoe being tied on securely is a sign of honor. If it falls off the car on the way to ricing, it's really a shame," she laughs. "You know if it falls off, someone will see you! Anyway, then you drive out there to your lake—you and your partner. You unload your canoe and drag it down to the shore, and it's already a workout. It's heavy and people are a lot more sedentary these days than they used to be. But a lot of these guys ricing on the reservation are pretty buff looking."

Ron drags the canoe to the water's edge and settles the boat. Before he gets in, he reaches into his pocket for a cigarette, crushes it in his fingers, and scatters the tobacco on the shore, a sacred traditional Ojibwe offering. "This is so we have a safe, dry, plentiful trip," he says, then gathers his gear and quickly balances his way into the boat.

"You get out there on the water, and it's misty. It's just this beautiful fog on the lake," Winona whispers, conjuring images with her words. "It's quiet. There's nothing except the birds. One guy stands in the back of the boat. He has a tall pole with a kind of fork on the bottom, about eighteen feet tall, made of cedar or some strong wood. Right in front is a person on their knees who's going to knock. And they have these two cedar sticks about thirty inches long, known as knockers. There are

Ron Chilton hears the harvest in our headphones.

a lot of jokes about that. *Bawa'iganoog* is their name, but everybody just calls them knockers, and then they laugh, you know. '**How's your knockers?**' A little Ojibwe humor."

Ron stands in back poling into the lake. The thick pasture of rice holds the canoe steady as he peers over the tall grass in search of brown hanging heads. Quietly he dips the pole into the water, hits bottom, and pulls. First one side. Then the other side. The canoe crawls through the rice.

"The person knocking the rice reaches out with one stick and bends the stalks of grain over the canoe, then sweeps the other stick across the heads. The ripe rice falls into the bottom of the canoe—tsst, tsst, tsst." Winona makes the light

tapping sound of grain hitting metal. "An armload of rice from one side of the canoe, an armload of rice from the other. Setting a steady pace, keeping a rhythm. Tsst, tsst, tsst. And if some falls into the water, that's better. You're reseeding the lake.

"The lake rice is diverse," says Winona. "Some looks like crow's feet. Some looks like a bottlebrush. That biodiversity is how the rice is able to hang on. It ripens at different times. So if you have a windstorm, it only blows off the green rice, leaving the red rice. One lake could get flooded and a crop wiped out, but the rice on another lake is okay because it's a little different variety that comes in later. That is how this rice has always been able to feed us.

"Now research universities and the paddy rice industry are domesticating varieties so the rice will be uniform and ripen at the same time. That's not a diverse crop; that's a mono crop. And they grow it in diked rice paddies, not on natural lakes. A lot of times they're using fungicides and chemicals, and they go in and harvest it with a combine. That is very different from two Indians in a canoe. They're trying to label it wild rice, but it's not wild rice. We call that tame rice, and it doesn't taste the same. **Our rice tastes like a lake. It tastes like a lake.**"

Ron's canoe carves a trail through the rice. The stalks "lay over" bent so that you can look back and see where you've been. It's peaceful hidden there in the tall grass with big, white swans flying overhead and river otters popping up all around.

"You try and be a little orderly about going through the rice because you don't want to make a mess of the lake, you know," Winona says. "You keep a rhythm. You've got the sound of the water lapping against the boat. You're talking kind of quietly and laughing sometimes, but it's a lot of work."

There are White Earth tribal members who are legendary ricers. Everyone knows who they are. They can harvest seven hundred pounds in a day to everyone else's three hundred pounds.

After several hours the canoe is heavy with a mountain of rice, and it's harder and harder to pole. "You bring your boat in," says Winona, "drag it up to shore, and lay the rice out to dry a little before you put it in gunnysacks and take it to the rice shed for finishing and then to sell. In harvest season, you can pick out the ricers on the road, their cars riding low with the weight of their load.

"For our guys, ricing is a way they get to be who they are," says Winona. "They're out there on the lake doing what they're really good at it. They know that. These guys come in, and they're all dusty and itchy, and they're happy. They really had a good day out there, and they feel proud."

WILD RICE ON THE LOWER EAST SIDE

Winona LaDuke traces her very life back to grain and poverty. Her Russian Jewish great-grandfather on her mother's side milled wheat in the Ukraine, until his windmill-driven business succumbed to a competitor with a power mill. Her grandparents immigrated to New York, which was where her mother, Betty, grew up and became an artist. Vincent LaDuke, Winona's father, was from a very traditional Ojibwe family up on the northern part of the White Earth reservation. He spent almost all his time in the woods.

"At one point my father became frustrated by what was happening on the reservation, the poverty and loss of tribal land," Winona says. "So he decided he was going to go sell wild rice in New York. He just took off in his old Indian car. I don't know how he got the idea, but he did. That's how he met my mother—selling wild rice on the streets of New York City forty-seven years ago. Isn't that strange how that works out? Forty years later, here I am selling rice and building windmills, doing the same thing as my dad and my mother's father."

Winona's parents eloped and drove across country to Los Angeles, where the westerns were being filmed. "He was a handsome guy," Winona laughs, "and he could ride a horse, and he looked like a real Indian, you know. So he was in all these westerns. That's what he did for a living. When I was little, my dad used to go hunting around Santa Barbara and Pasadena. We ate wild food all the time and wild rice from my dad's reservation."

When Winona first moved to White Earth, the price of wild rice was being driven down by the influx of cheaper paddy rice from California. She and Margaret Smith, now an eighty-seven-year-old tribal elder, got mad.

"You know, it's really hard knocking rice, and we thought they should give us a fair price. So Margaret and I, we'd go out there with our little bit of money hidden in our brassieres, and we'd offer the ricers more per pound. And those other guys bidding against us, they didn't know how much money we had. Kind of like

playing cards, like bluffing, you know—
we could have had a half a million dollars
as far as they knew. **Me and Margaret,
five thousand dollars stuck in our bras!**"

For the next four years Winona and
Margaret drove up the prices with their
little wad of bills. And Winona started
White Earth Land Recovery Project, not
only to improve the economics of the crop
for the tribe but also to protect the survival of wild rice itself.

"Our concern is that genetically modified rice is being grown in diked rice paddies in northern Minnesota," explains
Winona. "When they drain the paddies,
that modified rice seed goes into the public waterways and ends up in our lakes and
native rice stands. And we have a lot of

Margaret Smith and Winona LaDuke
received the Slow Food Biodiversity Award
in 2003 for their work with wild rice.

ducks up here—and they eat the rice. A duck cannot discern between paddy rice
and lake rice. So they carry the paddy rice to the lakes. That's how you get that rice
moving around. Over time the genetically modified rice starts crossing with the
native rice, and you get what they call nonshattering varieties. So a guy with traditional parching equipment cannot get the hull off or cannot get the rice to parch
right. So we are concerned about this contamination of our wild rice."

To Winona and to her tribal cohorts, wild rice is a historical food that deserves
preservation, just like the buildings around the country that footnote our past.
There are preservation associations to protect these landmarks from developers. The
White Earth Land Recovery Project set out to do the same for wild rice.

THE RICE SHED

The WELRP rice-processing shed is on a rutty dirt road about two miles off the paved highway, just past Winona's house on Round Lake. A hand-painted wooden sign at the turnoff says, "Native Harvest." A piece of board tacked at the bottom announces, "Buying Rice Today."

Old Impalas, pickups, and ancient Pontiacs line up outside the shed alongside the horse corral, their mufflers scraping under the weight of their rice sacks. On some days they're lined up all the way down to the gate waiting to sell. People find out by word of mouth. WELRP pays a good price, and they pay cash. Cash. That's a big incentive for people to do their rice processing with White Earth.

A stocky father and his teen-aged son pull in with three hundred pounds of rice in their trunk. The Chevy rides real low. In front of the shed, there's a big scale set up where the green rice is weighed. About one hundred sacks of green rice are piled just inside the shed, waiting to be finished.

Ron is in charge of the rice shed. His two sons, Mike and Eric, work there with him loading bags of rice. They all converge as the guys open up their trunk.

"Where ya been ricing?" Ron asks.

Ron Chilton and his sons, Eric (left) and Mike (middle), at the WELRP rice shed

You can sell your rice or pay to have it parched at the WELRP rice shed.

"Wild Lake and Blackburn," says the older man. Everyone stands around looking at the bags of rice for a long time. No one says much.

Ron opens one of the bags and scoops up a handful. "It ain't that small. That'll be a pretty good batch then. We're buying for a dollar a pound."

The ricer, Mike Levy, and his son load the bags on the scale. Between the two of them, they already have eight hundred pounds of finished rice stored at their house from this season. "We'll give some to relatives, we'll sell some, and we'll eat a lot," says Mike. "My wife has a thousand and one recipes for wild rice. She makes it with bacon and onions, with hamburger and mushroom soup, in salads. Hot dishes and cold dishes."

Mike began taking his son out ricing about four years ago. "He's still trying to out-rice me," Mike laughs. "He still can't do it. This old man can still out-rice him."

The boy speaks up. "Maybe when he's about sixty, I'll get him."

Mike Levy works nights as a security guard. In the summer he traps leeches and sells them to the fishermen for bait. "When leeching's done, ricing starts. After that, deer hunting and duck hunting. In the winter I trap and we'll take our fish house out on the frozen lake and we'll spear fish. Winter, I love winter. My wife is always getting mad because I like to go out hunting when it's blizzarding out. I always tell her it's a lot easier to sneak up on 'em."

The rice shed is loud. It's really loud. The old, beat-up tractor running the thrasher roars constantly. The motorized parching barrels are fired up and turning. Blowers scream, and rice dust fills the air. Out front, WELRP's old zebra-striped pickup truck revs its engine as it pulls a load of raw lumber to feed the fire that parches the rice.

"You know that old Johnny Cash song "I got a '47, '48, '49, '50 automobile?" asks Winona. "That's what that equipment is like down at the rice shed. Our crew patched the whole thing together out of thin air and spare parts. You got something that's been pieced together and made by five or six handy guys, and it's running off of a tractor. Our guys are handy."

LISTENING TO THE RICE

Pat Wichern loads three hundred pounds of rice into a large rotating barrel. He feeds oak and slabs of lumber into a steady fire burning underneath the big steel drum. Two metal paddles inside turn the rice so it doesn't burn on the bottom. This is wood-roasted, wood-parched wild rice.

Small and wiry, with large glasses and a long ponytail, Pat is focused on his job. "I can pretty much tell by the way the rice sounds in the barrel. When it's almost done, it makes a different noise, like a sizzling, hissing almost. Shhhhh, shhhhh, shhhhh. It's got that slap on the end when it falls over the paddle. When it's getting close, I just go stand by the barrel, and I listen to the rice."

Pat Wichern's job is sustainable communities coordinator assistant. "Or something like that," he says. "I'm the parcher. That's what we call it when you're cooking the rice. I cook on average eighteen hundred pounds a day, sometimes up to twenty-four hundred pounds."

Pat takes a long hand-carved stick with a small dipper lashed to the end. He reaches into the barrel and scoops out some rice. "If it gets too hot, it will pop. It looks like Rice Krispies. We call it popcorn rice. Then the whole batch is pretty much ruined."

Pat Wichern, The Parcher

This is Pat's eighth year parching rice. He used to live in Pipestone, making pipes for a while, but got tired of living in town. "I like it out in the country. When you're in town, you watch a lot of TV, and every time you want to go do something, it costs you money. Out here, if you want to go hunting or fishing, it don't cost you nothing.

"After about two weeks of cooking rice, **you see it in your sleep**," says Pat. "After twelve hours a day of this for three weeks, you know, you're ready to move on to corn or something." In the spring, during maple sugaring time, Pat is in charge of the draft horses that pull the stainless steel holding tanks by sled through the sugar bush. WELRP has a stand of maple trees that they tap for the syrup they sell along with their rice.

"We've got seasonal guys that help us during maple syruping," Pat says, "and we get people that help us pick the berries so we can make the jam to sell. A lot of people around here only work seasonal. They go from one job to the next, you know, with the seasons."

DANCING ON THE RICE

After Pat Wichern has parched the rice, it goes into a cooling box for about five minutes, and then Ed Barnett shovels it into the thrasher. Ed is a seasonal worker who works for WELRP during sugar mapling and comes on again at ricing time.

His thrashing machine is under a blue-tarp lean-to on the side of the ricing shed. It runs off an ancient tractor hooked up out front. Quiet and serious, with a thousand-watt smile, Ed feeds the rice through the thrasher for about five minutes a batch.

"A long time ago and still some today," Ed remembers, "people used to dance on their rice, you know, in their new moccasins. That was how they thrashed the rice back then to get the chaff, the hulls.

"When I was growing up," says Ed, "the whole community would get together to go out ricing, and it would be like a caravan. Everybody would just come right to the lake and help each other getting their boats out. The older women would fix meals on the shore for the workers. And it was something to see—the young helping the old and the old teaching the young how to do it through the whole process of gathering, harvesting, feasting."

Ricing season at Mitchell Dam, 1960s

FEASTING FOOD

Down at the rice shed, Winona has set up a little wild rice feast for the workers: rice and maple syrup cake she's been experimenting with and a casserole that fills a quart roaster oven. "Here in Minnesota, they call everything a darn hot dish," she laughs. "I just put together wild rice, some squash that I grew, and our buffalo meat. You know, a hot dish.

"With each new season we feast our foods. In the fall we have another ceremony when we do our corn and another when we do our syruping." At the feast, there is a prayer, and tobacco is offered.

"**It's not just about the food**," Winona explains. "You have to reaffirm your relationship to the creator by your singing and your dancing and your feasting and your harvesting. And it's not like a once-a-week thing. It's how you live your life."

Winona LaDuke and her ever-expanding tribe of collaborators have built the Land Recovery Project around the seasons of their region. "In a community that's one of the poorest counties in the state of Minnesota," says Winona. "I didn't want to try to bring some factory onto my reservation. They are always training and retraining our people for jobs that don't exist. And these guys go and try to work in a border town. They cannot get hired and are made to feel like they are not any good. So instead of trying to make up some economy that makes no sense to us at all, we decided to develop something that we're good at. And we're good at ricing, maple sugaring, hunting, farming.

"Our wild rice is the centerpiece of our culture, but what we're talking about here is how you get healthy. Your body and your community, they're all related. It's not something that you can go buy at the store, you know, your culture. You have to live it."

SUN BEAR AND WINONA

"When my dad, Vincent LaDuke, was selling wild rice in New York," Winona told us, "he met my mother, Betty, who was this really stunning artist living in a loft. She painted big paintings, and she was hanging out with all the hip, radical artists and socialists. And they fell in love. And my mom's Jewish parents didn't understand what my father was. 'He's not a goy. He's not a Jew. What is he?'

"So they ran off to Los Angeles, and my dad became a Hollywood Indian acting in the westerns.

"My dad had a gift. It was a spiritual gift, and a lot of people were looking for

Sunbear and Winona 1960 Betty LADuke

something at that time. And he became a New Age spiritual leader known as Sun Bear. He had an eighth-grade education, but he had this huge following of people that came out of California and then all across the country. He just believed that people should get back in touch with the earth. He had a set of teachings, and his teachings were kind of Ojibwe based. And he had this one saying that I always use. He said, 'I don't want to hear your philosophy if it doesn't grow corn.' And, he was right. He was saying to all these people with esoteric philosophies, 'Straighten up, you guys. Grow food.'"

Wild Rice

With its highly textured, uneven grain, caramel color, and nutty smell, wild rice is wildly different from "paddy," or commercially available, rice. "My wife has a thousand and one recipes for it, so I eat it every way," says ricer Mike Levy.

The following recipe for simple wild rice is from Native Harvest. As a rule of thumb, wild rice will triple in volume when cooked. For added savory flavor, you can substitute beef or chicken broth for the water.

1	**cup wild rice**
3	**cups water or stock**
½–1	**teaspoon salt**

Rinse the wild rice in three changes of hot tap water.

In a saucepan over high heat, bring the wild rice, water or stock, and salt to a boil. Reduce heat and cover. Simmer until the wild rice has absorbed the water, about 20 minutes.

MAKES 3 CUPS

Wild Rice Hot Dish

Hot dish is the essential Minnesotan casserole comfort food brought by Scandinavian immigrants in the 1900s. It's a dish with endless themes and variations, depending on what is in season, what has been caught or trapped, what's available through the government surplus food service program, or what's on your kitchen shelf—from fresh corn and peas to wild buffalo and frozen Tater Tots. In this Native Harvest recipe, this Scandinavian tradition meets the ricing tradition of the Ojibwe tribe.

1	cup wild rice
2–3	tablespoons oil
1	pound pork steak, diced
½	pound veal steak, diced
1	cup chopped onion
1	cup diced celery
1	can cream of mushroom soup
2	tablespoons soy sauce
1	cup sliced fresh mushrooms
1	can water or milk

Preheat the oven to 350°F.

Cover the rice with hot water and let it stand for 20 minutes.

Meanwhile, add the oil to a large sauté pan, and over medium heat, brown the pork and veal together. Remove from the heat and set aside.

Drain the rice and place it in a medium-size bowl. Add the pork, veal, onion, celery, soup, soy sauce, mushrooms, and water or milk and stir until blended.

Pour into a casserole dish and bake for 2 hours, or until golden brown.

MAKES 6 SERVINGS

Wild Rice Stuffing

1 cup wild rice

3 cups chicken broth

½ cup butter or margarine

1 cup diced celery

¼ cup minced onion

⅓ pound mushrooms, sliced

⅓ teaspoon salt

¼ teaspoon sage

¼ teaspoon thyme

Rinse the wild rice in three changes of hot tap water.

In a saucepan over high heat, bring the wild rice and chicken broth to a boil. Reduce the heat and cover. Simmer until the wild rice has absorbed the broth, about 20 minutes. Fluff with a fork and let it cool.

In a large pan over medium heat, melt the butter or margarine. Sauté the celery, onion, and mushrooms for 2 to 3 minutes until tender. Stir in the rice, salt, sage, and thyme. Let cool.

Stuff in the cavity of the turkey, chicken, or buffalo roll.

MAKES 3 CUPS, OR ENOUGH TO STUFF A 10-POUND TURKEY

Two Indians in a canoe

FLORENCE GOODMAN—
A TRIBAL KITCHEN VISION

The guys from the rice shed shuffle around on the porch of the Native Harvest store, smoking and joking in the early-morning drizzle. They've come down before work to muscle Florence's new one-thousand-pound stainless steel jelly-making machine into the kitchen. Florence Goodman, wearing jeans and a crooked smile, watches from the doorway as the guys, grunting and groaning, using sheer brute strength with no ropes or dollies, inch the mother-of-all-jelly-machines off the bed of the pickup and onto the wooden porch. It's old and it's used, but it works, said the guy up in Duluth who sold it to them.

Usually quiet and soft-spoken, Florence lights up at the idea of having a new machine in her kitchen. "I make jams and jellies, and I experiment a lot. Cranberry-plum jelly, that's a mixture. Plum-chokecherry. There's cranberry-chokecherry. I get my ideas from my taste."

In her sixties, with a smooth, wide face and soft, dark hair clipped back, Florence is the Native Harvest coordinator for White Earth Land Recovery Project. "I never meant to be a cook," she says. "I was never interested until they gave me a kitchen where I could be like a mad scientist."

Florence has had a string of jobs in her life—teacher's aide, nurse's aide. "When I first started here, I was a cleaning lady," she says. "Then I got to be the head of the garden. I hated to come inside. I hated to go work in the kitchen. But I learned how. I enjoy it more now. Kitchen work isn't as bad as I thought it would be, and I get to experiment.

"We buy from people on the reservation. People that need money. They'll go out and pick chokecherries, plums, whatever, and come sell them to us. We put a sign up: 'Buying Berries,' 'Buying Rice,' Buying This, Buying That. Then it's word of mouth.

"When I first started, I worked until three o'clock in the morning because I had to come up with three hundred jars of jam the next day so it could all go out to our mail-order customers. Between Thanksgiving and Christmas, it gets real busy."

Native Harvest sells Florence's jams made with honey along with wild rice, buffalo sausage, fry bread mix, hominy, birch bark baskets, and other Ojibwe crafts. The store with its community room and kitchen is on Round Lake, off a long stretch of empty highway thirty-five miles from the nearest town. But they have an online store that reaches the world.

Native Harvest is part store, part meeting room, part industrial-size kitchen. "The guys put in everything—all the big convection ovens, the big stove and blowers—and brought it up to code.

"We have a big kitchen, and already we are outgrowing it," says Florence. "We get restaurant orders, and we have a program for elder diabetics that we give good healthy food to. The health on the reservation isn't very good. So my job means a lot to me, you know, giving healthy food. The Native Harvest kitchen is free to tribal members who want to use it to make their own products to sell.

"The thing about this place is if you have a good idea, you can make it come true. They let you do that. You know, usually in a company just big people get their ideas in, but no matter who comes in, if they have a good idea, they get a chance to make it work. If you are interested, there are opportunities. Like, I wanted to go to art school, and I couldn't afford it. But here they have grant workshops and mentors. So I'm applying for a scholarship."

Florence is working on her scholarship, but right now it's the middle of chokecherry season, which is the same time as the ricing season. And the plums and cranberries are coming in. Enormous pots of jam simmer on the stove, and the walk-in freezer is overflowing.

When we went on air with *Hidden Kitchens*, we asked people what kitchen traditions were disappearing from their neighborhoods, their lives, from the planet. We never imagined that home cooking would show up on the endangered species list, but it did, in dozens of messages and in all kinds of ways.

No Measuring Cups or Spoons

"Hello. I am Barbara Rowland. I have been teaching foods and nutrition at Stadium High School in Tacoma for thirty-five years. In my classes I always require my students to cook something at home. In the last few years I've noticed that many students say they can't do the assignment. They have no measuring spoons or cups, or other kitchen tools in their homes. So I buy the equipment and send it home with them so they can cook. One girl in the class came to me and said she had never had a home-cooked meal. All the food her family eats comes from the deli. Somebody picks it up on the way home every day.

"The generation that just passed through my classes will sit around when they are old and remember fondly Tortino's frozen pizzas and Pepito's microwave burritos. They will not be remembering how Mama's house smelled with a pork roast cooking. We are losing generations of food memories—of what Gramma cooked, childhood memories of the house smelling good. Every day, cooking and the eating of good food at home is truly becoming a lost art. I think American culture ought to take a second look at that."

Iowa on a State of Emergency

"This is Lisa Stone. You mentioned wanting to know about things that are disappearing. The one thing that springs to mind is flavor. Along those lines, I would put the State of Iowa on a state of emergency for being able to find good food while on the road, but that's becoming the case everywhere. Our country's food has become so homogeneous, so bland. There are some tremendous exceptions to this, but mainly, it's true. And that loss of variety and flavor in food is something I mourn."

Very Cold War-ish

"Hi. This is Mitch Downing. The hidden kitchens I'm thinking about are on the Nevada test site. There are two kitchens: one in Mercury and the other is a very tiny kitchen/cafeteria at a location called CG-1. Both of them are very 'Cold War-ish' and very different. Accessibility may be an issue because they are government installations, but they do give tours. As a person from the younger generation, it gives me a feeling of what it was like back in the heyday when the test site had some thirty thousand people working there. Now it is much more like a ghost town. It is a part of history that is going to go away."

Jumping into Other People's Kitchens

"Hello. My name is Katie Bowles. I think you should do a story on my father, Craig Bowles. He is a small farmer in southeast Nebraska. He farms the same ground that his great-grandpa farmed. He is the kind of guy that is disappearing. We are moving away from getting food that was created by farmers who want to feed the world, and moving toward a system where the Wal-Marts and the manufacturers want to produce a product that is not necessarily nutritious.

"If my dad has said it once, he's said it a million times: He wouldn't mind growing corn for 1940 prices if he knew that every kid went to bed with a stomach full. And Wal-Mart doesn't care. That's why I have become an anti-hunger advocate and work with a Congressional Hunger Center and the Nebraska Appleseed Center. I think you should talk to my dad about showing people where their soybeans come from and how they should be produced before you think about jumping into people's kitchens."

Message #419 was received Friday at 11:46 PM

"My name is Makayla Shannon, and I'm calling from Denver, Colorado. I think I have a great story for your project. I'm not exactly sure what you would call it—maybe 'Hippie Kitchens' or 'Concert Kitchens.' They are definitely endangered, and they are found primarily at Phish shows or Grateful Dead shows. They consist of mostly vegetarian fare that hippies make on their own camp stoves in the parking lot and sell for cheap to hungry concertgoers. Things like 'Jerry Rolls' or grilled cheese, and my personal favorite is veggie burritos. The reason I think this is going extinct—and I've been to lots of shows, and I've really only seen it at Phish shows and the Dead, probably Bono and U2—is that Phish is no longer going to be around and the Dead doesn't tour so much any-more. And I just felt like they are endangered and they are really an integral part of concerts.

"It's truly amazing what some of these people do with just a camp stove. Probably a great place to chronicle the Hippie Kitchen would be at the Phish Festival in Vermont. The show is sold out, but I'm going, so if you'd be interested, I would be very happy to help you out."

Loving Ovens

"Hi, my name is Jeffrey Pitts. I know about some hidden kitchens that most every-body in America has no idea about. It all started at Woodstock. Every year since then, the counterculture in America—young kids and old hippies—all get together all over the United States, like a bunch of traveling gypsies, and they operate free kitchens and camp out in the national forests. Once a year they get together on the

4th of July, and they have a national meeting. There are as many as thirty or forty kitchens, cooking free food. The kitchens are usually a big bunch of tarps over some trees, and they build mud and rock ovens, and it is mostly vegetarian food and even vegan food. There are some kitchens that cook nothing but desserts and some that bake bread. They have names like 'Loving Ovens,' 'Tea Time,' or 'Coffee, Coffee'—hundreds of them."

Rainbow Kitchens

"Hello. I'd like to tell you about one of the most remarkable of hidden kitchens. There is an organization called Rainbow that splits the country up into fifteen regions, and each of those regions has a gathering in a national forest in their region once a year, and we feed everybody that shows up for free. The people come from a wide range of backgrounds, lifestyles, and value systems. You would think that an organization that is so beneficial would be something that would be embraced. But the reaction of the authorities is to try to shut down and make difficult the whole process of presenting these gatherings and having a safe place for people who are disenchanted with the regular lifestyle and goals in this society. The Forest Service has set up regulations specifically aimed at restricting and making these gatherings illegal. You might want to show up and help in this very noble effort. Thank you for your attention."

Burgoo
Mopping the Mutton

Message #4 was received Friday at 9:20 AM

"Hi, this is Ellen Birkett Morris. I'm calling about a Kentucky tradition, burgoo, which is a frontier stew they cook at the Kentucky Colonel's barbecue at the Kentucky Derby that raises money for good causes. There are ladies in fancy hats sippin' ice tea, old guys wearing really loud jackets. The governor is always on hand, greeting people and working the crowd. The fellow who puts together the thing every year is Billy Hearst, and he's over eighty years old. He was a hog farmer over in Nelson County. They begin cooking the burgoo in huge pots the night before. They stand there and stir all night long, and they know they are going to have a particularly good batch of burgoo when the cooking crew hears a plop in the middle of the night. Legend has it that there is a nest of black snakes in the trees above the kettles, and from time to time one of the snakes will climb out onto a limb to get a whiff of the stew and actually fall in."

Burgoo? That was a new one on us. And Ellen wasn't the only one calling the *Hidden Kitchens* hotline about it.

Message #36 was received Sunday at 9:40 AM

"Good morning, my name is Nancy Penrod. I was raised in Owensboro, Kentucky, on the Ohio River, and my deepest food memory is the Catholic Church burgoo picnics in the summer. Burgoo, B-U-R-G-O-O, served with barbecued mutton and chicken on the side. They cook the burgoo in big kettles and barbecue the meat in long pits all night long. Saint So-and-So's would have the picnic one weekend, Saint Somebody Else the next time, Our Blessed Mother the weekend after that, and it goes on all summer. No kidding. You need to go. Bye."

After the fifth burgoo message we figured this was a tradition to reckon with. Since we had already missed the Kentucky Derby, we called Nancy Penrod to thank her for the tip and tell her we were headed to Owensboro to make the parish picnic circuit. She said, "Hold everything, girls. If you get here next week, there are three burgoo events in one weekend. I'll pick you up at the airport and get you there. Meet me outside of Baggage. I'll be the blonde in the blue Expedition."

Nancy Penrod, a grandmother, a retired public health nurse, a cattlewoman, and a devoted public radio listener, became our guide for the weekend, leading us to the churchyards and fire pits of her hometown—to the story of a community stew that goes as far back as anyone can remember.

Cart for hauling gallon jugs of burgoo from the burgoo barn to the sales stands

The Expedition plies through the warm summer night. Nancy peers into the darkness. "Okay, it's somewhere off Highlands Drive across from the prison. You sisters see a sign for Highlands?" Nancy checks her notes. "We got a ways to go."

The neighborhoods roll by. Low, sturdy brick houses with nice lawns and cement backyards with swing sets and metal lawn furniture. Package liquor stores, elementary schools, car dealerships. All is quiet in this corner of western Kentucky, except for the huge glowing bonfire we pass, higher than a house, blazing and mys-terious. "Oh, they're cranking it up at Blessed Mother," Nancy says. "We'll head back here in a while."

"What do I remember?" she muses as we drive. "I remember the people cooking all night long and the fire and smoke, eating standing up off of two-by-twelves strung between trees, thick aromatic burgoo served in little cardboard boats with spicy barbecued mutton sandwiches on the side, lots of people that you hadn't seen since last year. It was the whole Catholic picnic tradition that was kind

Nancy Penrod called the NPR *Hidden Kitchens* hotline and demanded we come to Kentucky to delve into the mysteries of burgoo.

of like the glue that held that community together, and I'm not even Catholic!'"

On the outskirts of Owensboro, a hand-painted sign just off Highway 60 looms large in the headlights: "Burgoo—This Saturday—St. Pius X Cooking Team—Chickens $6.00." Nancy makes a hard right and guns it up the hill. "Now these guys here," she tells us in a low, confidential voice as we park the car and crank up the levels on our tape recorder, "they're kind of controversial. They do not stir their burgoo by hand."

3:30 AM, SATURDAY: ST. PIUS X PARISH

At the top of the rise, country music and light pour out of St. Pius X's burgoo barn, a shed constructed of aluminum that shelters a massive industrial kitchen customized for the cooking of one dish and one dish alone: burgoo. Men and meat mingle in the whirr of twelve huge cauldrons equipped with motorized stirring paddles.

"Hey, ladies! You found us!" shouts L. K. Burcham over the roar of mixers and grinders. "Let's get you some coffee, and I'll show you around." Mr. Burcham, a creased, kindly grandfather type wearing a red St. Pius X Cooking Team trucker hat, is in charge of the burgoo crew. It takes about nine hours to make a batch of burgoo, so it's not something you do alone if you can help it. You do it with your tribe or your crew, for your parish. This morning L.K. is overseeing about thirty guys who are cooking to help raise funds for the church.

Burgoo. The word belongs to western Kentucky, where the Ohio and Mississippi Rivers come together. It leaks across the river into Indiana and Illinois, sometimes traveling under other names, immigrating with Kentuckians and pioneers as they made their way north and west. "Most everybody has a regional soup," L.K. explains. "South of here they call it Brunswick stew. Over in Indiana and a little bit north you have turtle soup. Burgoo is ours. It's a slow-cooked stew that used to be made from what people had left over in the garden, vegetable-wise—tomatoes, okra, cabbage, corn—and what they caught or killed meat-wise—squirrel, deer, turkey, quail, anything that had legs or wings probably. Today, people mostly make it with a variety of vegetables and some tomato sauce stewed with ground-up boiled mutton and chicken. But our exact recipe's a secret here at Pius X."

The St. Pius X Cooking Team has been around for more than fifty years, and they cook almost every weekend to raise funds for the church or some needy cause. Mostly made up of successful retired local businessmen, as well as some younger working guys who have been "grandfathered" in, the crew has the clean-cut look of an Elks or Rotary Club devoted to stewing and grilling.

"These are our automated kettles," L.K. tells us as we peer into a vat of simmering red stew. "As of right now, we've just got our tomatoes and our beans in. We use Great Northern and limas. A lot of people don't agree with putting in limas," he laughs, "but that's what makes our burgoo the best. The ground-up

boiled meat is the last thing we put in it, then you'll really taste something."

The brightly lit shed houses a predawn frenzy of activity. Working at a high stainless steel table in the middle of the room, one man labors over boiled mutton next to a father and his young son, who are pulling apart boiled chickens that will soon be ground up and put into the stew. Near the burgoo pots, a fast-moving guy in a green apron has just finished grinding thirty heads of cabbage in an industrial-size electric grinder, and now he's moving on to potatoes. There are men washing vegetables, stacking containers, and emptying big barrels of garbage. Wrapped in our recording equipment with cords and wires dangling, we bob and weave to stay out of the line of traffic.

Every parish has its own theme and variation on this stew, and the burgoo battles have been raging for years. Debating the best recipe is as much a part of the tradition as making the stew. Walter Estes, an early bird who has dropped by the cooking shed to watch the action, pipes in. "It's like the difference in your wife's cake and your mother-in-law's cake and a cake at the store. Same is true of burgoo. Some is just a little smoother; some is mushy; some has more textured meat in it. Some has more visible corn or lima beans. Everybody thinks theirs is the best."

Charlie McKay, lively and good-humored even at 4:00 AM, is on duty watching over the waist-high vats of burgoo. A rotor suspended from the ceiling continuously sloshes the concoction. "If you don't stir burgoo, it will scorch in a heartbeat," he tells us. According to Charlie, St. Pius stopped hand-stirring about ten years ago, when a mechanically inclined parishioner got the big idea to automate, setting up paddles on rotors, enabling St. Pius to crank out more burgoo with less manpower. "We used to have to stand there all night long and stir by hand." Charlie points up at the retired eight-foot wooden stirring paddles hanging from the rafters, the ghosts of burgoo past. "Yep, that's how we stirred in the good old days. The guys at most of the other churches still do it that way and claim that the old ways are best. We know otherwise."

The Pius X Cooking Team is renowned in the parish picnic world. They're "grand champs" in the annual downtown Owensboro competition, with ribbons and trophies for burgoo and barbecue plastered and placed all around the edges of the burgoo barn, anyplace that won't get spattered.

Each year Owensboro kicks off the summer picnic season with a cutthroat community barbecue and burgoo competition in the middle of downtown. All along the main street cooking teams set up row upon row of portable barbecue pits. Last year some seven cooking teams competed for the Governor's Cup, including St. Pius X, Blessed Mother, Precious Blood, and Our Lady of Lourdes. The trophy goes back and forth between the teams year after year, and everyone in town knows the score.

In Owensboro, **where there are men stirring burgoo, there are men grilling meat.** We walk outside the barn and up the hill past the baseball diamond toward St. Pius's one-hundred-foot barbecue pits. The sky glows red as flames shoot up around the edges of a high tin roof. These are St. Pius's permanent pits, solidly built of brick with a shed roof to contain the flames and protect them in winter. A small group of men silhouetted in the glow from the pits, wield hoses to control the fire as cords of sassafras and hickory burn down to hot embers.

Danny Morris—lean, ruddy, and thoughtful looking—drinks a beer as he sprays big arcs of water onto the hot fire. "We just do it for the parish, and we do a lot of

Danny Morris tends the pits at St. Pius X.

charity," Danny says. "We'll take the chickens and burgoo down to the stand we have at the bottom of the hill here on Highway 60, and people will drive by and pick them up, and we always sell out. Today the money's going to the Boy Scouts and to buy flowers for the church. And Father Richard bought one kettle for the prisoners across the road." Redemption in a kettle. Even prisoners need to eat the local stew. It's part of who you are if you're part of Owensboro.

The Kitchen Sisters with the St. Pius X burgoo mobile

It's dark and quiet except for a train far in the distance and the crackling and hiss of the flames. "I've been doing this here for twenty-five years, I guess," Danny thinks back. "My dad used to take me with him when I was a small child to work at the picnics up there at Whitesville. We did the same things we're doing now—build fires, barbecue meat, and cook burgoo."

5:30 AM: BLESSED MOTHER PARISH

Nancy winds us through sleeping Owensboro toward the flames we had seen earlier. It's flat here. River-bottom country.

Near downtown, smack in the middle of a residential neighborhood, the Blessed Mother fire pits are blazing. Cars are lined up for blocks, and the burgoo barn next to the Catholic church is buzzing. Today is Blessed Mother's big annual fund-raising barbecue burgoo feed and carnival. In the early-morning light, a few guys are already hammering together booths in the parking lot. Later in the afternoon, they tell us, this whole area will be packed with people—"it'll be so crowded that you won't be able to move."

Inside the burgoo barn, Danny Thomas is already five hours into stirring and can barely move his arms, but he's not complaining. Danny, a small farm-boyish-looking guy in his early thirties, has been in charge of the burgoo crew for nine years. His father, who taught him the secrets of the stew, cooked at Blessed Mother for thirty years before him. "Here at Blessed Mother we stir the burgoo by hand," he tells us, "mainly for the fellowship, people being together, standing side by side. A fellowship of stirring. We have seventy-five-gallon kettles, each about fifteen feet apart. They are all fired with hardwood. It gets very hot in here—a lot of smoke—but you have to keep on stirring for as long as it takes, about nine or ten hours total." **One man, one pot.**

If you don't stir burgoo constantly, it will scorch in a heartbeat.

Flipping chickens and parboiling mutton at Blessed Mother

At Blessed Mother they stir burgoo the way it's been done for one hundred years—with long oarlike paddles that make a ninety-degree turn at the top of the kettle and jut out about five feet so that the man stirring can stand back away from the heat. "There are roughly seventy-five people working on burgoo in this barn and another thirty outside grilling meat," says Danny. "We'll be cooking about twelve hundred gallons of burgoo, twenty-five hundred pounds of mutton, one thousand pounds of pork, and eight hundred chickens."

Outside, the sweet smell of hickory wood and mutton clogs the fresh morning air. On the grassy area by the side of the church are the barbecue pits covered with an endless sea of mutton, chicken, and a cut of pork they call Boston butt. These are portable pits, grills set up on stands with sheets of corrugated steel around the bottoms. The guys put them up each year in the middle of the night, and by dinnertime the next day they're gone, with nothing left but smoldering ashes and burnt

Mopping the mutton

lawn. Manning the pits is dangerous work. One year a new guy fainted from the heat. Another year they melted the vinyl siding on the parish hall. Still everyone kept right on cooking.

The Blessed Mother Cooking Team is made up of big athletic guys in their forties and fifties who have kind of a rugged, beer-drinking look about them. They wear black-and-white "Blessed Mother Cooking Team" bowling shirts. These guys are well aware of the trophy now sitting over in St. Pius's burgoo barn and will be the first to tell you that they plan to take it away from them in next year's competition. Some of these guys barbecue almost every weekend during the long, warm summer, not just for the church but also for other causes—the volunteer fire department, their kids' sports teams.

Bob Newman is the grilling captain. "This team right here has been together for about twenty-five years," he tells us, peering through the smoke at several men who are expertly flipping sets of enormous flat grates, one on top of the other, with thirty-two chickens sandwiched in between them. These are tight partnerships, real moments of trust and dependence. You rely on the guy across from you to lift and flip the rack in unison without chickens flying all over the coals or the lawn—or over the person flipping.

"After your first year, you know what you want to do—mutton or chicken," Newman tells us. **"The mutton guys, they eat a lot of smoke.** They have to bend over the pit, and it gets real hot turning the mutton with a fork and mopping dip on

it with a cotton kitchen mop. Some of the guys don't like that. There's a little bit of competition between the chicken team and the mutton team."

"It's a personal choice," says Dan Stallings, a dark-haired, handsome man with a deep voice and a slow drawl. "Anybody can cook a chicken. It takes a little more work to do the mutton, and I enjoy the mutton. Mutton is my forte."

Dan Stallings is eating a piece of elk sausage he brought from

Blessed Mother Chicken Team

home and drinking a beer as he pokes and tends about twenty fat slabs of mutton on the grill. A charter member of the cooking team, he also does a lot of cooking in his own backyard. "I have my own kettle, and I do burgoo at home," he says. "It'll have deer meat in it, it could have some squirrels in it, maybe a hen, and it'll have mutton and cabbage. At the picnics we don't put wild animals in the burgoo, no squirrel or anything like that, because that meat's not USDA inspected."

It turns out Dan wrote a college paper about burgoo and has more theories about the stew than anyone we've met yet. "Burgoo is actually a Welsh stew that came from England or Wales," he tells us. "One of the books said that during the Civil War there was a Confederate cook with one of the brigades. He had a lisp, and he was trying to say 'bird stew,' because he was making a stew that had doves and quail and different types of animal meat in it. And it came out 'bur-goo' instead of 'bird stew.'"

The cake wheel, Blessed Mother Picnic

Upwind of the pits, a guy is setting up a line of band saws that they'll be using to cut the chickens and barbecued mutton into sizable chunks. Then an assembly line of workers wearing rubber gloves will weigh the meat and box it up for sale. "We start selling at 4:00," says Newman. "People begin lining up around 2:30 for the gallon takeout jugs of burgoo and the boxed-up barbecue— it goes fast."

Burgoo and barbecue. It's a man's world. But the women, too, are busy as bees. There's the auction, the quilts, making the pies and the side dishes, bottling the burgoo, selling, and serving. "All told, the Blessed Mother Picnic will probably bring in close to forty thousand dollars for the church," says Father Freddie, the red-haired, pie-faced pastor of Blessed Mother. He's a big supporter of the fund-raiser, not just for the money it brings in but also for the fellowship. He doesn't often see some of these men cleaned up at church on Sundays, but they're here, faithfully, at the cooking congregation by the pit.

1:00 PM: MOONLITE BAR-B-Q INN

Nancy heads us to the Moonlite Bar-B-Q Inn for our appointment with the burgoo guru of Owensboro.

As we drive past Kentucky Wesleyan College, we spot portable pits pulled up on the campus lawn, and a group of coeds in soccer uniforms flagging down motorists with hand-painted signs that proclaim: "Chickens $6—We Need Warm-Ups." There are lots of people buying chickens and hobnobbing with each other and with the guys who are barbecuing. Over at a place called Golfland, the United Brotherhood of Electrical Workers is having their annual union picnic, and there's a kettle of burgoo simmering while various local political candidates meet and greet the brothers. It's clear that the Catholics do not have a monopoly on burgoo and barbecue. Everywhere we turn it's being served up as the fast food, the community food, the takeout of Owensboro.

You might think that all of these parish picnics and street-corner burgoo stands would put a dent in Ken Bosley's Moonlite Bar-B-Q business, but you would be wrong. "All this cooking, it just makes people hungry for more barbecue," Ken tells us with a voice drenched in smoke. "Most of the time when there's a church picnic, it makes us even busier. People hear about it all week and talk about it, and they want barbecue and burgoo. Maybe it's too hot to go out there. Might be too big a crowd. May rain. So instead, they come here."

Family owned and operated for thirty-five years, the Moonlite Bar-B-Q Inn has grown over the years from a 30-seat roadside café to a 350-seat sprawling restaurant with a parking lot jammed full of cars. Democratic Party chairman and an Owensboro booster, Ken Bosley and his family have put this town on the culinary map with their legendary all-you-can-eat barbecue buffet and burgoo bar. President Clinton ate chopped mutton and burgoo here, and so did Jimmy Carter. Local NASCAR champions, the Waltrip brothers and the Green brothers, are regulars. Photographs memorializing these images cover the walls of the place.

At the Moonlite Bar-B-Q they cook ten thousand pounds of mutton a week, Bosley tells us. "We know most people outside Daviess County don't like mutton or don't understand mutton, or they think they don't want mutton," he admits. "Generally we tell them it's beef, and they like it. Mutton is a dressed fat ewe, about a hundred pounds. We just quarter it and throw it over a hickory fire and cook it about twelve hours. The smoke gives it a sweet taste."

"Mutton is what distinguishes Owensboro's burgoo and barbecue from the rest of the world's," Bosley explains. "When you say BBQ here, you mean mutton. And mutton in burgoo gives it that gamy taste. Keeps it original without the wild. You go fifty miles any direction and ask for mutton, and they will just look at you."

What is it about men and meat and midnight and a pit? "I just think people like to cook together," Bosley says. "Men especially like to barbecue outside and burn things up; it's a primal thing. The men here in Owensboro, they come together in cooking crews—it's like gangs. There are gangs of men here and gangs of men there, and there's a lot of competition. But, you know, it's towards something else, something greater. It's for the community, and the tradition holds people together."

The night is heavy and warm. We drive out of town past Pius X and the car dealerships, past big houses with big barns through the rolling hills, past Doodlebug Latham's country store toward St. Lawrence Church, to the oldest parish picnic in Daviess County with some of the oldest burgoo makers around. Nancy cranks up the radio. She likes it loud. "Blue moon of Kentucky keep on shining . . . ," she hums along. "You're in Bluegrass Country now, girls," she tells us. "That's Bill Monroe, The Father of Bluegrass. He grew up fifty miles from here."

As we turn off the main highway and curl back a long, narrow road into the shadowy picnic grounds, night is in our headphones—cicadas, crackling fires, Kentucky men's voices and laughter. The sweet smell of Boston butt fills the air.

The men of St. Lawrence parish stir, just as their fathers and their grandfathers did before them. It's a tradition that started more than one hundred years ago. In the light from the fire they appear almost ancient, even the younger ones, their faces sweaty from the blaze. In New York they have bar mitzvahs; in South Africa boys are sent to the bush. In Owensboro, Kentucky, a man's rite of passage is to join a cooking crew.

The St. Lawrence Picnic is a fund-raiser like St. Pius and a church bazaar like Blessed Mother, but truly, it's a homecoming. Parishioners, living in Florida or Philadelphia, make their way home each year for this reunion. When they leave, they carry back jugs of burgoo to savor through the months and cartons of mutton to eat on the plane.

Darrell Cecil, a concrete man by trade, is a St. Lawrence dip maker. Dip is the marinade they mop onto the mutton and chicken as it barbecues for hours on the grill. Like burgoo, the recipe for dip is a guarded secret within each parish. "Dip—it's a calling," Darrell tells us as he scoops out a taste of the greasy liquid into a small tin cup. You are called either to make dip or to make burgoo. Some men are born to mop mutton, some to the fellowship of stirring. In all, he tells us, they're making sixty gallons of dip to mop the meat for this year's picnic.

Darrell is vague when we ask him about the ingredients that make up the dip. "It's mainly lard, margarine, butter, and you got your lemon juice. And of course, your lemon cuts your lard, and your lard cuts your lemon. As far as writing down the recipe, the amount and all, I couldn't tell you. It's not a piece-of-paper dip. It's kind of handed down from generation to generation. But every generation wants to dabble a little bit."

Darrell keeps experimenting with the dip from year to year. This is Kentucky science, and tradition, too. Each time you make a batch, you recall the spirit and the heart of the man who bequeathed you his secret recipe. You may not have cash or property to leave your children, but the family recipe for dip or burgoo is a treasured legacy.

"An old man taught me how to make the dip when I was about ten," says Kevin Coomes, a young guy with a buzz cut who is stirring a large pot full of thin, pungent dip. "When I was eighteen, he said, 'Here you go,' and turned it over to me, and I've been doing it ever since." Kevin's two kids run in lazy circles on the hill above the pit. "As far as the cooking goes, it's mostly just men up here. My little girl here, she's eight, and she's probably the only girl who's been up here for several years. She's here 'cause it's my night to babysit. Mama's out!" he laughs. I mean, my son, it don't matter if Mama was home, he would have been up here with me anyway. But my daughter, she probably would have stayed home if Mama woulda' been home."

By day, Martin Higdon works for Commonwealth Aluminum; by night he's the head of the burgoo crew at St. Lawrence. Martin is working on gathering the memories of the older men who are, one by one, handing over the paddle. It's a long chain of burgoo that links these men and boys together. "I got drafted into it," Martin tells us. "A guy came to my house one day. He said, 'We need someone to take over the burgoo.' The other guy was getting up in years. And I said, 'Well, I'm

Father and son, John Johnson and Danny Johnson

the last guy you should be asking.' He said, 'You are!' So, here I am. I've been doing this now for twenty years."

John Johnson, an old-timer in coveralls, hovers around the younger men. His son is in charge of the whole picnic this year. Talking about the old days brings tears to his milky eyes. Nearby, his son, Danny, balances an armload of sassafras and stokes the fire under the dip.

"Good day, boy," he greets his son.

"What are you getting me into, Dad?" Danny says, eyeing our mic. "That's my dad," he tells us. "Finest fellow you ever want to meet."

John and his longtime dip-making buddy, Clemie Cecil, hang by the fire talking politics and war and peace, while Clemie steadily stirs. "There's people in the world that's hungry," John says to his friend passionately. "Around here you wouldn't realize that. We got all the food to eat and everything we need here, you know, and you take some of these foreign countries, they just don't have it."

Clemie, a farmer and millwright in his late sixties, thinks about this for a few minutes and responds quietly, "I think we need peace more than anything in the world. What's all this fighting, everybody aggravating the other?" Their voices and the spit and pop of the fire cut through the quiet of the summer night. The wind is picking up, and the tall ancient trees that ring the parish pits move and sway. It's beautiful and eerie out here in the green, rolling hills of Kentucky.

10:00 AM: ST. LAWRENCE PICNIC

The smoky, glowing altered state of the night has given way to morning. The congregation has come down from the hills to be together for the Sunday picnic—the young, the old, and the in-between. The huge overhanging trees shade dozens of makeshift booths displaying quilts and baby clothes to be raffled, tiny religious statues and holy cards for sale, funnel cakes, dart games, and the beanbag toss.

B-24, B-24—the bingo game is firing up. Long tables of kids and oldsters sit side by side under an open tent marking their cards as the day grows hot and the smell of the barbecue permeates the grounds. Nancy has found the cake wheel and is putting her money down on number 6—there's a jam cake made by St. Lawrence's legendary Edge sisters in her future.

Nancy Penrod and The Kitchen Sisters

Women carrying heaping bowls of potato salad and coleslaw bustle about tending the food counters. Lines of eaters stream by loading their bowls with burgoo, their plates with barbecued mutton and cornbread—eight dollars, all you can eat. Nobody sits, everyone stands as they eat at the high tables, shoulder to shoulder, in long rows.

We keep looking for Father Tony. We hear he's the engine behind this picnic. Finally at the end of the day someone tells us that's him up on stage, the big man that kind of looks like Waylon Jennings in a black shirt, cowboy hat, and jeans singing "Help Me Make It Through the Night" to the congregation fanning themselves under the dance pavilion.

Smoky clusters of exhausted men sip beer by the smoldering pits. "This is the only time during the year that I get to see some of these guys, you know. We're all so busy with our lives," says Martin Higdon. "You walk down to that pit in the morning, and you hear everybody hollering, and you know that they know what's got to be done. And they're here to do the job. I mean, once all is said and done and the meat's all sold and everybody's come together for a good cause, that's what it's all about. You've got to have that in one community."

Moonlite Bar-B-Q Burgoo

"If you went to fifteen church picnics, you'd have fifteen types of burgoo," says Ken Bosley, owner of the Moonlite Bar-B-Q Inn, a restaurant that is a kind of year-round festival of regional cooking. Every parish has its own secret burgoo recipe, carefully guarded in the spirit of fierce and friendly competition. The recipes aren't written but are passed down orally from father to son. In fact, the recipe is just a guideline. Ken generously shared Moonlite Bar-B-Q's recipe with us.

4 pounds mutton

1–3 pounds chicken, cut up

¾ pound cabbage, finely chopped

¾ pound onions, finely chopped

5 pounds potatoes, peeled and diced

2 cans (17 ounces each) corn or 2 cups fresh corn kernels

¾ cup ketchup

3 cans (10¾ ounces each) tomato puree

Juice of 1 lemon

¾ cup distilled vinegar

½ cup Worcestershire sauce

2½ tablespoons salt, or more to taste

2 tablespoons ground black pepper, or more to taste

1 teaspoon cayenne pepper, or more to taste

In an extra-large pot, bring the mutton to a boil over high heat in enough water to cover. Simmer until the meat is tender enough to fall off the bones, about 2 to 3 hours.

Once the meat is tender, drain it and discard the broth. Let the meat cool. When it is cool enough to handle, debone the meat and throw out the bones. Use a sharp knife to finely chop the meat and set aside.

Meanwhile, place the chicken and 2 gallons of water in another large pot. Bring to a boil over high heat. Reduce the heat and simmer until the chicken is tender, approximately 1 hour. Remove the chicken and set aside to cool. To the broth, add the cabbage, onion, potatoes, corn, ketchup, and an additional gallon of water. Bring to a boil over high heat, then reduce the heat and let simmer.

Debone the chicken meat and throw out the bones and skin. Chop up the chicken meat and set aside. When the potatoes are tender, add the chicken, mutton, tomato puree, lemon, vinegar, Worcestershire sauce, salt, black pepper, and cayenne pepper. Let simmer for 2 hours or longer, stirring often from the bottom as it thickens. Serve piping hot.

MAKES 3 GALLONS

Dip

Tart with vinegar and salty with spice, dip is a tangy basting marinade mopped on meat as it cooks. When you are feeding a parish, you can baste your dip with a mop; when you are feeding your family, you can baste your dip with a brush. This dip is especially good basted on chopped and sliced mutton. Thanks again, Ken Bosley, for this Moonlite Bar-B-Q recipe.

1 gallon water

1⅔ cups Worcestershire sauce

2½ tablespoons freshly ground black pepper

⅓ cup brown sugar

1 teaspoon MSG (optional)

1 teaspoon allspice

1 teaspoon onion salt

1 teaspoon coarsely chopped garlic

2 tablespoons salt

2 tablespoons lemon juice

1⅔ cups distilled white vinegar

In a large pot, mix all ingredients. Bring to a boil over high heat. Reduce the heat to medium and simmer until the sauce is reduced, about 20 minutes. Baste over the meat as directed.

MAKES ABOUT 1 GALLON

CAMPAIGN COOKING—
A POLITICAL KITCHEN VISION
(TO KNOW THE PEOPLE'S MOOD, YOU MUST EAT THE PEOPLE'S FOOD)

"If you are a true political junkie and want to eat well, I'd start in New England going to pancake breakfasts. Then I would work my way down the Eastern Seaboard. In Virginia I'd hit a shad-planking political dinner. Shad is a kind of fish that runs in the spring, and the plank that they put it on is wood, and it gives it a wonderful flavor. As you start heading into the Midwest, keep your eyes open for muskrat dinners. It's an acquired taste. I don't think I've ever heard of one that was held for someone running for an office higher than the town council or city level. I haven't seen a congressional candidate brave enough to have a muskrat dinner."

Margaret Engel, coauthor of *Food Finds*, has an eye for the food that rallies the nation's voters and a theory that some of the most authentic regional culinary treasures are to be found at political potlucks.

"If you want to taste America, you want to start low," Margaret tells us. "Local races really have sweat equity involved with them, and that means home-prepared food or food prepared in school kitchens. Once you get higher up on the food chain, so to speak, you're going to find people writing out checks to caterers.

"There's no correlation between price paid and quality of food. I've had some of the best political food at pierogi breakfasts in Cleveland, where you pay five dollars and get handmade pierogi. They're like doughy pillows filled with mashed potatoes or prunes or onions, and they're Ukrainian and Polish in origin, and they're slathered in butter, and they're really spectacular.

"Every time there is a regional favorite, you will see some sort of political event

President Lyndon B. Johnson and Vice President-Elect Hubert Humphrey, 1964 campaign

built around it. Like the big oyster festival in Leonardtown, Maryland, that falls right before the November election.

"Politicians tend to set up shop there and pass out literature. And they do try to eat the food at these events, because they are trying to be part of the community, and it's a very happy event. You don't find many grumpy people at the Pumpkin Chunkin' Festival in Delaware, for example. People are in a good mood, and that's exactly how the politicians like to present their case—to people who are in a happy, relaxed state of mind, and they're sitting at a table, not going anywhere."

Margaret is not just touting theory when it comes to campaign cooking. She's speaking from experience. "I was a political wife for eight years. My husband was on the county council, and the first thing I did when he told me he was running for office was buy a food processor. The name of the game in political food is 'How inexpensively can we feed the faithful,' because you are so grateful to volunteers

KITCHEN VISIONARY

and donors, but you are also trying to raise money. So there is a real juggling of what kind of food you can have.

"The typical political gathering, I've come to find out, is a table in the center with liter jugs of soft drinks and open bags of potato chips. That's the basic standard. So anything you can do to improve on that will make you quite popular. So we made a special effort to have unusual food and good food. We got a little carried away. One time I did a leg of lamb with apricots. It was just something that was big and could be cut up quickly. So we tended to feed people well, but we also did a lot of popcorn balls."

EDIBLE MEMORABILIA

"We are starting to see more and more food samples being given out by politicians," says Margaret. "The one we did the most was fortune cookies. 'Good fortune smiles on those who vote for Bruce Adams.' We did thousands and thousands of those fortune cookies and handed them out at political rallies and on election day.

"At both the Republican and Democrat conventions in 2004, the Kraft food company did special editions of their macaroni. One package had a big donkey on it, and the other one had a big elephant and it was labeled, 'Kraft Macaroni special edition for the Republican National Convention, New York, 2004.' And they shaped macaroni into elephants and donkeys. It's edible memorabilia.

"The best political event I ever went to was in western Maryland. There are always corn roasts, for both Democrats and Republicans, in rural parts of the state around fall election time every year. There were open grills with coals under them. They had the corn in the husk covered with burlap sacks, and they were wetting it down with a hose. There were speeches as people were eating.

"It was one of the best ways to inject civics and great corn at the same time."

"FOOD ON THE CAMPAIGN TRAIL IS A LOT LIKE THE NOMINEE'S BODY LANGUAGE OR A SPOUSE'S PERFORMANCE IN PUBLIC. IT SEEMS INCONSEQUENTIAL, YET THE WIZARDS IN TOUCH WITH THE DARK ARTS OF INTERNAL POLLING KNOW IT'S CRUCIAL IN SOME PRIMORDIAL AND AWESOME WAY. A CANDIDATE'S RELATIONSHIP TO DEMOCRATIC FOOD IS ALL ABOUT AUTHENTICITY, ABOUT BEING ONE OF US EVEN AS WE ELEVATE HIM BEYOND US: SIMILAR YET DIFFERENT. FOOD IS TO THE MODERN CANDIDATE WHAT A CHILDHOOD SPENT IN A LOG CABIN WAS TO NINETEENTH-CENTURY POLITICIANS—A METAPHOR FOR BEING IN TOUCH WITH THE LIFE OF THE COMMON VOTER. EVERY POLITICIAN NEEDS TO FIND A WAY TO PORTRAY HIMSELF AS COMFORTABLE AROUND DEMOCRATIC FOOD."

—EXCERPTED FROM "MORE PIE, MR. PRESIDENT?"
BY JACK HITT FOR THE *NEW YORK TIMES SUNDAY MAGAZINE*,
OCTOBER 17, 2004

America Eats

A Hidden Archive

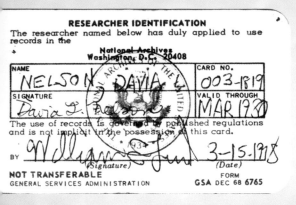

The Kitchen Sisters and archives go way back. In our early radio days in the 1980s, we spent hour upon hour plugged into the listening room at the National Archives in Washington, D.C., gathering historic audio recordings, old broadcasts, and oral histories that inspired some of the first Kitchen Sisters documentaries aired on NPR.

These audio elements were featured in stories such as "Route 66: The History of the Mother Road" and "War and Separation," a piece about life on the home front during World War II. And our series *Lost & Found Sound* was based on hundreds of early recordings that we never would have found without the guiding force of archivists around the country.

When we read Mark Kurlansky's book *Choice Cuts* and saw a reference to America Eats, a Works Progress Administration (WPA) project hidden away in the Library of Congress, we felt as if we were coming home. There, preserved in an archive, was a project done in the 1930s that sounded remarkably similar to what we were trying to do in *Hidden Kitchens*. Once again, the librarians and archivists of the nation were pointing the way.

In 1935, during the deepest dark days of the Depression, President Franklin Roosevelt came up with a radical plan to put people to work, meaningful work. It was called the Works Progress Administration, part of Roosevelt's New Deal program. All over the country, laborers were given jobs building highways and bridges, artists painted murals in public buildings, photographers documented the state of the nation, and writers chronicled the people and places that make up this vast country.

Some of the work done as part of these New Deal programs is legendary—Grand Coulee Dam, Dorothea Lange's photo of a migrant mother, the *American Guide* tourist handbook series that captured the history and spirit of the country during those years. But tucked away in the Library of Congress, stored in gray acid-free archival boxes, is a little-known collection of writings done by the Federal Writers' Project (FWP) between 1937 and 1941 called America Eats.

"WRITERS NEED TO EAT, TOO . . . "

Stetson Kennedy, like many people in the country, was flat broke in 1937 when he was hired by the Federal Writers' Project as Florida's state director of oral history and ethnic studies. Fresh out of college, he was put in charge of overseeing dozens

Stetson Kennedy, state director of oral history for the Federal Writers' Project in Florida, gathered stories for America Eats.

of writers throughout the state hired to collect oral histories, folklore, stories, songs, you name it.

"There was, of course, a hot debate in Congress about spending federal tax money on things like this," remembers eighty-nine-year-old Stetson Kennedy. "And someone said, 'Well, you know, writers and artists, they need to eat, too.' And so they passed the bill in 1935. But in order to get any WPA job, one had to qualify as being eligible for 'relief,' as welfare was first known. And you had to take a pauper's oath. And the pauper's oath said, 'Do you have any money, a job, any property, or any prospects of getting any of those things?' Since I didn't, I was eminently qualified, and I got the job."

As state director of oral history in Florida, Kennedy had plenty of willing applicants, as did regional directors all across the country. Some of the people who came to work for the FWP were accomplished and well known—Nelson Algren, Saul Bellow, Zora Neale Hurston. Some of the people were barely writers at all. You were paid $37.50 a week, no matter who you were.

"We had over two hundred people just in Florida, and for the most part they were middle-aged housewives with a high school education, if that. And of course, academicians worried about how these people would establish rapport with these 'folk' types they were talking to in the field. But our workers had no such problem. They could knock on any door, and the rapport was there because they were speaking the same language and came out of the same culture. No problem."

One of the projects Stetson and his writers worked on was America Eats, an ambitious endeavor to document how food traditions throughout the country brought people together and helped them retain their sense of who they were—even during the depths of the Depression. Far beyond just a list of recipes, this project was to delve into the stories of foods that were unique to specific regions of the state, to particular ethnic groups, various professions, churches, even to individual families.

The America Eats writings were to be gathered together into a seventy-thousand-word book, illustrated with line drawings and Currier and Ives prints. Slated for publication February 1, 1942, the book would tell the story of "group eating as an important American social institution." It would be a chronicle of what we ate from coast to coast and how our meals reflected who we were and where we came from. The book would bear witness to the waning days of home cooking, as mass-produced and convenience foods began to appear on our culinary horizon.

Mark Kurlansky, who also wrote *Salt: A World History* and *Cod: A Biography of the Fish That Changed the World,* stumbled upon the America Eats collection while researching his book *Choice Cuts,* a collection of food writing from around the world. For Kurlansky, the collection is a perfect time capsule, a treasure trove of information about how America really ate—not what went on in expensive public shrines to gourmet cuisine, but how people ate as family members, as inheritors of an ethnic or religious or regional tradition.

From the files of America Eats, archived at the Library of Congress

The annual Los Angeles Sheriff's Barbecue, 1930s

As he reads from a list of proposed America Eats stories, Kurlansky is amazed at the breadth of diversity revealed by something as simple as meals in America. "Ohio rabbit fries, Coca-Cola parties in Georgia, Florida's cemetery-cleaning pic-nics, foot-washing dinners all over the country. And in New England," Kurlansky notes, "they make a point of describing how baked beans and Indian pudding and gingerbread and all these molasses-based dishes are products of the slave trade. It was very anthropological. So much of what is written is written about the great chefs and great restaurants. The America Eats project was all about food as a part of culture and about following food to find America."

MISSISSIPPI EATS

No one knows exactly how much material the FWP collected for America Eats since the manuscripts are housed in several institutions around the country, but the impact of this material extends far beyond the specifics of any given story. John T. Edge is the head of the Southern Foodways Alliance at the University of Mississippi at Oxford, studying the link between what we eat and who we are. He got his start in the field digging through the state archives in Jackson. There he found a languishing little-known archive of more than three hundred pages of Mississsippi's contribution to America Eats that includes an unpublished Eudora Welty manuscript, a cookbook of local recipes called "Possum and Pomegranate," and various essays about fish fries, political barbecues, and other kinds of community food.

"You can feel Mississippi come to life in those unpublished pages," says John T. "There are the recipes, which are a kind of road map to the re-creation of a dish. And then there are the people. I'm interested in knowing who these people were, who stood at the stove on an August day in the Deep South in 1935 with sweat running down their back, stirring up a mess of gumbo. I want to know about their family and if this was a meal of celebration they were cooking or a food engendered by poverty. And the closest thing I've come to answering that is this America Eats material.

"There's one essay I really love about a political barbecue and a guy called Blue Bill Yancey, who 'had a head like a cypress tree.' This piece doesn't tell you the name of the politician who was holding forth from a stump. But you know a lot about Blue Bill Yancey and a lot about Old Cy Curtis, who sells lemonade from a plank nailed between two trees singing out, 'Ice cold lemonade, made in the shade and stirred with a spade, good enough for any old maid.'"

John T. reads about regional food the way another man might pore over a political biography. **A meal is never just a combination of foods on a plate—it's a key to unlocking the past.** It's a map of the country as sure as if it were hanging up in a classroom.

The stories have seeped deep into John T. Edge's imagination. He chants the names of Southern foods chronicled in America Eats as though each one is a link in a chain, carrying him back in time: "Hoecake, cracklin' bread, persimmon beer, possum and taters. All these recipes telegraph some meaning that says, 'I'm eating low on the hog, I'm eating close to the farm. They put a rosy glow on a hungry world.'"

FROM PEANUT FESTIVALS TO CHAIN GANGS

Stetson Kennedy traveled throughout Florida gathering his stories long before portable tape recorders were invented. **The recording device he used was the size of a coffee table** and required two men to lift it. He traveled with two automobile batteries to power it.

One of his America Eats pieces, titled "A Ton of Rice and Three Red Roosters," tells the story of a peanut festival in High Springs, Florida, that offered free chicken pilau. It also tells the story of segregation. In his field notes he wrote, "Folk from all the surrounding . . . came crowded into old automobiles and light

Boiling coffee at the Florida Peanut Festival

pickup trucks from which tow-headed children dangled their legs. In spite of the area's large Negro population, the only ones in attendance were those who assisted in the preparation of the chicken pilau."

One of the writers who worked for Kennedy on the Federal Writers' Project was Zora Neale Hurston, the African-American anthropologist and novelist. She had already

Women preparing chicken for the pilau dinner at the Peanut Festival in High Springs, Florida

won a Pulitzer Prize when she went to work for him in 1938—but she was hired, like Kennedy, as a "junior interviewer" and was paid even two dollars less each week because she lived in Eatonville, where the cost of living was lower than it was in Jacksonville.

"Working with Zora in those days of Jim Crow apartheid, it was unthinkable for a black/white team, much less male/female team, going around in public working on anything," says Kennedy. "So we had to send Zora ahead by herself to identify who we should talk to in the Florida turpentine camps, for example, where the

Zora Neale Hurston traveled the South collecting oral histories and folklore for the Federal Writers' Project.

workers lived hard, rough lives collecting sap from the trees and distilling it to make turpentine. Zora would go into the camp first, then I would follow up with a recording device and an assistant, both of us white. Zora had great difficulty, you know, with restaurants. She had to look for black restaurants. And there were almost no black hotels or motels, so she often had to sleep in her beat-up Chevy.

"You know, it was Zora Neale Hurston who said, '**I've been in sorrow's kitchen and licked out all the pots.**'"

Stetson Kennedy wanted no part of a culture that kept Zora Hurston out, and the longer he worked for the FWP, the more he saw it as a chance to say so. But the stories being gathered were supposed to reflect optimism, which was in short supply, and so there was little room for Stetson Kennedy's truth.

Peggy Bulger, director of the American Folklife Center at the Library of Congress, knows the stories behind the stories: "Stetson Kennedy was quite the rabble-rouser. He really wanted to write the truth. In Florida he wanted to write about racism, he wanted to write about the fact that it was one hundred ten degrees and one hundred percent humidity sometimes in Florida. That it wasn't the paradise that people thought of. He really wanted to write the truth in the state guidebooks. Well, obviously, the editors at the national office wouldn't have anything like that. So they cut out everything that wasn't positive. And it was to the chagrin of many of the writers who really wanted to tell a different story. The national office wanted to bring people's psyches out of the Depression, and they wanted to encourage tourism. They thought the only way to do that was to gild the lily."

Kennedy still remembers the stories and songs he recorded that reflected what life was really like for many in the state during the Depression:

"**One story I picked up was on the chain gangs** in the penitentiaries and prison farms. The trick was to keep these guys alive and working but with the least expense possible. That meant they were given very little food—and certainly no food of the flavorful, home-cooked variety. Well, I was recording a group of men, and they told me this was the chain gang theme song they'd come up with:

> *"I don't want no*
> *Cornbread, beans, and molasses*
> *I don't want no*
> *Cornbread, beans, and molasses*
> *At supper time, oh supper time."*

Stetson continued to chronicle and submit what he saw and heard in his home state regardless of how it was received back in Washington.

THE GOSPEL BIRD

Up north in Chicago, Nelson Algren joined the Illinois Writers' Project for the Midwest region that included from Indiana west to Nebraska, and from Minnesota south to Kansas. In 1935, he was a struggling artist, fifteen years away from winning the first National Book Award for his novel *The Man with the Golden Arm*.

During the Depression he was writing to pay his bills—stories about the Czechs and their *kolache*, the Poles and their special cakes and wafers for religious festivals, Serbian picnics and their barbecued lamb.

In one of his America Eats essays, Algren wrote:

> These are the foods of many nations, brought from many lands to nourish one land. They are all the old world ways which have gone to the great melting pot of the Middle west to come out from behind the counter of the all-night hamburger stand on U.S. 66 or in the quick-service businessmen's lunch on any downtown street in Minneapolis, Akron, or Omaha. These are the blue-plate specials that streamlined steaks and the laborer's lunch pail passed down an endless boarding house table, from a brave dressed in buckskin to a blue-turbaned voyager, from a coonskinned Yankee to a drawling steamboat man, from a Negro fish vendor to an Irish section hand. Many foods from many nations, yet one food, one nation. Many lands, one land.

Nelson Algren kept a copy of his American Eats writings, but in 1975, depressed and disillusioned, he auctioned off the contents of his Chicago apartment before leaving the city—not just furniture but photographs and his manuscripts as well. Algren's America Eats went to his friend, chef Louise Szathmary, who recognized its significance. It was published by the University of Iowa Press in 1992, after Algren's death. One chapter was entitled "Festivals in the Fields":

Spaghetti supper at Grape Festival in Tontitown, Arkansas, August 16, 1941

In southern Indiana as well as in southern Illinois, chicken is still referred to as the "gospel bird." This is a hangover from days when circuit-riding preachers came visiting. It was customary to serve the gospel man a chicken and hence, the name . . .

Libertyville, Illinois, holds gatherings which are both Serbian and American. The tables are covered with smoked ham, roasts that smell of garlic, spinach pies, rolled pancakes filled with preserves or cottage cheese, and apple strudel. . . . The youngsters commonly prefer the American dishes . . . mostly fried foods, sandwiches, sweets and cold soda water. . . . Sitting at the same table with their children, holding in their hands sizable chunks of barbecued lamb, the parents look at their American born children in wonder and dismay unable to understand an attachment to cold sodas and hotdogs eaten together. The American hotdog and the Serbian barbecued lamb are old rivals, representing two worlds. The fight has been going on for decades and is a fight for survival. Though it is not over, judging from what we see at Serbian festivals, the barbecued lamb is waging a losing fight.

MINERS' LUNCH BOXES

Another cache of America Eats papers turned up in Montana's State Archives at the University of Bozeman. "Whistleberries, Stirabout, and Depression Cake" was finished around 1940, after Edward B. Reynolds and Michael Kennedy had traveled the West, recording stories of migrants for whom food was the only vestige of their lives back home.

Mark Kurlansky has read the Montana papers. "It was a time when people were really looking at America in its vastness. There were a lot of immigrants, and there was a lot of inner-migration. The Dust Bowl, people from Oklahoma moving to California, people moving around because of unemployment and riding rails. There was this real sense of the country and the variety of cultures. Just by investigating what America eats, you learn so much about immigration, hidden history, and what this country was."

All a writer had to do to know a working man was to look into the man's lunch box. That traveling meal revealed where a man came from as surely as if the interviewer had asked the question outright.

> The most important duty in homes, boarding houses and cafes of mining camps is "putting up lunch buckets." Some restaurants advertise "Lunch buckets a specialty." Not only the miner's individual tastes, but his nationality is taken into consideration. . . .
>
> Conventional ham sandwiches, cake, fruit, and apple pie might comprise the contents of the American buckets. The Irish workmen might face the same array with one exception, the son of Erin would wash his food down, not with coffee, but with strong, black tea fortified with stirabout. In the Cornish miner's bucket would be a generous proportioned pasty and a few slices of yellow saffron bread . . .

The America Eats inventory of lunch boxes describes the dried fish and venison jerky beloved by the Finns. The Mexicans' preference for "hot tempered frijoles and tortillas," the Serbs' brisket and bread, and the Scots' haggis, a cold meat pudding cooked in the stomach of a sheep:

> The lunch pails from Italian or Austrian homes are sure to contain homemade red-and-white-mottled salami sandwiches with their throat-burning seasoning, a button of garlic and, perhaps, a whole Bermuda onion. Inevitably, there is Italian claret or "Dago Red." That is if some other miner has not found his way to the wine before the lunch hour. Hunting for "Dago Red" is a popular underground sport.

THE END OF AN ERA

By 1940, the newly formed House Committee on Un-American Activities was raising a skeptical eyebrow at the politics of the Writers' Project and its sibling, the Federal Theatre Project. The FWP argued that the America Eats project bolstered patriotism. In a memo one supervisor wrote: "If the book has a basic purpose, it is

This photo collected for the America Eats project shows a segregated barbecue at F. M. Gays Plantation, Alabama, 1914.

to make people appreciate a much-neglected aspect of our culture, the American table, as much as a few expatriates do the French. **If we can make Americans realize that they have the best table in the world, we shall have helped to deepen national patriotism.**"

But when war broke out, all talk of purpose ended, replaced with talk of victory. Stetson Kennedy and his FWP colleagues around the country were given only weeks to pack up and leave their offices. They piled as much as they could into boxes, found safe homes for the documents at the Library of Congress and in libraries and historical societies around the country, and America Eats and the Writers' Project succumbed to history.

The Depression brought America Eats into existence—and World War II caused it to disappear without ever being published. "All the WPA projects were replaced by the building of ships and tanks," reflects Mark Kurlansky. "It's an example of how war negates culture. What we eat and who we are and our culture are forgotten. Everything is redefined in military terms."

The stories intended to bring a nation together were dispersed into anonymity to be discovered a generation later by archivists looking to make sense of the past.

"Never before, or since, has a society decided to delegate a staff of its citizens on that scale to go out and record and preserve the culture," Stetson Kennedy says. "The Federal Writers' Project was an unprecedented effort, the largest documentary project ever undertaken in the United States to this day. We were well aware that we were doing something important, and here in Florida, and I'm sure elsewhere, we were like a bunch of kids on a treasure hunt. We were very excited whenever we found what we thought was a crown jewel. I feel it ought to be a responsibility of society to record and nurture its cultural assets."

Stetson Kennedy still lives in Florida, the state where he was born and where he has spent much of his life documenting the stories and voices of his region. He marvels at the rediscovery of the America Eats manuscripts. What did you have to eat? may not sound like a profound question until the great variety of answers are arrayed in front of the reader. Then it becomes clear: What did you have to eat? leads to larger answers about who we are, where we have been, and where we might head together.

"I feel it ought to be a responsibility of society to record and nurture its cultural assets."

—STETSON KENNEDY

HOPI CORN CEREMONY

COLLECTED BY EDWARD P. WARE, ARIZONA WRITERS' PROJECT, AMERICA EATS

On the twentieth day of the baby's life, up to which time the sun is not supposed to have shone upon it, the infant is washed in yucca root water and rubbed all over with cornmeal and the pollen of flowers. Wrapped firmly on its cradle-board, it is then carried to the edge of the mesa, with the mother in her bridal clothing and carrying an ear of corn in her hand. There, with the sun shining full upon it, the baby is touched with the ear of corn in christening, and the officiate high priest gives it its chosen names. Then the friends of the parents, and there will always be many, also touch the infant with the ear of corn, each in turn bestowing upon the baby such names as they wish it to bear. Thus it is that a newly christened baby may have fifty or even a hundred names.

The christening over, the entire procession marches to the home of the parents for the Christening Feast. And such a feast is truly a great event, a feast no Hopi family would even think of passing up.

The principal dish at the feast—and all foods are cooked out of doors—is mutton, roasted or stewed with corn and beans. Rich cornmeal pudding filled with peach-seed kernels and bits of mutton-fat baked in wrappers of cornhusks is always part of the feast. In season, green corn, tomatoes, fruit, and melons are served. While the guests eat, they make wishes for the baby and each person gives presents of food. Piki bread in gay colors surrounds the feasters.

Apple Pie (Old-Time/American)

Nelson Algren, who wrote *The Man with the Golden Arm*, also collected recipes and food stories from the Midwest for the America Eats project in the 1930s. Algren's work on the project was later published as part of the Iowa Szathmary Culinary Arts Series. The cookbook—part anecdotal, part cultural commentary—reveals the rituals surrounding life in the region—from the origins of the cakewalk to sauerkraut day to an apple peelin' party. This apple pie recipe comes from Algren's archives.

Instead of making 1 pie, this recipe makes 12 small turnovers, which are fried. This recipe also calls for dried apples which are boiled in the soaking water with the spices.

1 **cup dried apples**

½ **cup brown sugar**

½ **teaspoon ground cinnamon**

½ **teaspoon nutmeg**

¼ **teaspoon salt**

2 **piecrusts**

Soak the apples in water to cover overnight.

Remove all cores and boil with the brown sugar and cinnamon, nutmeg, and salt until it makes a thick sauce.

Cut the piecrusts into 6 wedges each. Spoon into each wedge just enough filling so that you can fold half of the wedge over the other half, pressing the edges together like a turnover.

Fry the individual pie wedges in deep fat at a fairly high temperature, turning once if necessary. Place on paper towels, sprinkle with powdered sugar, and serve warm.

MAKES 12 TURNOVERS

From "Possum and Pomegranate"

These recipes were collected by the Mississippi America Eats project for a cookbook that was never published, titled "Possum and Pomegranate." They came to us from the Southern Foodways Alliance. Many of the authors and cooks behind these recipes are unknown. These recipes appear as they were originally written.

Shrimper's Sauce

The fisherman out on the shrimping boat eats but one meal a day, and that's when the day's work is done. His recipe for shrimper's sauce has been handed down through many generations of fishermen. And although based on Creole recipes of two hundred years ago, it shows by addition of salt pork the Austrian influence among shrimpers.

½ cup cooking oil

1 cup chopped salt pork

3 onions, finely chopped

1 can (8 ounces) tomato sauce

3 cups boiling water

1 teaspoon chili powder

2 cloves garlic, minced

2 bay leaves

1 sprig thyme

1 teaspoon celery salt

Salt to taste

Black pepper to taste

Fry the chopped salt pork in the oil. Add the onions and fry but do not allow them to burn. Add the tomato sauce, then the boiling water, never letting the water stop boiling. Add the chili powder, garlic, bay leaves, thyme, celery salt, and salt and pepper.

Cook slowly for about 30 minutes, stirring frequently.

With the sauce made, the cook sets it carefully aside and looks over his supplies to decide what the meal will be.

Persimmon Beer

Remove the seeds from enough ripe persimmons to make a bushel of fruit without the seeds. Line a wooden keg with clean corn shucks. Mash up the persimmons with half a bushel of cornmeal and half a bushel of sweet potato peelings. Put the mixture in the keg and cover with water. Cover the keg and allow to stand until the taste is right, and then bore a hole in the top of the keg and draw off the beer. If you put a piece of cornbread in a cup and fill up the cup with persimmon beer, you'll have something highly satisfactory. Indulge cautiously until you learn your capacity.

Sweet Cucumber Pickles

It is better to have little finger-sized cucumbers, but as far as the taste goes, bigger ones cut into slices or chunks about 1" thick are just as good. There should be about 2 gallons cucumbers. Place them in a stone jar and pour over them 2 cups salt and 1 gallon boiling water. Let this stand for one week, skimming every day.

On the eighth day, drain well and pour over the cucumbers 1 gallon fresh boiling water. Let this stand for 24 hours.

On the ninth day, drain again and pour over a second gallon fresh boiling water. Add 1 table-spoon powdered alum. Let this stand for 24 hours.

On the tenth day, drain liquid off and pour over 1 gallon of fresh boiling water. Let stand for 24 hours.

On the eleventh day, drain water off and put the cucumbers in a clean stone jar or a preserving kettle. Prepare a syrup of 5 pints vinegar, ½ ounce celery seed, 6 cups sugar, and 1 ounce stick cinnamon. When this comes to a boiling point, pour it over the cucumbers. Let stand for 24 hours.

On the twelfth, thirteenth, and fourteenth days, drain and reheat the syrup, adding 1 cup sugar each day.

On the fourteenth day, pack the cucumbers in fruit jars and cover with syrup. Put rubbers and tops on the jars but do not screw tightly. Heat these jars of sweet pickles to the scalding point and seal.

You may think you would never be willing to undertake such a prolonged process, but if you ever get one sniff of these pickles, you will do anything necessary to get your pantry stocked with them. They smell like Araby the Blest, and they taste better than they smell.

Of the 2,879 minutes of messages that came pouring in, countless recalled childhood—land of food and memory.

Cherrystone Clams

"My name is Thea Lahti. My hidden kitchen story is this. When I was a little girl, my family lived fairly far out on Long Island. One day I was playing, and I heard a bell ring and saw a man coming along pushing a little two-wheeled cart. I thought maybe he was the ice cream man, so I ran down to greet him and said, 'Do you have ice cream?' He said, 'No, little girl. I am selling fish.' I said, 'Fish? No ice cream?' He said, 'Well no, but you can have one of these if you want.' And he shucked a cherrystone clam and said, 'You want to try?' and I said, 'Sure.' And I liked it and swallowed it down. And he said, 'Here, have another,' and he gave me as many as I wanted to eat. Once a week he would come by, and I would run down to greet him, and he'd shuck cherrystone clams as long as I ate them. I am sorry to say that there are probably no more **fishmen pushing little carts** through villages on Long Island anymore."

Waveland, Mississippi

"Hi, my name is Phillip Kehoe. Back in the late 1950s I got to spend a year living with my grandparents in Waveland, Mississippi, on the Gulf Coast. Every Sunday before dawn, my grandfather, my brother, and I would gather up the crab nets and walk down to the local Coleman Street Pier. We'd stop on the way and pick up a dozen hot glazed doughnuts, and then we would set our crab nets out and perpetually tend them. An hour and a half or so later you would have a number two washtub absolutely brim full of Gulf Coast blue crab.

"I don't know if it was by the weather, by the moon, or how she knew, but my grandmother always had a sense of when that bucket would be full. Here she'd come in her Hudson to pick us up and haul us home. We'd go home, and all through the morning she would boil seafood, and **the entire neighborhood would get together** and eat dinner that day—every Sunday. One family provided all the greens out of the garden. Another, the baked goods. It was always a great meal and a good time, one of my most cherished memories. I hope this adds to your kitchen collection."

"Dear Kitchen Sisters,

"When I was a child, my four sisters and I each were given one day a week on which we cooked dinner (seven days, seven people in the family). We had to plan for the shopping, and as a reward for cooking, the cook got to read part of a novel to the others while they cleaned up the dishes. This was not only a way to teach us life skills but also a way for my parents to, as my mom says, keep seven lives afloat at the expense of none. My parents had to suffer through ramshackle meals as we learned to cook. (My pièce de résistance was cutting hot dogs into inch-long pieces, carefully grating Cheddar cheese over them and broiling the platter. Voilà—the perfect dinner, served with a dainty china bowl filled with ketchup.) We were not allowed to complain or refuse to eat someone's cooking. My parents would say, 'This is the best bowl of defrosted vegetables we're having tonight!' In the end, they taught me not only how to cook but also grace and manners, and most important, how to work as an ensemble.

"**The system was called First Turn**, because the initial idea was set up as a democratic way to share special things—like sitting in the front seat or getting the first choice of a pie (and as a brilliant way for my parents to avoid our bickering). As I am the fourth sister, my day was, and continues to be, Thursday. And that means Thursday is always the best day of the week."

—Gabrielle Burton

When we opened up the Hidden Kitchens hotline, we pleaded, "Please don't tell us about your grandmother and her cooking." We know it sounds cold, heartless. Kitchens and grandmothers. The two are inextricably linked, but that's what we were afraid of. We knew that if we gave grandmother stories an inch, the hotline would melt down. It would be a flood, an endless sea of grandmothers and their cookies, pies, and advice. Fortunately for us, most of you completely disregarded our plea and called up not once, not twice, but three times to tell us about Grandma. Here are some kitchen stories even the hard-hearted Kitchen Sisters could not resist.

Message #671 was received Saturday at 6:00 PM

"Hi. My name is Nicole Johnston, and I'm calling in reference to my great-great-grandmother, Ellen Rocho, who started a box lunch company in Omaha, Nebraska, shortly after World War I called Rocho's Box Lunch. Her husband was in prison for embezzlement, and she had been left alone, penniless with four daughters to raise. She opened a rooming house and started making box lunches for her boarders. She started as a one-woman kitchen and ended up with a bakery and a fleet of trucks that supplied box lunches to local workers all over town. To me, it is amazing to

Rocho's Box Lunch delivery—Walter, Uncle Sam, and Marjorie—in 1924, Omaha, Nebraska

think of one woman who, while trying to figure out a way to support her family, in the end becomes one of the first industry leaders in baking and cooking in Omaha. Really, you have to call my grandmother, Marjorie Towey, and she'll tell you more."

The Food of Slaves

"Hi, my name is Richard Forhez. My grandmother was born and raised in Hungary and moved to the United States when she was young. When I was in sixth grade, we were living with her, and I came home with a cooking assignment for extra credit. We were studying the slave period in American history, and I decided to cook cornbread because it was the food of slaves. Being an Old World European grandma, she just kind of raised her eyebrow when I told her what I was doing. I got the ingredients and started to make my cornbread, and I burned it. By this point it was about midnight, and I was tired. So my grandmother said that I should go to sleep and that she would make the cornbread for me, again.

Mrs. Ellen Rocho's
Box Lunch business

"When I woke up in the morning, there was no cornbread. There were potato pancakes. My grandmother explained to me that when she was little and poor, people used to pick potatoes in Hungary and that this was the food of slaves. I was mortified and embarrassed, because I thought, now I'm going to have to go to school and try to explain to people why I brought in potato pancakes instead of cornbread. It didn't occur to me what she was saying. I really, truly just couldn't grasp at the age of twelve, what she meant. Many, many years later, I was just driving up the highway, and this whole thing flooded back into my memory, and I realized what she had done. She had shared this very personal thing with me—cooking the food of the slaves. She was already dead by then, so I didn't get a chance to thank her."

Big Grandma, Little Grandma

"My name is Douglas Weed. I have a story to tell about my two grandmas' kitchens. There was only one grandma at a time in my family. They rarely saw each other—didn't particularly like each other. I called them Little Grandma and Big Grandma in an accurate reflection of their physical sizes and the food on their tables. They each lived in small, obscure Pennsylvania towns.

"**Little Grandma ate no seeds, no salt, no sugar**, refused to make sauces, would not serve jams, berry pies, berry cobbler, berry pancakes. All meat was boiled or baked. Coarse whole-wheat bread was served with salt-free oatmeal for breakfast. Lots of plain boiled vegetables, canned sugar-free fruit for dessert. For a little boy in the 1950s, this was a tough assignment. Any meal at Little Grandma's house was a challenge. The solid, oh-so-plain food and not much of it.

"Big Grandma, by contrast, produced dinners to die for. Her table was covered with china serving bowls filled with chicken gravy, gravy-soaked biscuits, another with hot biscuits, two kinds of jam, honey still in the comb, the chicken in its own bowl, and milky coleslaw, a plate of ham, fresh fruit swimming in condensed milk. Big Grandma loved to make decorated two-layer buttercream-frosted cakes. Yellow, white, chocolate. You could have whatever flavor you wanted. She once made three different cakes for the same day. She baked pies, too, and homemade doughnuts. Frycakes, she called them.

"I loved my grandmas. Little Grandma was as sad and troubled as her food was plain. Big Grandma was as happy and as thoughtful as her table was loaded. Both lived into their eighties. Little Grandma died depressed and a bit demented. She lingered. Big Grandma died of high blood pressure and diabetes. A little artery blew up in her head. She fell to the floor dead in midsentence. No surprises for either, I suppose. They died as they lived—as they cooked in their nearly identical kitchens."

Message #34 was received
Thursday at 8:26 AM

"My name is Beverly Wege, and I live in a little town called Westmoreland, Kansas. My interest in cooking was greatly influenced by my mother and the neighbor ladies listening to *Radio Homemaker* programs that were broadcast from the Shenandoah, Iowa, area when I was a young girl. The Radio Homemakers had their start back in the 1930s, when stations were first going on the air and needed people to do live broadcasts.

Jessie Young broadcasting from her kitchen in Shenandoah, Iowa, home to KMA radio, the station that aired *Koffee Klatter*, a program that connected many women out on the prairie for years. From fellow broadcaster Evelyn Birkby's book *Neighboring on the Air*.

They helped spread the word about new cooking ideas, new food products, and they shared recipes with their army of devoted listeners.

"Household chores stopped when it was time for the recipes to be given. Children quickly learned it was a time they didn't bother Mom, and if they did, it had better be because someone was dying! If a neighbor had to miss a program,

they were on the phone to another neighbor as soon as possible to find out what had happened and what recipe they missed. I hated to see these programs end; they served to provide a continuity and a connection between the generations."

The Forager

Hunting and Gathering
with Angelo Garro

We met Angelo Garro nearly a decade ago, when we were working on *Waiting for Joe DiMaggio,* a Kitchen Sisters radio story about the return of Joltin' Joe at age eighty-three to his parents' village in Sicily. We needed help with some Sicilian translation, and a friend told us about a blacksmith from Sicily who lived in his forge, hidden down an alleyway in San Francisco, and who made artisan wrought iron and cured his own olives. He sounded promising.

Davia called Angelo out of the blue and asked him to listen to our tapes over the phone. He stopped everything he was doing to translate the recordings, and then invited us to the forge that evening for rabbit and polenta. We were in the midst of the mix of *DiMaggio,* so we didn't make it out that night.

A few months later the phone rang. "Are you coming for lunch or are you coming for dinner?" It was Angelo. The next day Davia spent a rainy afternoon eating lunch by candlelight. Everything was handmade by Angelo: the salami, the prosciutto, the pasta, the sauce, the wine, even the candlesticks.

The next week, after returning from hunting, he called to invite us to a wild boar dinner. Then a few months after that, we went foraging for fennel. That's when The Kitchen Sisters began following Angelo, as he follows the seasons, harvesting the wild, re-creating in wrought iron and in cooking the life he left behind in Sicily.

A ngelo!" Bob yells through the pine trees. "Shhh. Don't make any noise, Bob. Don't make any noise. Otherwise, the other hunters will be attracted." The two friends creep through the woods, looking for buried treasure on a steep stretch of California's coast. There's not a soul in sight, but you never know who might be there, lurking, trying to discover your secret spots. Quietly they press on, their boots squish the moist forest floor. Angelo Garro, his eyes peeled for porcini, is searching for supper.

"You have to look at the wet area of the trees, where there's dead stumps," Angelo leads in a loud Italian whisper. "They're hiding in the pine needle carpets here. You have to be focused. We're looking for porcini. And where there is a bubble, a little bump, there's a mushroom. Could be porcini, could be a poison one, so you have to be careful."

Born in Siracusa, Sicily, the son of a citrus merchant, Angelo grew up in the groves of oranges and lemons that

Angelo encounters some fellow Italian porcini hunters.

The Kitchen Sisters record Angelo in his kitchen at the forge.

his father exported to fruit sellers in Rome and Milan. "I was born in Sicily, and now I live in San Francisco," says Angelo. "In Sicily, I could tell by the smell what time of the year it was—orange season, persimmon season, then olive season. People used to pick olives and bring them to town, where they would crush them to make olive oil. The smells permeated the town where my grandmother lived."

Suddenly Angelo is down on his knees, dusting away the dirt. "Look! Bob! Bob! Come here!" yells Angelo, forgetting to whisper now. Years of foraging have taught him that porcini like two days of winter rain followed by one day of sun, which is what the Bay Area just had. "Wow. **Porcini bonanza!** Look how beautiful. Smell! If we find ten like this, tonight we can cook and make crostini mushrooms."

Angelo Garro—handsome, animated, compact, Sicilian—seems to have x-ray vision as he forages the forest floor. He doesn't just see a mushroom hidden beneath the pine mulch, he sees the meal he will make when he brings the porcini home to cook and the look on his friend Bob's face and on the faces of the ten other people he will invite when they eat porcini crostini back at the forge.

FORGING

Angelo Garro lives at the end of an alley in an industrial part of San Francisco, in an invented space that is his wrought-iron studio and his kitchen and his private, personal restaurant. But that is only the physical truth. His spirit lives in a much larger space, informed by **an ancient link between food and heart**.

"My place—how can I describe my place?" Angelo surveys the enormous welding tools, Italian olive picking baskets, branches of ripe grapefruit, the scanner and iPod, hunting catalogs, hand-wrought metal grapevines that fill the cavernous workshop he calls Renaissance Forge.

"This used to be a blacksmith shop and a stable in the 1890s, where all the gold diggers and cowboys used to bring the horses to shoe them and to fix their carriages. I do architectural wrought-iron work, which adorns beautiful homes. I forge elements for balconies, gates, staircases. And over here I built a kitchen off in the corner of the shop. So here, right in the forge, while the metal is warming, before I beat it up, I can just start a recipe. **If I feel inspired, I don't have to go far.**"

Angelo Garro working metal at Renaissance Forge. At right, a piece of his handcrafted gate.

Angelo in the olives

He taps a mallet lightly on a hot piece of bronze he is shaping on his anvil. "Listen to this one." A sweet metallic note rings out and mingles with the sound of the Puccini aria and the slam and pump of the hydraulic hammer. "Listen, it's like a soprano, like music. Each place on the metal has a different sound, you know. When iron was discovered in Europe, it was used to make weapons. But they also made beautiful gates, which is good. If I had been born back then, I would make gates, not weapons."

"Hey, Xavier!" Angelo calls out to a large, beaming Frenchman who bursts in without knocking. "This is my friend Xavier," Angelo says. "He just went dove hunting, and tonight we're cooking wild dove and polenta. His wife and kids are coming, and some other friends, too. Would you like to stay?"

Angelo met Xavier Carbonnet, an art dealer from France, on Ocean Beach at sunset, when the striped bass were running. Somehow the California coastline wasn't big enough for both of them. The Italian and the Frenchman began their friendship arguing about how and where to fish. Several hours and several bass later, the two went back to the forge to cook their catch. Twenty years later, they are still arguing, about how to hunt duck, how to cook dove, who should be president, whether Xavier's elk meatballs need more salt. "More salt? All you Sicilians know is salt. I want to taste elk, not salt," says Xavier.

Xavier heads back through the forge to the walk-in meat locker/wine cellar Angelo recently built and adds the doves to the forager's bounty: huge wild boar prosciutto, three barrels of homemade pinot noir, three baskets of olives curing in salt, a big beaker of homemade grappa.

"Angelo goes with the seasons," says Xavier. "If he has hunted a boar, there will be sausage making, and there will be prosciutto making. In the spring it's fennel. In the fall it's wine. In the middle of November, turkey hunting. In the rain it's ducks. If you come on a day like today, you don't know what you're going to see, or what you're going to eat.

"Angelo, what are you cooking today?" Xavier bellows from the fridge.

Angelo, his eyes shielded by welder's goggles, is pulling molten metal out of the two-thousand-degree kiln, creating the graceful curves of a bronze balcony. Lost in a seventeenth-century moment, he is brought back by the idea of a late breakfast.

"I can make you Sicilian poached eggs."

"Angelo is a center of gravity for people from just about every class and every job—plumbers, filmmakers, artists; women from every country flock here," Xavier tells us. "I've seen the most eclectic group of people come to the forge for lunch and dinner. And I wouldn't think of driving within five miles of the forge without stopping by."

Angelo moves with grace and precision around his industrial kitchen, pouring balsamic vinegar into a pan of boiling water on the stove. "I had a hangover one day, and I made eggs and accidentally put some vinegar into the water. You know, like you fight fire with fire, the same thing. You use vinegar to fight the wine. Most of the great science over the centuries is by accident, the people putting two and two together."

Xavier is starting a sauce for the doves as Angelo poaches. "The forge is like the Old Country," Xavier continues. "It's like a piece of Italy or Old Europe, frozen in time in the middle of San Francisco. It's just a very mysterious place. It's a metal-smith forge. It has just about everything from crab nets to bow and arrows; photographs of his children, family, and friends; old machinery; and tools. And there's a fig tree in the middle of it with fruit. The center of the forge is open to the sky, with no roof."

"This kitchen is in keeping with the Italian tradition," interrupts Angelo. "They always have a little open kitchen outside in south of Italy, because it's so hot you have to be outside under the big mulberry shade trees. So I try to recreate that in this little spot here in San Francisco in a fifteen-by-twelve kitchen."

He twists oregano off a dry twig, filling the air with scent. "This is imported from Sicily. Every time I use some, it makes me feel homesick. My grandmother used to tell me, '*Angeluzzu, vai, vai prendere oregano . . .* ' Go pick some oregano, we'll dry it. I'll give you some ice cream."

Angelo scoops out four perfect poached eggs, lays them on toast, drizzles Italian olive oil on top, and sprinkles each with oregano.

"Xavier, stop talking and eat while it's hot, *subito*."

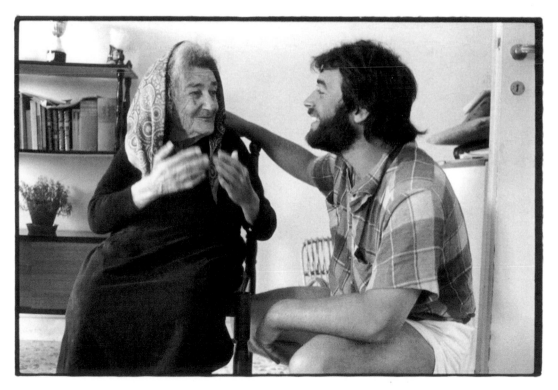

Angelo and his grandmother Sebastiana in Sicily

EELING

"Angelo got one!" The crowd cheers.

"Angelo, can I fish with you?"

Angelo Garro is surrounded by his apostles, fisherman, just like in the Bible. Most of them are under ten, the next generation of foragers swarming around him on the slippery rocks near Stinson Beach above San Francisco.

This is their second annual April eeling expedition, and Angelo is showing them the ropes, how to bait the bamboo poke pole with squid, how to find the

monkey-faced prickle-backed eels that lurk out of sight in the cracks, and how not to get knocked down by a wave. Another dozen adults, who have already learned these lessons from Angelo, are scattered in the shallows, stabbing the crevices in search of tonight's feast.

Angelo started his eeling tradition on his birthday a dozen years back. He and his friends gathered eels under the Golden Gate Bridge by day and grilled them on the beach by night. One year, someone brought along Alice Waters, the legendary founder of Chez Panisse, who has a love and appreciation for all things wild and foraged. Alice recognized a kindred spirit, and she and Angelo have been friends and kitchen collaborators ever since.

"Angelo is sort of the Pied Piper of this group of people in San Francisco, gathering them together and taking them out into nature to places we never thought to go," says Alice, negotiating the slimy boulders as she heads down to the tide pools with her poke pole. "We feel connected because of that, these trips. Whether it's out foraging in the hillsides for wild mushrooms or coming down here to the ocean and fishing for eels or picking grapes or harvesting olives or wild boar hunting—well, I haven't gone on a wild boar hunt—there's always something, every season. I can't separate spring from the fennel cakes, fall from the wild mushrooms. His seven-fish dinner at Christmastime is one of our big celebrations. It's Sicilian, but now it's become adopted, and it's our tradition as well."

"Whoa, that's a beautiful hole right here," Angelo yells exuberantly from a rock nearby. "**If I were an eel, I would live there.** You know, you can't have the seven-fish dinner at Christmas without eel. It's almost like turkey on Thanksgiving."

Peggy Knickerbocker, a cook and food writer, wades in to her waist. Peggy was one of the first people Angelo met when he moved to San Francisco some twenty years ago. She figures Angelo's eeling and foraging is the search for much more than food. "Angelo has this theory that when people do these things communally—like when you get together to peel the skins off of the eels or sit around sorting olives—you can figure out all your psychological problems. In Sicily, he says, there's no need to go to the psychologists. When you work with a group of friends and talk, it is not only relaxing, but it brings you together as a family of friends."

"Uh oh," Angelo yells. "Eel coming; I can feel it nibbling! You have to concentrate." He laughs and nabs one from its hidden hole. "I'm concentrating on the eel and the spiral pasta with baked eels in a fish stock sauce with parsley bread crumbs, garlic, and a few spoons of tomato sauce for coloring that I will cook for everybody tonight!"

FENNELING

It's November, and Angelo is driving home from Petaluma, where he's been helping some friends harvest and press their olives to make oil. The light is fading, and the heartbreaking Italian love songs of Adriano Celentano fill the Xterra as Angelo navigates the back roads. Even Angelo, Italian to the bone, can't bear this much tragedy. "I'm going to try to find some opera," he says, changing the music. "It's more cheerful."

Suddenly he hits the brakes and pulls over. "There's fennel. We're going to pick some dry fennel so that I can flavor my olives that are curing in the forge. Plus, the car will smell good all the way to San Francisco." In seconds, he's out of the car, wielding a pocketknife and cutting the dry branches that line the fence alongside a cow pasture.

"I pick fennel all over San Francisco in empty parking lots, in driveways, below the freeways. Urban foraging. I try to go to the reclusive places, off the beaten tracks. You drive around, see a beautiful spot, maybe it's somebody's backyard, and I knock on the door and ask, 'Can I pick your fennel?' Fresh wild fennel, *finnochio selvaggio,* like in the hills in Sicily. My grandmother gathered wild fennel every spring to make *polpete di finocchio,* fennel patties, little fried cakes with wild fennel, bread crumbs, and *parmigianno.* So when I saw fennel in

Angelo on an urban foraging expedition

California, I thought, 'Wow, that's just like in Sicily,' and I started to make it almost immediately."

When he was growing up in Sicily, Angelo never cooked. He ate what his mother and grandmother cooked for him. "In Sicily, men, if they go in the kitchen, they are teased. They say you are a *huomo in sottana,* a man with a skirt. The women—they just cast you away. 'Get out of here. This is not your place.' But, as an adult, after I moved away, when I came home from Switzerland and Canada to visit, I spent a lot of time with my mother in the kitchen as she prepared the meals. And when I was away, I would call back for recipes and cook from the memory of smell and taste trying to replicate what I left behind."

DUCK HUNTING

"Today, it is January, and we are here in Colusa to hunt ducks," Angelo proclaims. "Day" is stretching it a bit; it's actually two hours till dawn in a cold, wet duck blind in northern California's Central Valley. Xavier, Angelo, and their sixteen-year-old hunting protégé Cody are bermed into the duck blind **for the last day of the season**. "After that, we put everything to rest."

The men are proud of this blind. Cody's dad, a welder, customized the thing. It's a metal box, like a small trash bin, buried three quarters into a flooded rice paddy. Four stools inside sit in about six inches of mucky water, with spent shells and casings floating about. Twigs and branches have been made into a kind of canopy to camouflage the container from the thousands of ducks that pass overhead on their way to Mexico for the winter. Xavier has brought a thermos of the most perfect espresso, and the hunters take shots between rounds.

"We are in rice ponds," says Xavier. "They harvested the rice a few months ago, and then they flood these ponds, and we put a few hundred plastic decoys in the water. You have the decoys spread around to make the ducks think there are birds on the ground feeding. You're trying to trick them, fool them, intercept them."

They are not alone. Xavier figures there are two thousand hunters buried chest-deep in the valley. Angelo is blowing the homemade wooden duck callers that hang around his neck. "'**Kurkurk, kurkurk.' That's a coot.**" He is smiling now. He raises a different wooden whistle to his mouth and quacks, 'Eh eh eh.' That's a mallard green head calling the female." Angelo runs through his duck-call repertoire—puddle ducks, diving ducks, pintails, wigeons, cinnamon teals. His little concert has set off a volley of shots from hunters throughout the marsh who think Angelo is a duck.

"It's very nice to know birds, to know what surrounds where you live. How many people know the names of birds? So many people don't know the plant species or the bird species." Angelo's reverie is interrupted by Xavier's watch.

Kitchen Sister Davia reporting for duck-blind duty

"Goose, goose, overhead!" The men unload about nine rounds, but the geese are long gone. "We scared them away. That poor goose. He's got stories to tell."

"We never shoot at the leader of the pack," says Xavier. "Out of respect. This is the mother of those birds, the one that is knowledgeable, that can get the flock all the way to Mexico."

Xavier turns to Angelo; the cold water sloshes under their waders. The early-morning light peeks silver through the high clouds. "Angelo, why do we do what we do?"

"I think because we are a prehistoric people," he says. "We haven't shaken out the instinct of hunting like *Homo sapiens*, you know? We're kind of a living history. It's a very distant memory, something you feel familiar with. I can't quite explain myself what makes me hunt or kill an animal. It's something I grew up with. I am a duck hunter, but also I am a nature lover, and I don't see anything contradictory to love nature and love ducks, and hunt some of them and make this incredible dinner for my friends."

As Angelo talks, scattered gunshots pepper the dawn. "I think about death. I mean, death is part of life. To have a good heart, you have to be able to feel everything: death, crying, happiness."

"Birds coming!!" Xavier alerts the others. The men raise their guns. Several rounds later, Angelo has bagged a mallard. You can see a recipe rolling around his brain before the bird even hits the water.

"When I was a little boy in Sicily, there was a movie theater near my grandfather's, and I would go watch John Wayne westerns with the cowboys and Indians. I always thought, 'I want to go to America and live like the Indians.' And here I am. I have the passion of hunting, of foraging, the passion for opera, for my work, for the people I love. I have the passion of cooking, pickling, curing salamis, sausage, wine in the fall. This is my life. I do this with my friends. It is to my heart."

A SPRINGTIME SPECIALTY

Angelo Garro shares his grandmother Sebastiana's recipe for wild fennel patties. You won't find fennel, the beautiful, furry green that covers coastal California, in your produce section. It's too fragile and delicate for mass harvesting, but for a few weeks each spring, you can forage for it in and around San Francisco and anywhere that early Italian settlers may have sprinkled seeds. Angelo calls this "fenneling." Somehow with Angelo, most all his nouns somehow become verbs. After fenneling, it's time for mushrooming, then eeling. Come fennel season, Angelo gathers a group of friends and heads to a hillside or roadside or a freeway underpass for a fenneling foray. For Angelo's many friends, the first fennel patties of the season are a beloved rite of spring.

Fennel hearts are the bright green, furry pieces that are in the center of the green shoots of fennel. Unlike conventional fennel, which is about the familiar white bulbs, wild fennel is all about the greens; the white bulb and stalks are not visible. When you're gathering fennel, pick only the young fronds and lay them in a paper bag horizontally—all the tops should be pointing in the same direction. Keep them together in your hands as you wash them gently in a bucket of cold water.

Angelo Garro's Wild Fennel Cakes

Wild fennel fronds (the bright green interiors), enough to fill a large brown supermarket bag

3 eggs

1 cup high-quality hand-grated Parmesan cheese, such as Reggiano

1 cup coarsely ground bread crumbs (made from day-old bread ground up in a food processor or blender, not store-bought fine-grain bread crumbs)

1 teaspoon crushed red pepper flakes

Extra virgin olive oil

Peanut oil

Salt to taste

Black pepper to taste

Wash the fronds in cold water, swishing them until no dirt is visible. Working in batches, lay the fronds on a chopping board and finely chop about 8" of each frond.

Bring a large pot of salted water to boil over high heat and parboil the chopped fronds for 15 to 20 minutes. Taste to make sure they are tender. Pour them into a colander, allowing the fronds to dry in their own steam. Stir once or twice with a wooden spoon to help the cooling process. When the chopped fronds are cold, transfer them to a large mixing bowl.

Combine the chopped fennel with the eggs, cheese, bread crumbs, and red pepper flakes. Form into 2" patties.

Heat a cast-iron or nonstick frying pan with a very little bit of olive oil cut with a very small amount of peanut oil. Fry the fennel cakes on both sides until golden brown. Drain them on paper towels and sprinkle with salt and pepper.

The patties are best served warm to the friends you went fenneling with.

MAKES 20 TO 30 SMALL (HORS D'OEUVRE–SIZE) FENNEL CAKES

Sicilian Poached Eggs

Like most Italians, Angelo doesn't usually have more than cappuccino and a little crostini (toast) in the morning. But when he does eat breakfast, he might poach his eggs Sicilian style— topped with a drizzle of olive oil and a pinch of fragrant oregano.

2 cups water

1½–2 tablespoons red wine or balsamic vinegar

2 eggs

2 slices bread

Salt to taste

Fresh cracked pepper to taste

Extra-virgin olive oil

Pinch of fresh or dried oregano

In a shallow saucepan, bring the water to a boil. Add 1 tablespoon vinegar. Using great care, break your eggs into the boiling water. Cook for 1 to 1½ minutes.

Meanwhile, toast the bread. When done, remove the eggs with a slotted spoon and drain off any liquid (the yolk should be soft, and the egg white should be solid). Place the eggs over the toast and sprinkle with salt and pepper. Top with a drizzle olive oil, a dash of vinegar, and oregano.

MAKES 2 SERVINGS

Angelo's Porcini Pasta

Angelo forages for porcini mushrooms, but you can also buy porcinis in season at a farmers' market or good food store. To clean the mushrooms, carefully brush and wipe them. Don't put them in water as they will absorb it like a sponge. When cooking this pasta dish, Angelo makes his own homemade fresh linguine, but dried pasta works as well.

8	porcini mushrooms (1 to 2 per person)
1½–2	tablespoons olive oil
	Salt to taste
	Black pepper to taste
1	clove garlic, thinly sliced
1	pound fresh or dried linguine or fettuccine
	Italian parsley, minced
	High-quality Parmesan cheese, such as Reggiano

Using a damp cloth or a brush, clean the mushrooms. Slice the mushrooms vertically into pieces ⅛" thick.

Heat the olive oil over high heat in a cast-iron pan. Add the sliced mushrooms and sauté until golden brown. (Keep the pan hot.) Season the mushrooms with salt and pepper. Add the garlic and sauté 2 to 3 minutes more. Set aside.

Meanwhile, bring a large pot of water to a boil. Add a dash of salt and cook the pasta until al dente. Drain and divide the pasta among 4 plates.

Add the mushroom mixture to your pasta and sprinkle parsley on top with an additional drizzle of olive oil. Serve with Parmesan, but not too much.

MAKES 4 SERVINGS

After we aired Angelo's story, foragers started popping up everywhere, like mushrooms after a rain. Foragers and hunters are scattered across the backyards, hills, and woods of this abundant nation.

Veronica Williams,
the Mushroom Lady

From: Sharon Boorstin
Subject: The Mushroom Lady!

"I learned about Veronica Williams when I was on the Long Beach Peninsula in Washington, just across the mouth of the Columbia River from Astoria, Oregon, writing a story about women chefs of the region. They all get their wild mushrooms from Veronica, who forages every day in the very wet, moss-covered forests there.

"Veronica drives a mud-spattered red BMW with 'ALL WILD' on the license plate—the name of her mushroom-foraging business, which supplies many of the top restaurants in the area. Veronica refuses to take anyone with her when she goes into the woods so they won't find her secret spots. It's been said that she always dresses her best so that if something should happen to her and people find her body, she'll look respectable."

From: Douglas Smith
Subject: Hunting and Foraging with Angelo Garro

"Hi, Sisters. My FM dial was parked on NPR before dawn this morning as I left my house in Red Lodge, Montana. I was off for a hunt in one of our magical little enclaves, where the grasslands of the Great Plains erupt suddenly into the Rocky

Mountains. As I drove to my special spot, I was most pleasantly surprised to hear your feature on Angelo Garro. In the midst of an NPR universe dominated by people suspicious of hunters and guns, suddenly we were treated to a portrait of a vibrant Sicilian who is both an avid hunter and a gourmet cook. Furthermore, he was granted airtime to explain that he sees no conflict in being both an animal lover and a hunter.

"In the duck blind you captured the hunter's respect for his prey and his intimate knowledge of each waterfowl species' unique voice. You also did not succumb to political correctness and actually recorded the sound of the firing shotgun. Good on you—hunters are not ashamed of ethically and humanely taking a wild creature.

"I felt an uncanny identification with this story. Some of my most treasured hours are spent trekking the Montana foothills, shotgun in hand, with my **two talented bird dogs, Braindead and Jerry Lee**. When I take a wild creature, I feel an obligation, almost reverence, toward this wonderful gift of nature, which demands that I put forth a special effort when I prepare an animal I have killed for the table.

"Last week I made lasagna—from scratch! Please don't underestimate the commitment necessary for a bachelor to dedicate three hours to boiling noodles, simmering tomato sauce, grating Italian cheeses with unpronounceable names, pressing garlic, and washing a dizzying array of pots and pans. Would this near-heroic culinary undertaking have occurred in the absence of my handmade venison Italian sausage as a prime ingredient of the finished dish? Not in a million years!

"The vast majority of hunters are ethical, dedicated outdoorsmen and environmentalists who savor the game they harvest as table fare.

"Unfortunately, there exists a tiny minority of unethical 'slobs with guns' who are often the hunters most visible to the nonhunting public. On behalf of the many hunters who listen to NPR, thanks for a fascinating and positive story."

—Douglas Smith, Red Lodge, Montana

A Secret Civil Rights Kitchen

Georgia Gilmore and
the Club from Nowhere

"Hey, my name is John T. Edge, and I live down in Oxford, Mississippi. I'm calling about a woman y'all need to know about. Her name is Georgia Gilmore. She was a cook in the 1950s in Montgomery, Alabama, and when I think of hidden kitchens, I think about the story of her back-door restaurant, her secret kitchen that fueled the Civil Rights Movement."

The restaurant Georgia Gilmore operated out of her home was hidden, all right, because if it had been a real restaurant, it would have been illegal. Blacks and whites couldn't eat together in Montgomery, Alabama, and throughout most of the South in the 1950s. John T. Edge, who called in to tell us about Georgia Gilmore, is the director of the Southern Foodways Alliance at the University of Mississippi.

"Our region is heavy with history," said John T. "I see food and time at the table as a way toward reconciliation, and Georgia's kitchen epitomized that."

We listened to John and decided to make a pilgrimage to Montgomery to chronicle the legacy of this secret civil rights kitchen.

Montgomery, Alabama, 2005. A 1954 city bus crawls past the state capitol. A handful of tourists are aboard for a tour along the city's "civil rights trail"—the Rosa Parks Museum, the church where Dr. Martin Luther King preached during the bus boycott, Governor George Wallace's office, and a half dozen other historic spots etched into the memory of Montgomery. Just a little ways off the route sits a modest brick house in a working-class neighborhood—Georgia Gilmore's place. It's not on the civil rights tour. Not yet. But Mark Gilmore, Georgia's son and a former city councilman, is working on that.

"Her house is on the historic register," says Mark Gilmore, the keeper of his mother's story. "Did you see the plaque in the yard?—'Georgia Gilmore, 1920–1990—a solid, energetic boycott participant and supporter . . . her culinary skills contributed to the cause of justice.' Yeah, Mama could cook. She was a stone cook."

"Georgia's food was cooked on the mama level, and Georgia was like Big Mama—the Southern-type big mamas—she took on the personality of ten or fifteen of them," remembers Reverend Al Dixon, who knew Georgia and her cooking well. Reverend Dixon, a disc jockey on WAPX, the black radio station in Montgomery, used to eat at Georgia's most every day. "She would listen to your problems, and she'd give you her ideas. But everybody could tell you Georgia Gilmore didn't take no junk! If you pushed her too far, she'd say a few bad words, and if you pushed her any further, she'd hit you!"

"She was swift on her feet," Councilman Gilmore concurs. "Mama weighed about three fifty, four hundred pounds, but she could move. And if she got on your head, she weighed about seven hundred pounds. 'Cause Mama didn't play."

People came to Georgia's for the cook as well as the cooking. "Folks just loved to hear her talk, loved to hear her joke," says Reverend Dixon. "She could talk on everybody's level, from the preachers to us disc jockeys. She was what we called a hip person. Aware, awake, alert, know what's going down, know what's up, with old folk and young people alike. And she was a confidante; she would even give you advice on how to keep your woman."

Georgia Gilmore came up working hard, first as a tie changer for the railroad, then as a midwife delivering babies in the black community. And for years she cooked at the National Lunch Company, a white-owned restaurant in downtown Montgomery, where the law required a partition to separate the counter into two areas, one for whites and one for blacks. "My sister and I used to work down at National Lunch Company with Mama, washing dishes," Mark remembers. "And when she had to leave to go deliver babies, we would fill in cooking."

Juggling jobs and raising six kids on her own, Georgia had her hands full. But that didn't keep her from "feeding half the church" and becoming a local fried chicken legend.

"During that time Georgia Gilmore was doing some catering for Dr. Martin Luther King, who was new in the area," remembers Nelson Malden, a barber who worked in Georgia's neighborhood. "I started cutting Dr. King's hair in 1954, when he first came to town. And when his friends or VIPs would come, he would always have Mrs. Gilmore cook up a batch of chicken. Her house was about three blocks from the parsonage where he lived, and whenever I saw her walking by with a big basket or crate of food, I knew pretty much where she was going."

Georgia Gilmore at Her Stove

"My mama cooked pound cake, German chocolate cake, red velvet cake, 7-Up cake, sour cream cake. All kinds of cakes, she could make 'em. She could make the peach pie and the banana pudding that would make you slap your brains out."

—MARK GILMORE

A SECRET CIVIL RIGHTS KITCHEN

Georgia lived on Centennial Hill most of her adult life, in a thriving, close-knit African-American community of black-owned businesses, grocery stores, beauty shops, and gas stations on Montgomery's east side near the state capitol. Alabama State, the first state-supported black teachers college in the United States, was only a few blocks from Georgia's. And so was the Biltmore Hotel, the nicest and largest lodging that accommodated blacks. Everyone would stay there when they came to town—ministers, visiting professors, and musicians like Sam Cooke, Brooke Benton, and others passing through Montgomery on tour. One town, two worlds until December 1, 1955.

"YOU CANNOT BE AFRAID"

On December 1, 1955, when Rosa Parks was arrested for refusing to give up her seat on a segregated city bus, word traveled fast through the Centennial Hill neighborhood. Georgia was at work at the National Lunch Company and heard the news on the radio. Staff members at Alabama State printed up flyers, the ministers got the word out from their pulpits, and the newspaper picked up the announcement: Mass Meeting at Holt Street Baptist Church, Monday Night, 7:00 PM.

"You know, you take things and take things and take things," Georgia Gilmore said some thirty years later, "and we were dealing with a new generation. And this new generation had decided that they just had taken as much as they could."

The town exploded. That Monday night, Georgia and four thousand others descended on Holt Street Baptist Church for the meeting. No one had expected such a turnout, and with the crowd overflowing into the street, they set up speakers outside so all could hear. "A lot of people at that time didn't know too much about Dr. King because he was just a local pastor," Nelson Malden remembers. "But the night of that first mass meeting, he got up to speak, and he was so eloquent one of the ladies turned to me and said, 'The lord has sent us a savior.' That man could speak, make your hair stand on end."

"I never cared too much for preachers, but I listened to him preach that night," Georgia later told a reporter. "And the things he said were things I believed in." That night, Dr. King was elected head of the Montgomery Improvement Association (MIA), a new organization formed to fight injustice and to lead the bus boycott.

Georgia got involved in the MIA right away the best way she could—by cooking. She'd make up baskets of food—her legendary fried chicken, tubs of macaroni and cheese, desserts—and bring them to the Monday night mass meetings. Organizers could always count on her to fix food for marchers and protestors.

In the early months of the boycott, the city of Montgomery accused Martin Luther King and the MIA of conspiracy for inciting the boycott. Defense lawyers called in witnesses from the community to help disprove the charges. Georgia was among those who took the stand.

She told the court she had taken the buses all her life, since she was a little girl growing up in Montgomery. But one day in 1955, just two months before Rosa Parks was arrested, a bus driver had rudely ordered her to get off the bus and reboard at the rear, even though she'd already paid. At first, Georgia refused. The driver yelled, "Nigger, get out that door and go around to the back." When she finally did as he said, he shut the back door and pulled away before she could get back on. That was the day Georgia started walking. She had not gotten back on a bus since.

"You cannot be afraid if you want to accomplish anything," Georgia said. **"You got to have the willin', the spirit, and above all, you got to have the get-up."**

News of Georgia's testimony was in all the papers, and her photo was on the front page of the *Chicago Defender.* That's when things got hard. The National Lunch Company fired her. The insurance company would not renew her homeowners' insurance. She was paying the price for her activism.

When Georgia told Reverend King she'd been fired for her involvement in the boycott, he urged her to start cooking on her own and even gave her the money to buy pots and pans as well as to make repairs to her house.

REV. KING'S OWN STORY

virtual stage with much of the world looking on. Included in the cast of the controversial trial was Mrs. Thelma Glass, (extreme left) president of Women's Political

Council of Montgomery. She leaves court after testifying. Star performer at the trial (second from left) was Mrs. Georgia Therese Gilmore, witness for the defense. S h e

stands on courthouse steps with Attys. Fred D. Gray and Ozell Billingsley. Mrs. G i l-more, 36, the mother of six children and a midwife by profession declared: "W h e n

they count the money Negro dimes ain't no different from white!" Ministers attending the trial (second from right) included Rev. W. J. Powell, Old Ship AMEZ church; Rev.

T. H. Bonner, CME church; Rev. Solomon Seay, A.M.E. Z. church; Rev. T. R. French and Rev. Leroy Bennett, both AMEZ ministers, and (rear) Rev. Edmond Rogan, C.M.E.

church, and Rev. R. Ewing Tricher, Louisville A.M.E.Z. church, Reluctant witness for the defense (extreme right) Mrs. Jeannetta Reese covers up from cameraman as she

hurries across street during trial. She has avoided sitting with the rest of spectators because of her role in informing on Atty. Fred D. Gray.

Chicago Defender
WORLD'S GREATEST WEEKLY

51 Years of SERVICE

15¢ and WORTH IT

Copyright 1956 by the Robert S. Abbott Pub. Co., 3435 Indiana Ave., CAlumet 5-3656

CHICAGO, ILLINOIS—SATURDAY, MARCH 31, 1956

THIS PAPER CONSISTS OF TWO PARTS — PART O

"Star performer at the trial (second from left) was Georgia Theresa Gilmore, witness for the defense. She stands on the courthouse steps with Attys. Fred D. Gray and Ozell Billingsley. Mrs. Gilmore, thirty-six, the mother of six children and a midwife by profession declared, 'When they count the money Negro dimes ain't no different from White!'"

—*CHICAGO DEFENDER*, MARCH 31, 1956

"She started fixing a little food at our home and selling it," Mark Gilmore recalls. "Word got out that Mrs. Gilmore was running a catering service out of her house on Dericote, making lunch and delivering it." She made stuffed pork chops, meat loaf, bread pudding, and sweet potato pies. The local doctors' offices, the teachers from the college, the secretaries, and the beauty operators all began ordering from her. The folks working at the capitol asked for Georgia's white meat and bacon, collard greens, and black-eyed peas. And every day she got a call from a black worker at a white-owned laundry on Decatur and High Streets, ordering up lunch for the laundry's twenty-five black employees.

With a house full of kids, a kitchen full of orders, and the phone ringing off the hook, Georgia cooked. Mark and his brother would deliver the food around town in Georgia's old Chrysler, or sometimes she'd deliver it herself. Pretty soon she was making three hundred to four hundred lunches a day.

As Georgia's take-out business grew, students and locals started showing up at her house wanting to eat lunch on the spot. They'd squeeze in around her oak trestle dining room table or eat sitting on the couches in Georgia's living room while she cooked and fussed in the kitchen.

Ninety-four-year-old Johnnie Rebecca Carr, president of the MIA since 1967, remembers Georgia's place as if it were right there before her, as if her friend Georgia were in the other room still frying for the Movement. "She turned part of her home into a dining area, but it was not an official restaurant; it was kind of a secret place."

Martin Luther King was a regular at the brick house on Dericote, just up the street from where African-American funeral director and legendary civil rights activist Rufus Lewis lived. King would bring guests for lunch and hold meetings at Georgia's place, some of them

"Georgia Gilmore's place, it was very important having a place of that caliber to go for food. You know, a lot of things have been settled over a cup of coffee or a cup of tea."
—ACTIVIST JOHNNIE REBECCA CARR

secret meetings. "Dr. King needed a place where he could go," Reverend Dixon explains. "You know, he couldn't go just anywhere and eat. He needed someplace where he could not only trust the people around him but also trust the food. And that was Georgia's."

At one point the city came around and wanted to shut Georgia down, condemn her house. "I'll never forget it," says Mark. "Dr. King stood up in the middle of the floor and said, 'Mrs. Gilmore, get a contractor and get everything checked out.' And he helped her remodel."

BEELINE FOR GEORGIA'S

The kitchen was small, and Georgia was large, but it all seemed to work. She'd get up at 4:00 in the morning to get things prepared, handwrite the day's menu for the tables, and be ready for lunch, always cooking and tasting, tasting and cooking.

"About noon we knew to make a beeline to Georgia Gilmore's place," remembers Reverend Thomas E. Jordan, pastor of the Lilly Baptist Church, who grew up playing with Georgia's children and later became a regular at her home restaurant. "A lot of times you'd have to wait an hour to be fed. You had a clientele that would sit around a regular-size dining room table and hold conversations on a daily basis. And people might not know each other at first, but through sitting there each day, they became friends, black and white. People like Morris Dees with the Southern Poverty Law Center and people from his office. A lot of the white lawyers and doctors would come in."

"And as these would leave, another set would come, just like a Methodist communion table," describes Althea Thomas, organist at Dexter Avenue King Memorial Baptist Church. "Sometimes there would be about four professors, clerical workers, and a policeman or two." And if the place was full, people would just stand up and eat, sometimes right in the kitchen. Georgia would be cooking chops, and she'd take one right out of the grease and put it on your plate.

Georgia's son, City Councilman Mark Gilmore

"Stuffed bell peppers. Barbecued ribs, fried fish, and spaghetti in meat sauce," Mark Gilmore recites the names of his mother's specialties with a reverence usually reserved for church. "She would have chitlins with slaw and take the hog maw and cut it up in 'em. Ma'dear could cook it, man. I call her Ma'dear because she was dear. Sometimes she would run out of food, and they'd say, 'Mrs. Gilmore, what you got left?' She'd say, 'Baby, I don't have nothing but these chicken backs.' They'd say, 'Well, fix them with some of those corn muffins and some of that good buttermilk.' The DAs, the senators, and the congressmen, they'd all come."

DR. KING CALLED HER TINY

"Dr. King called her Tiny; she called him Heifer, or Whore. That's right. She called nearly everyone who came in Heifer or Whore, including Dr. King. 'Come here, little heifer, and get your dinner,'" Mark laughs. "And she called the governor Guvs. 'Come here, Guvs.' 'Mrs. Gilmore, what'd you say?' And they'd kill themselves laughing."

She was funny, but she was big and she was tough. She was not a woman you wanted to cross. "She used to talk about that nonviolence thing," says Reverend Dixon. "I heard Georgia say, 'I couldn't take some of the things y'all take.' And she meant it. At one time she socked up a white garbage man over there because he would not come into her yard to pick up the garbage like he did in the white folks' yards. After that, it was established—don't mess with Georgia."

Georgia was not one to back down, especially when it came to her family and her turf. When her son Mark was beaten up by police for walking through a

Protestors, Montgomery, Alabama, circa 1964

"white only" park one evening on his way to the hospital where he worked, she and her son sued—*Gilmore v. City of Montgomery*—and they won.

THE CLUB FROM NOWHERE

The bus boycott lasted 381 days, longer than anyone had imagined it could, and Georgia cooked straight through. She put herself at risk every time she opened her front door for her customers. "Fear was everywhere," remembers Montgomery historian and writer Richard Bailey. "That was a bad time, a frightening time. And it took a lot of nerve and courage on all those people's parts. You were fighting the legal system and custom, and I don't know which was larger. During those days you would not admit that you were a member of the NAACP; you wouldn't admit that you were a member of anything that had anything to do with civil rights. You did nothing to debunk the status quo."

People were fired from their jobs for supporting the boycott, harassed by the police for driving boycotters to work, and there were bombings throughout Georgia Gilmore's neighborhood—at Dr. King's residence, outside one of the Monday night mass meetings, at the cabstands near the Biltmore Hotel.

The Movement needed money to buy station wagons and pay for gasoline for a flotilla of cars that had been pressed into service to carry boycotters to and from work. It takes a certain kind of person to look at a pie and see a weapon for change. That's the kind of person Georgia Gilmore was.

"Georgia just got it into her mind that she was going to raise money for the Movement," remembers Johnnie Carr. "And if Georgia was raising money, she was doing it through food. She started up a group called the Club from Nowhere."

Georgia baked pies, and she found other women to do the same. Maybe you couldn't attend a meeting, maybe you didn't have a lot of money to give, but most every woman in Montgomery back in 1955 did have a great recipe for 7-Up cake, red devil cake, or peach pie. That's where Georgia came in. She organized a grass-roots bake-and-carry operation—the women would bake at home and carry the goods to beauty shops, corner groceries, cabstands, or liquor stores to be sold throughout the community. Many people, both black and white, were afraid to openly support the boycott, so **the club remained anonymous—from nowhere.** No one but Georgia knew who actually baked or bought the food.

With her underground network of cooks and fund-raisers, Georgia Gilmore helped fuel and fund the Civil Rights Movement in Montgomery. Each Monday night at the mass meeting, Georgia would turn in the money she'd raised that week with her cadre of cooks. "Dr. King would preach," Mark tells, "then they would take up a public offering, and Mama would say here's so many hundreds of dollars right here, and the whole place would go wild, everybody cheering and shouting. She'd just bring the house down. She'd hand over more money than anyone else in Montgomery."

GEORGIA'S TABLE

The Civil Rights Movement was Georgia's calling for thirty-five years, and food was her tool for social change. As the Movement grew and took hold, Dr. King continued to rely on Georgia's place as a combination meeting room and social hall. "He brought Robert Kennedy, President Johnson, Governor Wallace," Mark remembers. "All of them—black, white, presidents, plumbers, Ray Charles, Aretha Franklin—all had a chance to eat at my mother's table."

In the spring of 1990, seventy-seven-year-old Georgia Gilmore was up early cooking for the twenty-fifth anniversary of the march from Selma to Montgomery, cooking even though time had taken its toll on her, cooking even though her children worried that she might have another one of her seizures and end up burning herself at the stove. But for Georgia, cooking was as much a part of the Civil Rights Movement as marching was.

"She was getting ready to cook heavy, to help feed the people," Mark remembers. "She was fixing these big tubs of macaroni and cheese and fried chicken. We were getting ready to meet everybody at the capitol. That was when she died.

"After the funeral at the visitation, when the people all came to the house, we served the food she had fixed for the marchers. Nobody could fix it better."

"I think Georgia Teresa Gilmore was one of the unsung heroines of the Civil Rights Movement," reflects Reverend Thomas Jordan. "She was not a formally educated woman, but she had that mother wit. She had a tough mind but a tender heart. You know, Martin Luther King often talked about the ground crew, the unknown people who work to keep the plane in the air. She was not really recognized for who she was, but had it not been for people like Georgia Gilmore, Martin Luther King Jr. would not have been who he was."

Georgia's Legendary Sweet Tea

This sweet tea was served to Martin Luther King, Sam Cooke, Bobby Kennedy, and the laundresses and schoolteachers of Montgomery, Alabama, who gathered around the Gilmores' table. Georgia's son Mark says, "When she served this tea with her cornbread, nobody could refuse."

2 **cups cold water**

3 **family-size tea bags**

1 **cup sugar**

Lemon juice to taste

Place the water in a pot and add the tea bags. Bring to a boil. Remove from the heat and let it sit. Pour the warm tea into an empty pitcher. Add the sugar and stir until the sugar is dissolved. Add the lemon and let it sit overnight in the refrigerator.

MAKES 2 CUPS

Georgia Gilmore's Homemade Pound Cake

When we asked for one of Georgia Gilmore's recipes, this is what Mark Gilmore told us. Now we know why they call it pound cake.

1 **pound butter**

2 **cups sugar**

6 **eggs**

1 **teaspoon vanilla**

A little milk

2 **cups flour**

First blend the butter and sugar together in a large bowl. Then add the eggs, vanilla, and milk. Add the flour and blend together.

Lightly grease a tube pan. Pour in the batter and bake at 350°F for 1 hour.

Turn it upside down—let it cool and then cut it. Thin slices or thick slices, however you want.

MAKES 15 SERVINGS, ACCORDING TO HOW THINLY YOU SLICE IT

Martha Hawkins's Fried Chicken and Collard Greens

Inspired by Georgia Gilmore, Martha Hawkins opened a restaurant in a house in Montgomery, Alabama, in 1988. Growing up, Martha had heard about Mrs. Gilmore and how she gathered blacks and whites together and tirelessly cooked for her community, and she dreamed about someday doing the same.

When at twenty-four she found herself single and on welfare with four boys to raise, she got determined. She saw Georgia's recipes printed in the town paper and decided she would learn them. She called Georgia, who gave her encouragement, and Councilman Gilmore helped her by picking up her pies and cakes and selling them at the capitol so she could get a leg up and open a restaurant. Mark calls Martha "Little Georgia Gilmore," because the spirit and soul of her food brings his mother to mind.

Fried Chicken

3 cups vegetable oil

1 chicken (3½ pounds), cut into 8 pieces

2 tablespoons salt

1 teaspoon black pepper

2 cups all-purpose flour

In a large, heavy skillet, heat the vegetable oil over medium-high heat until very hot but not smoking.

Toss the chicken well with salt and pepper. Place the flour in a bowl and add the chicken to coat. Shake the flour off the chicken and place it in the hot oil. Cook for 7 minutes, turning once. Adjust the heat so that the oil stays hot but doesn't begin to smoke. Reduce the heat to medium-low and cook for 15 minutes, turning occasionally.

MAKES 3 TO 4 SERVINGS

Collard Greens

2 ham hocks

5 cups water

3 pounds collard greens

1 large onion, chopped

1 medium bell pepper, chopped

Salt to taste

Black pepper to taste

In a large pot, simmer the ham hocks in the water for 1 hour, covered.

Meanwhile, cut up the greens. Wash them in cold water, carefully lifting the greens out of the water and transferring them to a colander, then back to the sink of fresh water. Repeat the procedure.

Add the greens to the ham hocks and water. Stir in the onion, bell pepper, and salt and pepper. Cook until greens are very tender, about 1 hour.

MAKES 6 TO 8 SERVINGS

SHOE-BOX KITCHEN

Several times during this project, when we asked people what hidden kitchens conjured for them, we were told "shoe boxes." Until desegregation really took hold, there were next to no places for black families, traveling musicians, or a black businessman on a road trip to stop and have a meal. Most long trips were made with a shoe box full of home-fried chicken and a slice of pound cake, or some other easy-to-eat and filling food, brought from home and eaten on the road or under a shade tree because African-Americans were denied public accommodations and facilities.

Beginning in 1936, the annual *Negro Motorist Green-Book* listed restaurants,

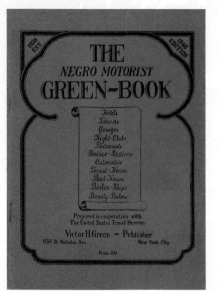

lodging, and other businesses that welcomed African-American travelers. One purchaser told Victor H. Green, the guide's originator, that "it would prove to mean as much if not more to us as the AAA (American Automobile Association) means to the white race."

Cleora Butler's Baked Fudge

Cleora Butler learned to cook from her mother, Martha Thomas. Their home in North Tulsa, Oklahoma, was a favorite destination for Cab Calloway and other black entertainers who often ate in private homes when traveling through the segregated South and Southwest.

In the 1940s Cleora and her mother would bake some 150 small pies a day in her kitchen to help supplement her family's income. By the mid-1950s she had opened her own successful catering business.

In *Cleora's Kitchen: The Memoir of a Cook and Eight Decades of Great American Food*, Butler recounts her life story and celebrates other African-American women who cooked for a living. Mrs. Butler's recipe comes from Barbara Haber's book *From Hardtack to Home Fries*.

4   eggs

2   cups sugar

1   cup (2 sticks) butter

4   heaping tablespoons
    cocoa powder

4   rounded tablespoons flour

1   cup pecans, broken into
    large pieces

2   teaspoons vanilla

    Whipped cream

Preheat the oven to 325°F.

In a medium-size bowl, beat the eggs. Add the sugar and butter and beat well again.

In a small bowl, sift together the cocoa and flour and add the pecans (meats). Fold the cocoa mixture into the butter mixture. Mix in the vanilla.

Pour the mixture into a 9" × 12" × 13" Pyrex dish or tin pan.

Set the dish in a pan of hot water (enough water to come ½" to 1" up on the sides of pan). Put the dish, still in the pan of hot water, into the oven. Bake for 45 minutes to 1 hour, until the fudge has the consistency of firm custard with a crust on top. Serve each piece with a dollop of whipped cream.

MAKES 9 TO 12 SERVINGS

It was an homage to a legendary Texas pit master, which we read in a newsletter on the flight back from Georgia Gilmore's, that made us want to honor some of the fallen kitchen heroes we've heard about and the traditions that may fade with them.

IN MEMORIAM: LARON MORGAN "The Central Texas barbecue family lost one of its most accomplished pit masters on November 6, 2004. Laron Morgan, co-owner of Elgin's Crosstown BBQ, died of an apparent heart attack at the age of fifty-one. The Elgin native had worked in the barbecue business around Elgin, a town that was declared the 'Sausage Capital of Texas' by the state legislature in 1995 . . . Laron Morgan loved his family, feeding people barbecue, and spending time with his beloved hunting dogs . . . "

—FROM THE NEWSLETTER OF THE SOUTHERN FOODWAYS ALLIANCE, MARCH 2005. THIS OBITUARY ORIGINALLY RAN IN THE *AUSTIN CHRONICLE*.

Message #157 was received at 4:23 PM

"This is Marilyn Fosberg. I heard *Hidden Kitchens* on NPR on the day that Margaret Gingrich died at about age ninety-five. She was always in charge of making **bologna sandwiches for funeral dinners**. This is a food tradition that is dying out. The little town of Britton, Michigan, is a ghost town now, but when my father owned a store there, he always donated ring bologna to the women that made the sandwiches. You ground up the bologna, added homemade pickle relish and salad dressing, not mayonnaise. You served this on white bread with coffee and iced tea to the people who came back to the funeral dinner. It's a tradition that is dying out here because the women are getting too old and the young women are not doing it. And they're delicious sandwiches."

"My grandmother was Mary Bridges. Mary used to make pies for families of people who died. On the day of her death, we began to receive pie plates. At first, we didn't really take notice because all these pie plates were empty, but as the day went on, we realized that they were her pie plates that she had given out to her community when someone had died. Before the day was over, we had received nearly fifty empty pie plates, all with her name on the back."

A Root Beer for Louie

Mineko Gallic pours a root beer into the San Francisco Bay as an offering to her late husband, Louis Gallic. The two swam together in the icy waters almost daily until he died at age ninety-five. "After our swim he liked to drink a root beer," says Mineko, who was raised in Tokyo. "In Japan when you know someone is fond of a certain food, it is offered to them after their death."

ERNIE SILVA: 1918–2005 One of The Kitchen Sisters' longtime inspirations was Ernie Silva, my dad—a cook par excellence and a pack rat. In our early days at radio station KUSP, it was in Ernie's garage, which held everything you could ever want or imagine, that we came across our first home recording, the infamous "Louie Letter." That homemade record, made by a woman for her husband who was overseas during World War II, launched The Kitchen Sisters' quest for archival audio and inspired so much of our work and radio-producing style.

Five years ago, Ernie moved into the commune where I've lived since The Kitchen Sisters first started working together back in 1979. It was a tough move, leaving his home of fifty years in Oakland. He'd had a heart attack, my mom had Alzheimer's, and he found himself, at age eighty-one, alone, in a commune with six other opinionated adults and four strong-willed, active kids.

But Ernie, in his own way, rose to the occasion. His joy was cooking. And even when it wasn't his night to cook, he helped prep, clean up, and when he could get away with it, supervise.

Opinionated and stubborn, he prided himself on never spending more than twenty-five dollars on his dinner night. He'd get the Wednesday ads and drive to every market in town to see how things looked before making even one purchase. He cooked hearty meals with a Portuguese flare. He loved dinnertime—the noise, political arguments, and eight-way conversations that have held our motley group together for twenty-five years despite ourselves.

Ernie died in February. It was on a Wednesday, his night to cook. I know that made him sad. A few days later, I found a handwritten cookbook he'd been working on, tucked away up in his room—Beets ala Silva, BBQ Holy Ghost Style, *Carne de Vinho e Alhos,* Dorothy's Only Banana Nut Bread. On the last page of the book, Ernie noted—"feeds twelve people average."

—Nikki Silva

From Ernie Silva's commune cookbook—
"Feeds Twelve People Average"

Dorothy's ONLY
BANANA nut Bread

(Note)
Dorothy says!
The riper the Bananas
The better the Bread—.

2½ cups flour
Tsp salt
2 Tsp Baking ~~Powder~~ soda
1 cup Veg oil
2 cups sugar
2 cup mashed VERY Ripe Bananas
about 6 medium
4 Eggs slightly Beaten
1 cups chopped walnuts

Oven 350°
Grease 2 Loaf pans 8½" x 4½"
Stir and Toss the flour salt & Baking soda.
in a large bowl mix oil, sugar, mashed bananas
eggs + nuts. Add the dry ingredients and mix
Till batter is well blended
Pour into greased + floured pans approx 1 hr.
Baking time checking after 45 min.
Remove from oven + let cool in the pans 5 min
Turn out onto rack to cool completely

(81)

In Minneapolis it's the Kitchen of Opportunity, an operation that transforms food destined for garbage bins into three thousand meals a day for the homeless. In Detroit it's Forgotten Harvest, serving seven million meals a year to the hungry. And in Ventura, California, it's a loner named Emiline Johnson, ladling soup and handing out blankets from her beat-up van under the freeway. In just about every town in America, there's a place where some enterprising individual or organization is grappling with the deep issues of our time through food.

The *Hidden Kitchens* hotline buzzed with news from these problem solvers, risk takers, and humanitarians. In Berkeley, California, the Edible Schoolyard at Martin Luther King Jr. Middle School is a garden and kitchen classroom that provides children a beautiful spot to connect to the land, to learn to grow vegetables and eat the delicious, healthy food they've raised free from fast-food vending machines. In Washington, D.C., Central Kitchen has galvanized the nation's capitol, providing four thousand meals a day to those in need, while offering culinary arts job training to those without home or work.

We've come to think of the hundreds of stories that have come to us as more than messages. They are a call to action. We salute these local kitchen heroes who help keep the planet a bit greener, our food a little tastier and healthier, and their cities more compassionate and full of life.

A Kitchen with a Soul

"This is Julie Emnet calling from Missoula, Montana. The hidden kitchen here is the Poverello Center. It's off a side street. There are no signs, no menus, no maître d', just hungry people joining together for a meal and enjoying one another's company. With Mike Landman at the helm and one paid staff member, it is the area's only emergency shelter and soup kitchen serving three meals a day, 365 days a year. It's truly a kitchen with a soul . . ."

"Hello, my name is Cathy Bernear. I'm the health service specialist for Head Start in Spokane County, Washington. I want to remind NPR that Lyndon Johnson started Head Start as a nutrition program for children who are hungry. We continue to meet this need for children today. Our kitchens are everywhere: community centers, churches, schools. They provide children with a daily opportunity to have a family-style meal where they get to serve their own food and participate in conversations ranging from talk about how sad it is that their puppy died to is there a God? Is their grandma with God?"

"Hello, my name is Linda Strauss. I'm calling not about a kitchen but about a place where people come to gather around food. It's a cooperative farm program in Millersville, Pennsylvania, where the horticulturists all have developmental disabilities and the project is supported by shareholders from the community . . ."

Support the Harvest

"My name is Hilary Baum. I'm calling with a kitchen story about how our community neighborhoods in New York come together through food and CSA, community supported agriculture. We have over a hundred households that gather together to support the harvest of a network of ten to twelve farmers who bring us our food every week for twenty-two to twenty-four weeks a year."

The Food Project

"Hi there, I'm Nikki Lamberg from the Food Project in Boston. A group of teenagers in Boston is working hard to make the process of how food gets from field to table more transparent. These youth are farmers, but they're not what you might think of as farmers. After all, this is metro Boston. They are black, white, Latino. They are affluent, low income. Yet they are the changing face and the future of the environmental movement . . ."

SHERIFF MICHAEL HENNESSEY—
A PRISON KITCHEN VISION

"All you have to do is watch some of the old prison movies, and you'll see that every jail riot starts in the dining room."

Sheriff Michael Hennessey knows this—he tells us this—yet the head of the twentieth largest jail system in America has agreed to allow two San Francisco chefs and their crews to come into his jail with knives and forks and organic vegetables and teach forty women prisoners how to cook healthy, affordable food, which they will sit down and eat together.

"People who run jails are either naturally suspicious and paranoid or paid to be that way. And I will say that this class has made some of my staff even more suspicious and paranoid. That's the constant yin and yang of providing programs in jails and prisons. The safest thing to do is to provide no programs whatsoever, to lock someone in her cell twenty-three hours a day and let her out for one hour of recreation. That's the safest thing. But that's not necessarily the best thing for the community."

Dimpled, Irish, almost cherubic looking, you'd never pick him out of a lineup as sheriff. Mike Hennessey started as a lawyer, representing prisoners and developing a prisoners' legal services program. Then he decided to stir things up—he ran for sheriff. He's been elected seven times by the city and county of San Francisco. Hennessey is known for his daring, some call them "wacky," ideas.

"I hire really crazy people who come to me with really crazy ideas," he says. "And my job is to merely say yes or no. You just bring in good people, and you let them know that this is an environment that is open to innovation and experimentation, because my general feeling is that the way jails and prisons have been run traditionally, they really don't work. So we should be trying to do things differently."

At the San Francisco jail acupuncture is available to inmates, they have a condom distribution program, and they have a garden project directed by Catherine Sneed, which has become a model organic garden project for prisons around the nation. "Gardening is marvelous," Sheriff Hennessey says, "because you can plant a seed and ninety days later you can have a completed product, a beautiful plant or a vegetable that you can eat."

Chefs Larry Bain of Acme Chophouse and Traci Des Jardins of Jardinière approached Hennessey about the idea of doing a cooking class inside the jail. **They call the project "Nextcourse."** There was a small teaching kitchen that had been designed into the new jail. It had never been used. Hennessey decided to put the kitchen and the San Francisco chefs together with the jail's Sister Program, a successful education project for women inmates with substance abuse problems.

Nextcourse is offered as a combination cooking class and math class. When we visited, half of the women were in the kitchen stirring pasta sauce and washing organic greens in enormous stainless steel bowls. The other half were in the adjoining meeting room analyzing the cost differentials between vegetables bought at Safeway, the farmers' market, and the corner convenience store. They were also having a taste test. Which was better—the organic Mutsu apple or the Red Delicious from Safeway?

"These chefs have restaurants where the meals are very nice and very expensive and

Sheriff Michael Hennessey

have very high-quality ingredients. I've eaten at both their restaurants. But most of these women, when they get out, are going back into very poor communities. They may be on food stamps and shopping at the local Quick Stop. They won't have a car, and **they can't spend a couple hours dawdling at the farmers' market looking for the best radicchio.** Many will be living in an SRO, single-room-occupancy hotel rooms, where they'll have to sneak in a hot plate or be using a communal kitchen where the forks and knives that were there yesterday won't be there tomorrow. So Larry and Traci and their staff have had to gear their skills and techniques to fit the lifestyles most of these women will face when they get out."

A cluster of about six women in the Nextcourse class are talking and laughing together while they work with the chefs preparing their meal. A small, wiry woman of about twenty-two is tearing up lettuce for a salad. Her name is Angel, but everyone calls her Shorty. "I don't really grocery shop," she tells us. "When I am hungry and I want something to eat, I will go get a bag of chips or a candy bar at the liquor store. That's it. I don't cook. I eat mostly fast food; I just order my food, get it, and go. Burger King and McDonald's. That's mostly what I eat."

"We are in jail, and that is a depressing thought," relates Tamara, a quiet, tall woman, a mother of two children in her midtwenties. "For myself, I have been here for six months, so this kind of helps you escape it. I could barely go to sleep last night because I'm, like, 'We've got cooking class tomorrow.' A lot of us here, we haven't been in society for a long time, and we haven't done regular, normal things. It's all focused on the criminal act. So when you come and do some cooking, it kind of helps bring you back into what life used to be like before you started doing the stuff you did before you came to jail. Food kind of brings people together. No matter what color, size, anything like that. When everyone comes together at once, it is refreshing."

Cooking in jail is not just a classroom activity, it's happening everywhere. "I can tell you a hundred and one ways to cook Top Ramen," pipes in Pam, a lanky, gap-toothed twenty-year-old at the end of the table. "My favorite is hot ramen with refried beans and cheese with tortilla chips mixed in—we call it a burrito. You just have to be creative with the microwave and with hot water."

The women call these concoctions "spreads." The ingredients come from the commissary and vending machines—Top Ramen, Slim Jims, jalapeño poppers, Cheetos, crumbled together inside the Cheetos bag with hot water then microwaved—"it's kind of the greenhouse effect." A spread serves about two people.

Last time Pam was in jail, she made a little cookbook. "I called it 'The Betty Crocker of County Jail Eight,' " she tells us. "I sent it to my mom. It's got things like how to make Alfredo over Ramen by crushing up potato chips on top of the noodles. And we made apple pie. I think my mom's still got it."

Sheriff Hennessey says there's always a lot of unauthorized cooking going on in jails. "You may know that you can make alcohol from an orange, some bread, and a little sugar—and prisoners do. In our jail system it's called pruno. There's a very famous poem, in fact, by a man on death row in which he alternates lines between the speech the judge read when he was sentenced to death and his recipe for how to make prison alcohol.

"I do have to tell you, though, that poem is in a book of prison writing that we use in our school classes, but I made them take that poem out. It's the one act of censorship that I think I've ever done because I don't want to give this recipe to prisoners. I don't want them making alcohol and getting drunk and causing distur-bances. That's just not cool.

"Shall I read it? I'm not going to read it all, though, because I don't want your listeners figuring this out. But here's a poem called 'Recipe for Prison Pruno,' by Jarvis Masters.

"Take ten peeled oranges

> *Jarvis Masters, it is the judgment and sentence of this court*

One eight-ounce bowl of fruit cocktail

> *That the charge information was true*

Squeeze the fruit into a small plastic bag

> *And the jury having previously upon said date*

And put the juice along with the mash inside

> *Found that the penalty shall be death*

Add sixteen ounces of water and seal the bag tightly

> *And this court having on August 20th, 1991*

Place the bag into your sink

> *Denied your motion for a new trial*

And heat it with hot running water for 15 minutes

> *It is the order of this court that you suffer death . . .*

"And the poem goes on from there. It's really a beautiful piece of writing."

As you leave Sheriff Hennessey's office, you pass by a collection of about twenty large documentary black-and-white photos. At first glance they look like museum photos of primitive art or some ancient culture's kitchen and hunting tools. But at closer look you begin to make out bed parts, plastic combs, mop handles, pieces of pipe that have been sharpened, twisted, melted, and wrapped by hand into shanks and weapons—prison contraband.

"We had a college student who wanted to do a law-enforcement-related photography study of guns and badges," says Sheriff Hennessey. "That was until she realized that they all looked the same. So I suggested she take a look at the contraband, jail-made weapons that have been confiscated from prisoners. And she did a remarkable portfolio of these objects, photographed so beautifully."

Hennessey wants to show us one photo in particular—it's his idea of a hidden kitchen. "This one is sort of food related. It's an electrical cord that's been turned into a stinger. You plug in one end, and you stick the insulated wires on the other end into your coffee to heat it up. That was confiscated from an inmate. It was used as an illegal coffeemaker. When you're in this business, it leads to different views of art and life."

Message #78 was received
Wednesday at 2:22 PM

"My name is Arissa Errens. I have a friend who created the most amazing kitchen. He was in prison at Angola State Penitentiary, our state penitentiary here in Louisiana, for thirty-one years. Twenty-nine of those years he was in solitary confinement, basically as a political prisoner, because he was a Black Panther who started a chapter of the movement with two of his friends. They had become a sort of cause célèbre, known as the Angola Three. Somehow, in solitary confinement, he managed to create a kitchen out of Coke cans and toilet paper, and he'd make pralines. He learned how to make these candies from his friend, Cap Pistol, who was in the prison at the time. My friend's out now—they decided they had made a mistake for locking him up for so long. And he's selling his candies as a way to help raise consciousness about political prisoners. He calls them Freelines. If you want to know more, I can get you in touch with him."

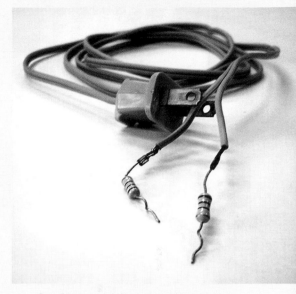

Confiscated from an inmate, a stinger is a modified electrical cord that you stick into a cup of coffee to heat it up.

STORY #10

Milk Cow Blues

The Apple Family Farm and the Indiana Cow Share Association

"FOOD HISTORY IS AS IMPORTANT AS A BAROQUE CHURCH.
GOVERNMENTS SHOULD RECOGNIZE THIS CULTURAL HERITAGE
AND PROTECT TRADITIONAL FOODS. A CHEESE IS AS WORTHY OF
PRESERVING AS A SIXTEENTH-CENTURY BUILDING."

—CARLO PETRINI, FOUNDER OF SLOW FOOD

Slow Food—if there's one organization that's inspired our thinking about lost and endangered kitchen traditions, it's this international organization that supports, protects, and celebrates small farmers and disappearing regional foods. Founded by Italian Carlo Petrini in response to the opening of a McDonald's near Rome's historic Spanish Steps in 1986, Slow Food brings together people from agricultural communities around the world to share ideas and grapple with issues of biological and cultural diversity, hunger, poverty, and sustainability.

No place was that more evident than at Slow Foods' conference, Terra Madre (Mother Earth), that we attended in Turin, Italy, in October 2004. Imagine a gathering of five thousand shepherds, beekeepers, fishermen, farmers, nomads, cattle breeders, community cooks, and cocoa growers—not to mention the Prince of Wales—people from more than 130 countries meeting in Italy for four days to talk via simultaneous translators in seven different languages about food—its traditions and its future—a kind of United Nations meets Woodstock meets the County Fair meets Martin Luther King's historic march on Washington.

The delegates to this global gathering were a sight to behold. Brazilian tribesmen with feathers pierced through their chins shared their beans with organic shrimp breeders from eastern Java. Kyrgyzstani yak herdsmen with gold teeth and high-peaked felt hats traded tips with the camel-milk producers from Mauritania. Abalone divers from Palau mingled with the black-headed sea bream fishermen from Oaxaca,

Mexico, while a cattleman with such pride in his hay, he brought it all the way from Texas and showed it off to anyone who would look.

During the course of Terra Madre, some one hundred cheese makers from countries throughout the world met in a high hill town an hour or so outside of Torino. Most of these small producers of unpasteurized milk and artisan cheeses have been criminalized by their governments, caught in the modern raw-milk cheese wars raging around the globe. These farmers were gathering to share their methods and wisdom and the ancient techniques used to age cheese in caves, on wood, with leaves, and ways to approach their individual legal dilemmas in a united way.

In the midst of the cheese conversations, we met Debbie Apple, a dairy farmer and cofounder of the Indiana Cow Share Association, whose small herd of Dutch Belted cows and the milk it yielded had recently been slapped with a cease and desist order after a neighbor had secretly turned her family in.

You wouldn't think you would go all the way to Italy to find a story in Indiana, but we did. We decided to follow Debbie home to McCordsville and see what was going on in the hidden hearts of Indiana dairy farmers.

I t is against the law in Indiana, as it is in most other states, to sell raw milk. We are a pasteurized nation as far as the law is concerned. The issue of raw milk is the kind of thing that sends health officials scrambling for complaint forms and turns people into zealots. Debbie and Mark Apple had no idea of this when they began to share the bounty of their cows with a handful of neighbors who came clamoring for raw milk.

"My name is Debbie Apple. I am a farmer and farmer's wife." Debbie lives with her husband, Mark, their two children, and her mother-in-law on their flat expanse of a cow farm in McCordsville, Indiana. The Apple Family Farm is almost 250 acres of cattle, sheep, goats, chickens, ducks, dogs, and cats in a sea of fast-disappearing farmland and fast-appearing gated communities and malls that sprawl south from Indianapolis.

Dressed in a long denim skirt and Frye boots, looking handsome and practical, Debbie Apple is not exactly the first person you'd finger for a lawbreaker. You might peg her for running the bookstore in town or cast her in the part of the rugged, pretty pioneer mother in a Willa Cather story, but you wouldn't cast her in the role of rebel.

"It never entered our minds that this was illegal. Neighbors were asking us to provide these products that they couldn't find elsewhere," says Debbie. "We were already doing it for ourselves, so we just expanded our own family food to feeding other families."

Then someone warned the Apples that what they were doing might be illegal. "We got some conflicting information," Debbie recalls. "Some people said we could put a sticker on it that said, 'Not fit for human consumption' or 'Pet milk.' But when we talked to our county agricultural extension agent, he told us point blank that it is against the law in Indiana to make raw milk available, trade it, sell it, or deliver it."

There is, however, one provision in the law: If you own the cow, then you can drink the milk. "So we decided if these people wanted milk, they would have to buy the cow. We would milk it for them."

Forty families wanted milk, and at that point the Apples had only four cows. So they decided to offer shares in each cow, as many as twenty shares per animal. That would give everyone at least a gallon of milk every week. "We set up the Indiana Cow

Debbie and Mark Apple and a Dutch Belted cow

Share Association, and we charged fifty dollars for a share. We decided that with milking just once a day and with feeding grass instead of grain, we were going to get about twenty gallons a week from a cow. We figured out a boarding fee and what our costs were, and everybody was very happy with that." At least that's what they thought.

THE APPLE FAMILY FARM

When the whole idea of cow sharing came about, Debbie and Mark had just recently moved back from Tennessee to Mark's family farm in McCordsville to try to make a go of it. They hadn't planned on starting a dairy farm. That's what Mark's dad had done in the 1960s, and it had driven him into debt and despair. Mark and Debbie had a vision of developing an organic farm, a self-sustaining operation growing crops for market and raising a few animals.

The Apple Family Farm goes back three generations of Apples. Mark grew up there, but as farming became more and more difficult and farms all around were being swallowed up by urban sprawl, Mark's father encouraged him to go to college to pursue another course in life rather than take up the family farm.

Mark's mother, Jo Apple, remembers those hard days in the 1970s, when prices for milk were dropping drastically, prices for equipment were skyrocketing, and she and her husband faced some serious decisions. **"We had lots of headaches and lots of Holsteins,"** she tells us. "We were milking so many cows, and just keeping up with the milk inspectors and all the health and sanitation regulations and the feeding, it just became too much. Finally, my husband did the books one year, and we realized that we would have made more money if we'd just sold the grain that we were growing to feed our cows. So we gave up the dairy, got rid of all the cattle, tore out the fences, and began running it as a crop farm—soybeans and corn planted all the way out to the road. We sent our two sons to college, because we just didn't think that our farm could support three families. It wasn't supporting us."

At the time the older Apples were turning to crops, Mark and Debbie were working on the road on the Christian music concert circuit with Amy Grant, Michael Smith, Johnny Cash, and Waylon Jennings, selling T-shirts and tapes. When they weren't on the road, they were living in a Victorian in Nashville with about seven acres of land, their "farmette," as they called it. After the birth of their first child, Debbie's interest began to shift from touring to her family and the land. They got

Rayna Apple has mastered the sound of every animal on her family's farm.

sheep because Debbie likes to knit. They got chickens because then they'd have eggs and Debbie likes to cook. And they started growing their own food—organically because as a mother Debbie had become more and more concerned about what she was feeding her family. As Mark's parents were struggling to maintain the family farm, Mark and Debbie began developing a vision for the farm where Mark had grown up.

"Mark and Debbie came to talk to John, my husband," remembers Jo. "They had a plan for the farm, bringing back livestock, phasing out chemicals, going organic. But when you've been a conventional farmer for years, there's a lot of mindset. 'If we're not going to put chemicals on these weeds, we're going to have weeds everywhere,' my husband would say. You just can't imagine that the crops will grow, because you think the weeds are going to take over. My husband just didn't see it."

Mark Apple, beard and glasses, the kind of guy you might expect to meet in the band room at school rather than a milk barn, remembers the conversations he had with his dad during that time. "We were trying to share all of our ideas with him, but by saying that we wanted to do something different, it was like I was saying he wasn't doing it right. He was having a really hard year, and we didn't want to make it harder, so we let it go."

When tax time came around, the numbers were worse than any of them expected. "It was such a rough year financially; it was just tearing at my husband," remembers Jo. "Then the Saturday before taxes were due, we were having lunch together, and he said, 'Call Mark and Debbie. I think they should come here and start on this farm what they're doing in Tennessee.' I couldn't believe it. I was so excited, and I tried to call the kids and tell them, but I didn't reach them."

Three days later, on April 15, with a lot of taxes due, John Apple had a heart attack and died. Debbie and Mark were on the road and didn't receive the message inviting them to come live and work on the farm until after his death.

Five months later, Mark and Debbie moved with their young son, Brandon, into one of the houses on the family farm in Indiana. Mark's mother, Jo, continued living on the farm as well in the house that her mother-in law had moved out of

Recording the Apple family chickens

nearly fifty years ago to make way for her when she first married John and moved to the farm. It's a full house, full of knickknacks, her two pianos, and a heap of sheet music. She now shares it with her other son, Paul, and his family who have also moved back home to work on the farm.

"When we first came back," Debbie remembers, "Mark didn't

really have any desire to get back into the dairy business. It kind of happened to us rather than us really planning. We started with the sheep and chickens, then we added cattle, **then we bought Belle,** a milk cow, for ourselves. We brought her home on the Friday after Thanksgiving, and on Saturday morning she gave us a calf."

It didn't take long for people in their close-knit Christian community to realize the Apples had a dairy cow and direct access to fresh milk. "I remember being at a meeting one night, and they went around the circle asking, 'What do you do for a living?' And I said we had a farm, and the room just got real quiet. One lady said, 'Do you have a dairy cow?' And when I said we did, everybody started talking at once saying, 'Can we get milk from you? Can we get milk?' They had all read a book called *What the Bible Has to Say about Healthy Living* and knew about the health benefits of raw milk." At 8:00 the next morning, three of those women were at the Apple's milk barn with their glass jars. And that's how it started.

CEASE AND DESIST

Dr. Bret Marsh, Indiana State Veterinarian, works for the state's Board of Animal Health, and since 1995 his department has been responsible for watching over the safety of animal products as well as the animals themselves. Raised on a farm, Dr. Marsh speaks in a mild and measured tone about raw milk and the Apple Family Farm.

"I first became aware of the Apple Family Farm from a local news article that indicated that they offered raw milk. The first call I received about this was actually from a dairy producer. He was quite upset. 'I didn't think we could do this in Indiana!' he yelled at me at the time. I said we would look in to it. There are some potentially harmful pathogens in these raw-milk products that can cause diseases such as tuberculosis and brucellosis—and that's the compelling reason for the pasteurization laws in the States. So we sent guys out to the Apple place to investigate."

The newspaper article that had mentioned the Apples was publicizing a farm festival weekend, inviting the community to visit area farms. Most of the farms on the tour grew grains and soybeans, so the organizers wanted to include the Apple Family Farm because it is one of the few dairy farms remaining in the area. There was only one line in the story that mentioned raw milk. But that's all it took.

"The local farmers put pressure on the Board of Animal Health to come and shut us down, and they did," recounts Mark. "They served us a cease and desist order in November 2002."

"It was such a scary thing," Debbie remembers. "When Mark told me they were at the farm serving him the cease and desist order, the first thing I did was pray."

The idea of **raw milk strikes a nerve** in farmers, health-regulating agencies, and consumers. Federal and state regulators and many others see raw milk as a hazard

The Apple Family Farm

because it harbors bacteria that can cause salmonella poisoning, tuberculosis, listeria, and other diseases. Pasteurization, a process that heats the milk and kills the germs that can cause these diseases, has become standard practice for commercial milk production. Raw-milk advocates believe that much of the nutritional value of milk is destroyed by pasteurization and that with proper handling raw milk is safe. Many of these people believe raw milk has health and curative powers, and a small group of them are proponents of it because they believe the Bible instructs them to eat a diet of unprocessed foods. Regardless of what people believe, or where they stand on the issue, the commercial selling of raw milk is currently illegal in most states.

"Our first thought was, let's just quit," says Mark, "try to stay out of trouble. But there were aspects that just made us angry. We're not lawbreakers. **We're not selling drugs.** This is not cocaine, crack, marijuana—this is milk. People want this. This is healthy. This is good for our kids. How can this cause so many problems?"

The Apples invited their friends and fellow cow share owners over to the farm to discuss the cease and desist order. They talked nearly all night, going back and forth about their options and what approach to take. Around 2:00 in the morning, the Apples decided that they would keep the cows and fight the cease and desist order.

"Raw milk, especially for a dairy farmer, is a big change," Debbie says. "It goes against everything they've been taught. It's really turning the whole system on its head—not just the question of whether or not to pasteurize but also selling straight to the public instead of going through a processing plant. I think there is a connotation that sometimes the government knows better, the processor knows better, the big corporations know better. It seems there is very little that is left in the hands of the farmer anymore." When the Apples began bypassing the system, selling directly to the public and making money on a product that many felt was unsafe, it got other farmers in the area upset.

For a while, the cow share owners were afraid to come by to pick up their milk, afraid that they'd get the Apples in even more trouble. During that time Debbie made a lot of cheese with her gallons of unclaimed milk. But one person continued to come, ninety-five-year-old Genevieve. "She would call and say, 'Debbie, this is Genevieve. Has the government come to take my milk away yet?' Genevieve had paid for her share of the cow, and she wanted her milk. She too was nervous and would have somebody drive her from the nursing home late at night, when she thought no one was watching, to come and get her milk."

Debbie and Mark went through the proceedings with the Board of Animal Health, who reviewed the issues. "We had so many people praying for us. Many people that get milk from their cows here are Christians, not all, but many," Debbie explains. "A lot of them wrote letters and sent faxes to the government. I think it must have amazed the board, because a lot of the letters started out, 'I have a master's degree . . . I have a PhD . . . and I can make my own decisions.' There were physicians, people that worked for Eli Lilly, attorneys for the hospital. The matriarch of the Republican Party in Indiana, she was a cow share owner!"

"When we met with Bret Marsh and the other members of the state committee reviewing our case," Debbie reflects, "we didn't try to change their minds to think that raw milk is the healthiest thing that God ever gave us. We just tried to get across the fact that these **people had a right to choose**."

Over the next few months the Apples met with the Board of Animal Health, and it was determined that they could continue their cow share program as long as there was no question about who owned the cow. "We had to make it very clear that the families and individuals getting milk definitely owned the cows," says Debbie. "However, we're still under the cease and desist order—three years later! There's still a lively debate about the issue, and they're still trying to figure out how best to deal with the situation."

DUTCH BELTED

In a one-acre corner of a thirty-acre pasture stand a dozen curious-looking cows, huddled together "for security," Mark says. Cows like to be together, not spread out all over the place. Imported by P. T. Barnum in the late 1800s because of their unusual markings, these Dutch Belted cows are all black with a wide white band around their middles. **"They look like Oreo cookies,"** says Mark, who often gives tours to school groups who come out to the farm to see where milk comes from. Mark says that the Dutch Belted were a popular breed up until the 1920s, when farming practices changed from being grass based to grain based. Dutch Belted are a small and compact breed that do well on grass but can't compete with the enormous grain-fed, spotted Holstein cows, who have been bred for size and productivity.

Mark enjoys rare breeds and hopes to protect them from being lost—from the Dutch Belted cows to his Scottish Highland beef cattle, who have long horns and

Grass-fed Dutch Belted cows

long hair and look as if they're wearing shaggy coats. Both breeds flourish on grass alone. In addition to producing raw milk, the Apples are well known in the area for raising grass-fed beef.

Passionate about his grass, each day Mark goes out with a stick to measure the height of it before pasturing the cows in a particular area. "I get my seed from a couple of Amish farmers here in Indiana who sell very high-tech grasses from Holland. It's good grass for making milk, mostly rye and white clover, which the cows love. The milk is very sweet, and the taste changes somewhat through the season as the grass changes. In my estimation, my belief, this grass makes for the best-tasting milk."

Standing close to the herd, especially with headphones on, you can hear huge tufts of grass being pulled out of the earth and the noisy sound of chewing. The music of the hand-forged cowbells Debbie just brought back from Italy clatter with each mouthful. Once a day, these grass-fed cows give grass-fed milk to music that fills the milking barn—*Bolero,* Rimsky-Korsakov's *Scheherazade,* Vivaldi's *Four Seasons* pour out of the boom box soothing the herd. Mark says a relaxed cow is a high-yield cow. And for two generations the Apple family farmers have been relaxing their cows to music. Before the grain came, **Mark's dad milked his herd to Southern gospel** and church music played on an eight-track.

CRANBERRY COTTAGE

Debbie Apple had earned a culinary degree, had developed a regular clientele for the milk, and had also harbored a secret desire to have a little shop that sold nice things. When people dropped by to pick up their milk, they'd ask if the

Debbie Apple in the Cranberry Cottage

Apples sold any soap or honey or other things, and that was all the encouragement Debbie needed. She and Mark transformed a trailer that had been on the property since 1964 into Cranberry Cottage, a combination dairy, meat market, grocery store, and craft supply, linen, and gift shop. They sell their own farm products there as well as their friends' and neighbors' products.

Jennifer Moss, a nurse practitioner, found Cranberry Cottage through the Internet. She lives twenty minutes away, where there are few farms but many subdivisions. "It seems like we are miles and miles away from the farms, so it's kind of nice to find this here, plus the kids enjoy seeing the cows. Today I'm buying eggs, chocolate milk, some cheese, a couple of pairs of knitting needles, four rib-eye steaks, and two ground round packages. There aren't many places in the world you'd see knitting needles and rib eye in the same pile."

"We're probably the only trailer in Indiana that has salt that's twenty-five dollars a pound," laughs Debbie, "Celtic sea salt. And we sell a boatload of cod liver oil. We have it in regular, mint, and new citrus. My children take it every day, and so do I."

The beef is organized by cut in the freezer. "The first shelf, we have all of our lamb chops, T-bones, leg steaks. We have all of our ribs frenched for a nice presentation. Then we have our two-inch-thick porterhouse steaks. This is the serious meat-lover's special."

Debbie homeschools her two kids, Rayna and Brandon, and is often busy with the farm, so Cranberry Cottage is primarily self-serve, on the honor system. Customers just help themselves, fill out a receipt, and put their money in the cash box. On occasion Debbie let's people run up a tab and pay when they can, when "their husbands get a job or when they don't have cancer anymore."

SOUL-SEARCHING

One afternoon, about a year and half after the Board of Animal Health imposed the cease and desist order on the Apples, there was a knock at their door. Standing on her porch was a man Debbie had never seen before. "You don't have to talk to me if you don't want to; I will totally understand" were his first words to her. There before her was the neighbor who had turned in the Apple Family Farm to the state.

"My heart was pounding," remembers Debbie. "I was there by myself."

The man asked Debbie if they could sit and talk. Something about him made her say yes. They settled at the picnic table for a conversation that lasted more than two hours. He confided that he couldn't make it farming anymore and, as a last resort, had come to her for advice. "I could tell he was at the end of his rope," says Debbie. "He talked about his son. He told me his boy was sixteen years old, bagging groceries, but that his heart belonged to farm. The way things were going, though, with milk prices so low, the farm could barely support one family, let alone two. He was very humble, and I could see that this was a difficult thing for him to do."

The farmer told Debbie that he had initiated the complaint about the Apple's raw-milk business to the state's board out of jealousy and desperation. After reading about them in the newspapers and realizing they were selling raw milk for probably three times more than he was getting for his processed milk, it just hadn't seemed fair. Now he was here, on their porch, asking not only for forgiveness but for advice as well.

"I really believe that if there had been anybody else he could have gone to, he would have gone there," says Debbie, "but he didn't know anybody else who was doing this type of diversified farming and distribution except us."

The farmer asked Debbie to explain their cow share program, and he wanted to know about how she ran Cranberry Cottage. He didn't want to sell raw milk, but he had been thinking maybe he'd like to try the cow-sharing idea with pasteurized milk. He said there was a little building on his farm that might even work as a store, and lately he'd been thinking about raising chickens so that he could sell eggs, and maybe he could sell meat for a friend who raised hogs and honey for a friend who kept bees.

"He was a very proud man who had done a lot of soul-searching," Debbie reflects. As we talked, we discovered that our sons are just a few years apart and that really we both wanted the same thing, to make sure there is a farm for our sons."

Debbie showed him their cow share contract, and they toured the farm and Cranberry Cottage and the milk house. "It was so amazing to have this man who had turned us in, a dairy man with so much experience, here on our farm. I was able to ask him questions and get advice about dairying and how to do things. It almost made me feel like I had Mark's dad here."

In a strange way, Jo Apple understands the man's desperation and his betrayal of a neighbor. "When you're a farmer, you feel this passion to feed the world, you really do. And you feel the responsibility when your sons want to farm and carry the family name in that way. It's tragic and sad when you realize that what you are doing is just not going to work. So I could relate to this gentleman in this way. We have to find ways of making it work."

On Saturdays the Apples join with other farmers in the area at Traders Point Creamery Farmers' Market, where they sell their grass-fed beef.

Debbie and her kids are starting to pack up their grass-fed chops and steaks to take to the Traders Point Creamery Farmers' Market thirty miles away in Zionsville. Debbie stops. "That farmer, he needed to make a change. It's a story that is happening all over the country. Farmers that are on the verge of throwing in the towel are saying, 'Okay. I can't afford a sixty-thousand-dollar combine. I have to do something else. Maybe I'll get some cattle and see if I can just sell them to my neighbors.' That's just how it starts."

RAW-MILK COVEN IN NEW YORK CITY

Indiana isn't the only state grappling with the questions surrounding raw milk. We interviewed Frederick Kaufman, professor of English and journalism at the City University of New York and author of *A Short History of the American Stomach,* about his experiences gathering information for a Talk of the Town story he wrote for the *New Yorker* about raw milk.

"Milk is basic, it's primal. Mother's milk is the ultimate hidden kitchen—the giver of life. Milk to the ancient Hebrews is life incarnate. And it's a highly volatile substance in terms of people's spiritual attachments to it. I think that's part of the reason there's this big deal about milk.

"I infiltrated a raw-milk coven in New York City. It was a cold evening in Hell's Kitchen in a basement of a large apartment house. The Mennonite farmers had already arrived from Pennsylvania with their big cold packs full of their raw-milk contraband—their feta cheese that had not been aged for sixty days, and their raw milk that they had had to label 'Not Fit for Human Consumption.'

"When I got there, they were discussing the payoff to the driver. The person who is providing the milk cannot actually transport the milk across state lines. This is one of the difficulties of raw-milk consumption in New York City. It's kind of like the old Prohibition stories. The Mennonite farmer cannot come in with his milk. He needs a driver with a car to deliver the goods. It has to be a separate person. That's the law.

"After they paid off the driver, they set up shop. A secret list server sends out the word about where the drop-off is going to be to this raw-milk group that orders online. There were all walks of New York life lined up waiting to get their shipment of milk, cheese, and whey—housewives, computer programmers, musicians, little girls in princess costumes, dads, real estate brokers.

"The sale of milk in New York City has been highly regulated even as early as 1763. It was not allowed to be sold in the markets in New York City. In other words, for you to obtain raw milk in New York City, you have to go through the same kind of legal finesse as you do in Indiana. You have to sign a contract that says, 'I own the cow, or I own milk that you are processing for me. You're not delivering it to me, because I've already bought it.' They're on a fine legal line.

"Pasteurization is the process of heating milk up to a certain temperature for a certain amount of time and then quickly cooling it off. This kills off certain bacteria that find a home in milk. Milk is a very fruitful substance, and it gives life to a lot of different organisms. Some of these organisms are healthy to humans, some make no difference to humans, and some that find a congenial home in milk can be deadly to humans, causing diseases like listeria, tuberculosis, and diphtheria. That is part of the reason that pasteurization became the norm starting in the twentieth century in the United States.

"The dairy industry is huge. There are about four large dairy companies that control more than eighty-five percent of the milk market. Part of the issue raw-milk people have is that they see pasteurization as a way agribusiness gets around its faults. Businesses may be run poorly, they may not be sanitary, and pasteurization is a way to hide those faults. Raw-milk supporters feel that if these farms were run cleanly and run well, there would be no need for pasteurization on this level and for legislating pasteurization. If you talk to people who are serious about raw milk, they will tell you that they only will drink raw milk from a small operation that runs a very clean shop. Everybody is aware of what bacteria on a cow's udder can lead to."

Grilled Lamb Chops with Honey Glaze

In addition to raising grass-fed beef, the Apples raise grass-fed lamb. Grass-fed meat is leaner than grain-fed meat and higher in healthy omega-3 fats. Here, Debbie Apple shares her recipe for grilled lamb chops with honey glaze. For the best flavor, marinate the chops in the refrigerator for at least 2 hours or, better yet, overnight in the refrigerator (you can make these chops a day ahead). Debbie recommends you seek out a local beekeeper whose honey is fragrant with the flowers and foliage of your area.

¾ **cup dry red wine**

¼ **cup olive oil**

3 **teaspoons chopped fresh oregano**

2 **teaspoons minced garlic**

2 **teaspoons red wine vinegar**

½ **teaspoon salt**

½ **teaspoon ground black pepper**

8 **½"-thick, grass-fed lamb chops**

2 **teaspoons honey, preferably local to your area**

In a large bowl, mix together the wine, olive oil, oregano, garlic, vinegar, salt, and pepper. Add the lamb chops and let marinate for at least 2 hours or overnight in the refrigerator.

To grill, fire up the grill or the broiler and put the lamb chops on, basting them with the marinade until they are medium-rare, about 10 minutes. Add the honey to the marinade and use a brush to mop the chops just before removing them from the grill or broiler.

MAKES 8 CHOPS

Apple Farm Crème Brûlée

The first time Debbie made crème brûlée with her own cream and free-range eggs, it was an epiphany. When she talks about this recipe on her farm tours, people look at her cows in a new way, then ask for the recipe. Debbie adapted her crème brûlée from a recipe by Patricia Wells.

1 vanilla bean

1 quart heavy cream

½ cup sugar or vanilla sugar (see note)

6 large egg yolks from organic free-range chickens

½ cup firmly packed dark brown sugar

NOTE: To make vanilla sugar: Scrape the seeds from 4 vanilla beans and combine the pods, seeds, and 4 cups of sugar in a jar. Cover securely and allow the vanilla sugar to infuse for several weeks. Use in place of regular sugar when baking desserts.

Preheat the oven to 300°F.

Cut the vanilla bean in half lengthwise and use a small spoon to scrape out the tiny black seeds into a heavy saucepan. Add the cream and the vanilla pod halves and cook over medium-high heat to the boiling point. Remove from the heat, cover, and set aside to steep for 15 minutes. Remove the vanilla pods and set aside.

In a medium size bowl, combine the sugar and egg yolks and whisk until well blended. Mix in the vanilla cream until blended.

Place 6 shallow 6" round ramekins in a large roasting pan. Pour the cream mixture into the dishes. Add enough boiling water to the roasting pan to reach halfway up the sides of the baking dishes. Place on the center rack of the oven and bake just until the mixture is set in the center but still trembling, about 30 minutes.

Refrigerate for at least 1 hour and up to 24 hours. Remove from the refrigerator, sieve the brown sugar evenly over the top of each baked cream, and glaze under the broiler for several seconds until the sugar forms a firm crust. Watch carefully to see that it does not burn. Return the custards to the refrigerator to chill until a crust has formed, about 15 minutes. Serve and enjoy.

MAKES 6 SERVINGS

Francis Coppola and Lawrence Ferling

"FRANCIS COO
FOR NORTH BEAC

Francis Coppola personally cooks an Italian
benefit North Beach Citizens, a neighborhood
to homelessness.

With music, dancing, and plenty of foo
Sunday December 2, 200

Basement of Saints Peter and Paul Churc
666 Filbert Street, San Francisco.

Free parking in the lot next to the chu

Francis will serve antipasti, rigatoni
with meatballs and sausage*, salad,
dessert and wine at family-style long
tables. Please join us to eat, drink,
dance and enjoy the community we share and l

"The way to a community's heart is
stomach. Coppola's pasta and his home
straight to the heart of North

Lawrence Ferlinghetti

TO DECEMBER 2nd PASTA FESTA:

The Fellowship of Food

I f there is a single, unifying theme to the hours of stories and messages we've gathered, that theme is not about food but about fellowship. It is really this that lay beneath most of the stories, the hidden thing that happens in the best of kitchens—something is shared. It happens between two people late at night and in small towns among neighbors. It happens in large communities among friends and among strangers. The secret ingredients are important, and the way it all tastes, but more important is what the food evokes—a memory, a bond, a good story.

Message #797 was received Friday at 8:59 AM

"Hi, my name is Mary Brazauskas Parnell. I was raised in a traveling three-ring circus that performed all over the United States. My mother was a trapeze artist, my father was the manager, my sister performed on horseback, and I rode the elephants. The cookhouse flag went up on our big tent three times a day, and we all gathered together from our circus community, every nationality, and ate our meals together.

"As a youngster, I would go with my father to shop at the grocery store, and we would buy carts full of breads, milk in huge quantities, and fruits and vegetables for the animals. When we hit major cities like Chicago, we'd go to the Armour factory and get sides of beef. If there was a celebration like a wedding, the show would stop, and we'd barbecue whole cows and have an incredible feast for two days.

"No matter what had happened, if a tornado took the circus tent, if an animal got loose, if we were up all night in the mud tearing down the tent, we gathered on those big picnic benches and came together to eat. It was an incredible experience. How much I rejoice in that community kitchen."

We listen and marvel at how this simple ritual of sharing a table can create family, even among the most unlikely people—in a kitchen as big and raucous as a circus tent or as quiet and intimate as two people sharing a meal from separate worlds.

Message #14 was received Friday at 9:07 AM
"Hello, my name is Gabrielle Burton. I used to have a job as a cook for a wonderful man in Boston, a sort of classic WASP, old-style New Englander. He was about eighty-three, and when I left he was ninety-something. Dr. Harris would pick me up at college, and we'd wind our way through the cobblestone Cambridge streets, at slower and slower speeds as he aged, to go shopping for dinner, stopping at the small neighborhood grocer, putting two pieces of fresh fish or two chicken breasts on his charge account.

"Part of the evening was sitting and eating with him and sharing stories over dinner—me telling him about my college life, Dr. Harris reading me poetry, playing me records of John Cage or some classical music, someone he wanted me to know about. It was a remarkable way of **connecting across the generations.**

"I think young people seem to be increasingly isolated from anyone over the age of sixty in any real way. It seems to me that this is being lost. This is my small kitchen story, and I wanted to share it with you."

These small kitchen stories about the private traditions of family, natural and created, contain big ideas about how we can connect, how these connections lessen isolation, and how they can delight and bind, and even forge community. People will go to great lengths to find each other, and food is often the way they get there.

Message #341 was received Tuesday at 5:21 PM
"Hi, my name is Cindy Van Vreede. I'm calling from Milwaukee, Wisconsin. I'm a lesbian, and almost every lesbian community in the country comes together regu-

larly through potluck dinners, and Milwaukee is no exception. In fact, I went to Google and typed in 'lesbian potluck history' and came up with over seven thousand hits. It's sort of like **when three lesbians get together, it's a potluck. . . . "**

The man cooking burgoo at a kettle in Kentucky called it the fellowship of stirring, standing side by side with your neighbor, making something that links you to the past, present, and future of your community. These kitchens connect us in ways that are not always obvious—to each other and to the land itself.

Eating lunch at branding, Grayson Ranch, Quinn River Line Camp, 1978

Message #223 was received Friday at 5:08 PM
"Hello. This is Margaret Fitzgerald Evans. I was born and raised in the Mississippi delta. My father was a small-town doctor who began his practice in the 1940s. Many of his patients were poor and paid him for his services in homegrown vegetables. I remember well waking up on a sweltering, humid Mississippi summer morning with paper bags full of ripe corn, beans, tomatoes, turnip greens, cucumbers, green peppers, peas, and everything else imaginable piled up on the porch. We ate our dinner at noon every day—hot plates of vegetables, cold bowls of salad, and piles of steaming rice. My daddy always said the delta grew cotton and vegetables

that were out of this world. My father taught us **respect for the hardworking farmer.** *We knew that they left the vegetables on our doorstep before daybreak out of pride. We never saw their faces, but Daddy knew who they were and what they did for us. Thank you for listening to my story."*

There is the fellowship that comes from tending and feeding each other, and there is the fellowship that comes from listening. This need to be heard and understood and recognized seems as powerful as the primal need to feed and be fed. Food and story are a way to kinship with someone whose face you've never seen, whose work you don't know, whose experience is not your own—and a way of discovering perhaps that you share more than you realize.

"Hello, my name is David LaChance at Mount Holyoke College. Here at the college we have a kosher halal dining hall, which means that all of the food served there can be eaten both by observant Jews and by observant Muslims. It brings together these two groups on our campus to literally break bread together. The dining hall was opened here on September 13, 2001, at the request of students. It was their idea to have such a place. It is a powerful reminder of the connections between these two very ancient faiths."

In strange and simple ways, food can cross a line; it can cut through politics, race, religion. Civil rights activist Georgia Gilmore looked at a pie and saw a weapon for social change. So many other people around the country see the same power in *kolaches,* clams, ramps, burgoo—a way to raise money to build a library, fund a fire department, feed the hungry, take care of our elders and our children. In the right hands, in the right region, even a barbecued muskrat has earning potential for some social cause or political candidate.

THE POWER OF AN UPSIDE-DOWN CAKE

Messages and leads continue to pour in, and we continue to listen in wonder at the power of a kitchen story to reconnect someone to their past, or to a stranger. One call in particular struck a chord with us, and with NPR listeners, and we've received dozens of calls and letters in response.

Message #112 was received Tuesday at 5:30 AM

"Yeah, this is Bill Whan. It's 5:30 Eastern, and I'm currently on duty in the Air Force, **out on the runway monitoring F-16s.** *John Miller's story really got to me. You know, the Vietnam soldier who got the pineapple upside-down cake meant for some other guy, who called looking for the guy's parents in Connecticut to thank.*

"The common thread with me was during the deployment in '96 during the Bosnian conflict, I received a care package of assorted baked goods and cookies and the like. It was 'To any soldier.' I was really touched by the anonymous nature of it all, and I ended up developing a pen pal relationship with the son of this particular family in New Jersey. I'm from Detroit. And I really felt the emotion in John's Miller's voice, and I wanted you to know that it has touched me. The spirit and **the inherent good nature of human beings** *will never cease to inspire me. I wanted to pass that along to you and thank you very much for putting him on the air. I hope his quest to find that family works out, so that package sent more than thirty years ago is somehow fulfilled for him. Thank you again."*

So many different kinds of people called in about that one pineapple upside-down cake. People with databases in Connecticut willing to search for the name of the family, veterans, mothers, bakers. Why? Why did it resonate so deeply? This simple, sweet act of baking, of strangers tending one another during hard times, of civilians supporting a soldier during an ambiguous war, and a soldier's wish to repay that kindness cuts deep into the fabric of who we are and who we want to be.

Another message came through loud and clear on the *Hidden Kitchens* hotline. We are each other's keepers. We are *all* hungry if any of us is hungry. And many across the nation are taking matters into their own hands—from The Cooking Club in Los Angeles that works with women living on skid row, to Meals on Wheels, to the Head Start kitchens that feed our nation's poorest children, to Judy Davis's Aunt Ethel.

Message #721 was received Saturday at 10:35 AM
"My name is Judy Davis. I'm calling about Aunt Ethel. **My Aunt Ethel's knishes were famous.** *Not just in the family, not just in the Jewish play school where she was the lunch lady, and not just in Levittown, Pennsylvania, where she and Uncle Irv lived for 40 years. Ethel's knishes were known across the country. She didn't market them, and she didn't put her recipe on the Internet. She just shared them.*

Aunt Ethel and her knishes were known countrywide.

"She shared them with whomever they got to know at whatever campsite, at whatever national forest they happened to be vacationing in at the time. In the early years, she and Uncle Irv camped in a trailer with a pop-up tent. By the time of their retirement, it was a prized motor home. But whatever the vehicle, it always contained a freezer stuffed with knishes. It was an annual treat hearing Irv tell about how Ethel fed knishes to camping neighbors who'd never met a Jew in their lives, much less tasted such a delicacy. Knowing Ethel's gregariousness, her **won't-take-no-for-an-answer style,** and the incredible flakiness of those savory potato-stuffed morsels, it was not surprising to hear how often such strangers became fast friends, meeting regularly at one site or another for decades.

"Ethel was a maverick in her immigrant family's world. Over the years she endured much criticism and ridicule from her sisters and brothers-in-law in order to follow her American-born playboy of a husband. Unlike any of her sisters, she knew how to have fun. She knew how to play cards, take trips. My God, she even knew how to enjoy the outdoors. For all the rest of the family, the outdoors was dangerous. Driving on a highway anyplace you didn't have to go was crazy. Swimming in a cold pond with live fish was unthinkable. Most of all, exposing your daughters to a world outside the Jewish neighborhood was downright playing with fire.

"Ethel could be kosher and a camper. She could share her husband's love for adventure, and she could make him stop at every kosher butcher and synagogue along the way. She could schlep the two sets of pots and pans (one for dairy and one for meat) from campsite to campsite, and she could make friends with strangers. It was those strangers-turned-friends, Northerners and Southerners, blacks and whites, Jews and gentiles, who were there at her funeral. There with their love for Ethel and their wonderful stories about how much fun they had together and about how much they were going to miss those knishes by the campfire."

There are elected officials, and then there are the people that elect themselves the keepers of their community. A lot of the latter found us over the last few years. Like Aunt Ethel, these people aren't satisfied with the way things are going. They see a way to make things better, and often the way they get there is through their kitchen rituals and traditions.

Message #212 was received Friday at 9:09 AM

"This is Larry Lagattuta. I own the Enrico Biscotti Company in Pittsburgh, Pennsylvania. We are Italian, and we make biscotti and other Italian pastries. We are one hundred years behind the times here. We cook on wood, and we have a big brick oven that's about two-thousand-year-old technology.

"That's not why I'm calling. Why I'm calling is to tell you about a bread class that happens on the last Sunday of every month. People from all over the city come to join us—fathers, daughters, mothers, sons, sisters, brothers. Everybody gets together and makes bread.

"We bring them here, and we have a big throw-down breakfast for everyone. We teach them about the history of bread, how it's made and why it's made the way it's made. What we find is Americans have pretty much lost touch with the tradition of making bread. We then get our hands dirty and actually make bread in the brick oven. Okay, maybe we drink a couple of bottles of homemade wine while it's being baked.

"Everyone gets to take their bread home at the end of the day. There is this great companionship that begins here. These people who are making bread with us seem to have lost some of that family connection. I think it is an American phenomenon, with everybody being so busy, people tend not to join around a table, a communal table. That's what we provide here, and it's an amazing process. I think if we don't bring it back, we're going to lose this tradition and then lose part of ourselves."

The Family Table, Texas, circa 1940s

What happens to a culture when it loses some essential part of itself? People are telling us that home cooking and the family table are on the endangered species list—small farmers and producers are, too—and that these age-old practices and ways of life, cornerstones of our civilization, will become extinct if we don't stop and take notice and protect and preserve them.

THE COMPLICATED HEART OF THE NATION

Over the time we've spent gathering these *Hidden Kitchens* stories, our microphone has become a kind of stethoscope, listening to the complicated heart of the nation—in the plazas of San Antonio, the racing pits of NASCAR, the ricing lakes of the Ojibwe, over the hard road of hunger that led George Foreman to boxing. We have been baptized in dip, shown secret recipes that have been passed down from father to son, and witnessed micro-rivalries across the country over sauce and grilling techniques. We have come to wonder how can there ever be peace in the world when we can't even agree on how to barbecue. Yet, in some ways this is our only hope, that we can disagree about barbecue and still stay connected.

More than ever, America is portrayed as a nation divided by race, politics, economics, war. But our tape recorder and answering machine are picking up another part of the story. All over the country there are people who are concerned about embracing and creating traditions that bring about understanding and appreciation in their families, neighborhoods, and the world.

Perhaps these small kitchen stories are not just about stories but are a kind of guide, a way to travel through daily life—with eyes open to the hand-painted signs on the side of the road, to thinking about where the money we spend for food is going, to spotting a pit being fired up in a churchyard and the picnic that will soon follow, to farmers' markets, to community kitchens—to taking in all these scents and stories as they mingle and merge into one bigger American story.

America Eats, they called it back in the 1930s. We named it *Hidden Kitchens* in 2004. If we are lucky, fifty years from now some other nationwide collaboration will come along and stare into the fire pits and soup kettles of the nation and ask some of these same questions: Who glues your community together through food? Who is cooking on your corner? What traditions are vanishing from your neighborhood, your family, the planet? They will stop and ask these questions, and if they are as lucky as we are, they will get invited to eat, to sit at the table and hear a story, to learn a recipe. It's the food, but more than that, it's the fellowship. This improvisational, ingenious, imaginative cooking—new and old, a spirit that can't be suppressed—alive across America. Food is our universal language; it's what we have in common. When in doubt, cook.

NO ONE WHO COOKS, COOKS ALONE

The Kitchen Sisters began some twenty years back, inspired by two brothers. We close with a little kitchen inspiration from a pair of sisters. No relation to us, but then again, we're not related to each other either. Except that we are.

Emmy Bengtson and Mary Ann Waltz are sisters who cook at the local Elks Club in Shenandoah, Iowa. Jennifer Seydel called the *Hidden Kitchens* hotline to tell us about them:

"They're notorious, both for their cooking and their humor and as the glue for many family and community functions. I think they're both somewhere in their seventies. They prepare meals for weddings, athletic banquets, funerals, political events for Republicans and Democrats in the area, and cook for up to five hundred people without thinking twice. All you have to do is walk into their kitchen, and you can catch up on everything. Every Thursday they just cook for whomever shows up. They are known for their fried chicken and scalloped cabbage specialties that they cook on the

Emmy Bengtson and Mary Ann Waltz are sisters from Farragut, Iowa, who cook at the Shenandoah Elks Club.

first Sunday of the month. My husband and I are new to this community, and we have wondered what will happen—who they'll pass the torch to."

We might have to go see Emmy and Mary Ann before they pass on the torch. We've never had scalloped cabbage or even been to Iowa, and anyone cooking for Democrats, Republicans, funerals, and weddings knows something about how to create community and mark the rituals of life through food.

Lea Eggnog

What do you do when you have two recipes for the same family favorite? "There were eggnog recipes descended from both sides of my family, and the recipes warred every Christmas," says Jay Allison, our kitchen curator. "I don't think anyone ever wins a war like that."

This recipe for eggnog from Jay's Granny Lea via his mother, Barbara, is a star contender. Mrs. Preston Lea, wife of Governor Lea of Delaware, made great batches of this eggnog for the governor's entertaining at Christmas.

Make this recipe several days ahead as the taste improves with age.

12	eggs
4–7	teaspoons sugar
1	cup brandy
1	cup Jamaica rum
2	cups milk
2	cups heavy cream

Separate the eggs. In a large bowl, whisk the yolks to blend and whisk in the sugar, according to how sweet you like your nog. Slowly add the brandy and the rum, whisking as you go. (Granny always said that the liquor "cooked" the eggs.) Stir in the milk and heavy cream.

In a separate bowl, beat the egg whites until they form soft peaks and then fold them into the yolk mixture.

Pour into jars. Refrigerate overnight. When you're ready to serve, remove a jar from the refrigerator and then stir again, to blend in the froth, which will have risen to the top. Add more milk to thin it a little, as you wish. (Barbara thinks it is better a little thinned.) Keep refrigerated.

MAKES ½ GALLON OR 18 SERVINGS

Czechoslovakian Moon Cookies

"My name is John Patterson. I'm calling from Baltimore, Maryland. In the Episcopal church where my mother was a member of the Ladies Altar Guild, they took on adopting an immigrant family, the Jaraslava Pouska family. They found a house for them, furniture, and so forth. And as a thank-you gift, Mrs. Pouska would come every year, just after dark on December 5th, the eve of St. Nicholas Day. She would sneak up to the house, and we would hear a loud 'boom, boom, boom' on the door. No matter how fast we dashed, we never saw who delivered the wrapped carton with a return address that simply stated, 'Saint Nicholas.' Inside, there would be a special tin of Czechoslovakian moon cookies and a poem to members of our family. It was a tradition the Pouska family had brought with them from the outskirts of Prague to our small American town.

"At Mrs. Pouska's funeral we learned that she had left each member of the Altar Guild the recipe for Czechoslovakian moon cookies in her will. In my twenty-five years as a teacher, I have told this story each year to my students and given each of them a Czechoslovakian moon cookie on St. Nicholas Day, a day that truly speaks of the generosity from one to another. Now, when those former students invite us to their weddings, we give them the recipe and a serving tray for Czechoslovakian moon cookies. From a simple tin of cookies Mrs. Pouska's generosity and thanks has spread from family to family, from teacher to student, and friend to friend, one moon cookie at a time."

FROSTING

2 **tablespoons butter**

½ **pound 10X confectioners' sugar**

Almond or vanilla extract, Stroh rum from Austria, or imitation rum flavoring

1 **tablespoon milk, or more as needed**

COOKIES

6 **ounces chocolate bits**

½ **cup English walnuts**

¾ **cup butter**

⅞ **cup sugar**

4 **eggs, separated**

1⅜ **cups flour**

Preheat the oven to 350°F. Grease a 10" × 15" × ½" jelly-roll pan.

To make the frosting, cream the butter and sugar together in a small bowl. Flavor with droplets of extract or rum to taste. Add the milk, using more if needed to make the frosting creamy but not runny. Set aside.

To make the cookies, in a coffee grinder or food processor, grind the chocolate bits and the walnuts to a powder and set aside.

In a large bowl, cream together the butter and sugar. Add the egg yolks, nuts, and chocolate powder.

In a separate bowl, beat the egg whites until stiff. Carefully fold the egg whites into the batter and then lightly fold in the flour (do not overmix).

Spread the batter evenly in the jellyroll pan so that the dough is approximately ¼" to ½" thick. Bake until lightly browned (10 to 15 minutes, or when a toothpick inserted in the middle comes out clean).

Spread the frosting on the cookies while still warm so that the frosting soaks in a bit but forms a nice glaze. Let cool completely.

Using a thin-edged water glass (a cookie cutter is too shallow), start at one corner of the jellyroll pan and cut one "full moon," then move over ½" to cut a crescent moon, then continue until each row is finished.

For a gift, present them in a tin in layers, divided with waxed paper or aluminum foil, with a full moon in the center and crescent moons in a circular fan surrounding it.

MAKES 3 DOZEN COOKIES

Le Polpette della Mama:
Francis Ford Coppola's Homeless Meatballs for 500

Who glues your community together through food? In San Francisco's North Beach, once a year it is Francis Ford Coppola in collaboration with poet Lawrence Ferlengetti. Coppola started a neighborhood organization, the North Beach Citizens, to help the homeless in the Italian neighborhood where his film company, American Zoetrope, is based. For the last four years, he has gathered the community in the basement of St. Peter and Paul's Church for a family-style feast that raises money to support the services the group provides.

This meatball recipe came from Francis's mother. The trick to cooking for 500 is to cook in batches. For this event, Francis's kitchen crew makes the meatballs in 17 batches. Divide the ingredients accordingly.

The sauce is made in one big pot. In addition to using good-quality canned tomatoes (Francis uses di Napoli), the secret to making good tomato sauce is an excellent extra-virgin olive oil.

MEATBALLS

85	pounds lean ground beef
60	pounds ground pork
34	pounds onions, chopped
34	ounces garlic, finely chopped
26	pounds fine bread crumbs
170	eggs
34	ounces parsley
51	pounds Parmesan cheese
	Salt to taste
10	ounces black pepper
15	ounces red pepper flakes

To make the meatballs, in a large bowl mix together the beef and the pork. Add the onions, garlic, and bread crumbs. Add the eggs, parsley, Parmesan, salt, black pepper, and red pepper flakes. Use your hands to mix all the ingredients together. Combine well.

Take about 3 ounces of meat to form a meatball slightly larger than a golf ball.

In a large sauté pan over very high heat, add olive oil until there is ¼" in the bottom of the pan, and heat it until almost smoking. Fry about 10 meatballs at a time, turning them on all sides to brown them all over. They do not need to be cooked through entirely. You will eventually put them in the sauce to continue cooking.

TOMATO SAUCE

51 cans (6 pounds, 6 ounces each) whole plum tomatoes (such as di Napoli)

1½ gallons extra-virgin olive oil

8 pounds onions, chopped

2 pounds fresh basil leaves

14 ounces salt (or to taste)

10 ounces black pepper

15 ounces red pepper flakes

5 bottles (750 milliliters each) red wine

51 pork chops

26 ounces sugar

136 ounces tomato paste

GARNISH

Parmesan cheese

Fresh basil

To make the sauce, open the cans of tomatoes. Strain the tomatoes and reserve the juice.

In a large saucepan over medium heat, heat the olive oil. With a wooden spoon, stir in the chopped onions, add the pork chops, the basil leaves, salt, black pepper, and red pepper flakes. Sauté until the onions are clear. Add the red wine and the crushed tomatoes to the mixture. Cook for 15 minutes at a boil, stirring constantly, adding the reserved tomato juice as needed. Add the meatballs and the pork chops and reduce the heat to low and simmer for 40 minutes. Stir often so as not to scorch the bottom, but gently so as not to break up the meatballs. The pork chops will begin to crumble off the bone and become part of the sauce.

Use a slotted spoon to remove and discard the pork chop bones and remove the meatballs, setting them aside.

Stir in the sugar and the tomato paste and cook for another 30 minutes, or until the sauce is thick.

To serve, ladle the sauce over individual bowls of pasta and top with 2 meatballs. Sprinkle with Parmesan and fresh basil.

MAKES 1,000 MEATBALLS

Verta Mae Grosvenor's Scripture Cake

Verta Mae Grosvenor, one of our great colleagues at NPR, is one of the best storytellers we know. For Verta Mae, food and stories go together like hand and glove, and a recipe is just another way to tell a story. Here, she shares her "Grandmamma" Sula's recipe and story for scripture cake. Verta Mae, who is also a cookbook author, says the cake is a Southern tradition that she associates with Christmas and family homecomings.

Each ingredient in the recipe corresponds to a passage in the Bible. For instance, "spices" refers to 1 Kings 10:10: " . . . never again came such an abundance of spices as these which the queen of Sheba gave to King Solomon."

Verta Mae nicknamed this favorite holiday dessert "Till We Meet Again Cake" and says it tastes just as good whether or not you look up all the passages.

"A RECIPE IS JUST A STORY WITH A GOOD MEAL AT THE END."

—PAT CONROY, WRITER

SCRIPTURE CAKE

1 Samuel 30:12	2	cups raisins
1 Samuel 30:12	2	cups figs
Genesis 24:17	1	cup hot water
Judges 5:25	1	cup butter
Jeremiah 6:20	2	cups sugar
1 Kings 4:2	3½	cups sifted flour
Genesis 42:11	1	cup walnuts, chopped
Isaiah 10:14	6	eggs, separated
Exodus 16:31	3	tablespoons honey
1 Kings 10:10		Spices to taste
Leviticus 2:13	½	teaspoon salt
1 Corinthians 5:6	2	teaspoons baking powder

Soften the raisins and figs in the water and set aside. When softened, chop the figs.

In a large bowl, cream the butter and sugar and stir in half of the flour. Add the walnuts, raisins, and figs.

In a small bowl, beat the egg yolks, then stir in the honey.

In another small bowl, beat the egg whites with a pinch of salt until they stand in peaks.

Sift the remaining flour with the spices, salt, and baking powder. Add the mixture alternately with the yolks and honey to the sugar mixture. Fold in the egg whites lightly. Beat with an electric mixer, if possible. Turn the batter into a large rectangular pan lined with waxed paper.

Bake at 375°F for about 50 minutes, or until the cake is browned on top and begins to stand away from the sides of the pan.

MAKES 15 TO 18 SERVINGS

Resources

BOOKS

Algren, Nelson. *America Eats (Iowa Szathmary Culinary Arts Series)*. Iowa City, IA: University of Iowa Press, 1992.

Alperson, Myra. *Nosh New York: The Food Lover's Guide to New York City's Most Delicious Neighborhoods*. New York: St. Martin's Griffin, 2003.

Bailey, Pearl. *Pearl's Kitchen*. New York and London: Harcourt Brace Jovanovich, Inc., 1973.

Branch, Taylor. *Pillar of Fire: America in the King Years, 1963–65*. New York: Simon & Schuster, 1999.

Cogan, Jim, and William Clark. *Temples of Sound: Inside the Great Recording Studios*. San Francisco: Chronicle Books, 2003.

Cunningham, Marion. *Lost Recipes: Meals to Share with Friends and Family*. New York: Knopf, 2003.

Edge, John T. *Apple Pie: An American Story*. New York: G. P. Putnam's Sons, 2004.

Edge, John T. *Fried Chicken: An American Story*. New York: G. P. Putnam's Sons, 2004.

Editors of *Saveur* magazine. *Saveur Cooks Authentic French*. San Francisco, Chronicle Books, 1999.

Egerton, John, ed. *Cornbread Nation 1*. Chapel Hill and London: University of North Carolina Press, 2002.

Elie, Lolis Eric, ed. *Cornbread Nation 2*. Chapel Hill and London: University of North Carolina Press, 2004.

Engel, Allison, and Margaret Engel. *Food Finds: America's Best Local Foods and the People Who Produce Them*. New York: Quill, 2000.

Fisher, M. F. K. *The Art of Eating*. New York: Macmillan, 1990.

Foreman, George, and Joel Engel. *The Autobiography of George Foreman*. New York: Villard Books, 1995.

Gabaccia, Donna R. *We Are What We Eat: Ethnic Food and the Making of Americans*. Cambridge, MA: Harvard University Press, 1998.

Goyan, Pamela, and Kathryn Sucher. *Food and Culture in America: A Nutrition Handbook*. New York: Van Nostrand Reinhold, 1998.

Graham, Elon. *A Cookbook for Kids Written by a Kid*. Richmond, VA: Self-published, 2004.

Haber, Barbara. *Hardtack to Home Fries: An Uncommon History of American Cooks and Meals*. New York: Simon & Schuster, 2004. (Cleora Butler recipe)

Harmon, Katharine. *You Are Here*. New York: Princeton Architectural Press, 2004.

Knickerbocker, Peggy. *Olive Oil: From Tree to Table*. San Francisco: Chronicle Books, 1997.

Kummer, Corby. *The Pleasures of Slow Food: Celebrating Authentic Traditions, Flavors, and Recipes*. San Francisco: Chronicle Books, 2002.

Kurlansky, Mark, ed. *Choice Cuts: A Savory Selection of Food Writing from Around the World and Throughout History*. New York: Ballantine, 2002.

Lelievre, Roger A., ed. *Know Your Ships 2004: Guide to Boats and Boatwatching: Great Lakes and St. Lawrence Seaway*. Sault Ste. Marie, MI: Marine Publishing Co., 2004.

Martins, Patrick, and Ben Watson. *The Slow Food Guide to New York City Restaurants, Markets, Bars*. White River Junction, VT: Chelsea Green Publishing, 2003.

Masumoto, David Mas. *Epitaph for a Peach: Four Seasons on My Family Farm*. San Francisco: Harper Collins, 1996.

McKenna, P. K. *Ships of the Great Lakes Cookbook: Discover Their Culinary Legends*. Creative Characters Publishing Group, 2001.

Nabhan, Gary Paul. *Coming Home to Eat: The Pleasures and Politics of Local Foods*. New York: W. W. Norton & Company, 2002.

Nader, Nathra, and Rose B. Nader. *It Happened in the Kitchen: Recipes for Food and Thought.* Washington: Center for Study of Responsive Law, 1991.

Nestle, Marion. *Food Politics: How the Food Industry Influences Nutrition and Health.* Berkeley: University of California Press, 2002.

Pollan, Michael. *The Botany of Desire: A Plant's-Eye View of the World.* New York: Random House, 2001.

Seay Sr., S. S. *I Was There by the Grace of God.* Montgomery, AL: New South Books, 2006.

Schenone, Laura. *A Thousand Years Over a Hot Stove: A History of American Women Told Through Food, Recipes, and Remembrances.* New York: W. W. Norton, 2003.

Scher, Paula. *Make It Bigger.* New York: Princeton Architectural Press, 2002.

Schlosser, Eric. *Fast Food Nation.* San Francisco: Harper Collins, 2001.

Strachwitz, Chris, with James Nicolopulos. *Lydia Mendoza: A Family Autobiography.* Houston, TX: Arte Publico Press, 1993.

Sutton, David. *Remembrance of Repasts: An Anthropology of Food and Memory.* Oxford: Berg, 2001.

Terkel, Studs. *Talking to Myself.* New York: Pantheon Books, 1973.

Trillin, Calvin. *Feeding a Yen: Savoring Local Specialties, from Kansas City to Cuzco.* New York: Random House, 2003.

Unterman, Patricia. *San Francisco Food Lover Guide.* Berkeley: Ten Speed Press, 2005.

Walsh, Robb. *Legends of Texas Barbecue Cookbook: Recipes and Collections from the Pit Bosses.* San Francisco: Chronicle Books, 2002.

Walsh, Robb. *The Tex-Mex Cookbook: A History in Recipes and Photos.* New York: Broadway Books, 2004.

Willinger, Faith H. *Eating in Italy: A Traveler's Guide to the Hidden Gastronomic Pleasures of Northern Italy.* New York: Morrow Cookbooks, 1998.

ARTICLES, BLOGS, AND PERIODICALS

Andrews, Colman, ed. *Saveur* magazine.

Association of Independents in Radio, publishers. *AIRSPACE: Journal for Public Radio Producers.*

Behrens, Steve, ed. *Current: The Newspaper about Public Television and Radio.*

Food Museum Blog. www.foodmuseum.typepad.com

Gladwell, Malcolm. "The Trouble with Fries: Fast Food Is Killing Us. Can It Be Fixed?" *The New Yorker,* March 5, 2001.

Hitt, Jack. "More Pie, Mr. President?" *The New York Times Magazine,* October 17, 2004.

Huntley, Dan. "Cooking with NASCAR." *Idaho State Journal,* August 22, 2004. www.journalnet.com/articles/2004/01/21/features/food01.txt.

Mintz, Sidney W., and C. M. Du Bois. "The Anthropology of Food and Eating." *Annual Review of Anthropology* 31 (2002): 99–119.

Newton, Maud, blog. http://maudnewton.com/blog/

Petrini, Carlo, ed. *Slow: The Magazine of the Slow Food Movement.*

Smirnoff, Marc, ed. *Oxford American* magazine.

Wolfe, Tom. "The Last American Hero Is Junior Johnson. *Yes!*" *Esquire,* March 1965.

INSTITUTIONS AND ONLINE SOURCES

The Apple Family Farm
www.applefamilyfarm.com

Center for American History at the University of Texas at Austin
www.cah.utexas.edu

The Chez Panisse Foundation
www.chezpanisse.com/cpfoundation.html

D.C. Central Kitchen
www.dccentralkitchen.org

The Edible Schoolyard
www.edibleschoolyard.org

Esperanza Peace and Justice Center, San Antonio
www.esperanzacenter.org

The Food Museum Online
www.foodmuseum.com

Forgotten Harvest, Detroit
www.forgottenharvest.org

The Garden Mosaic Project at Cornell University
www.gardenmosaics.org

Goosefoot Acres
www.EdibleWeeds.com

Heritage Foods USA
www.heritagefoodsusa.com

Hidden Kitchens
www.hiddenkitchens.org

Highlander Research and Education Center
www.highlandercenter.org

The Kitchen Sisters
www.kitchensisters.org

The Lee Brothers Boiled Peanuts Catalog
www.boiledpeanuts.com

Library of Congress: America Eats
www.loc.gov/exhibits/treasures/tri098.html

Nashville Public Library Civil Rights Collection
www.library.nashville.org/Newsevents/
Civil%20Rights%20Room/civilrightsroom.htm

The National Archives
www.archives.gov

Native Harvest Catalog
www.welrp.org/nativeharvest/nativeharvest.html

New York City Municipal Archives
www.nyc.gov/html/records/html/about/archives.shtml

Nextcourse
www.nextcourse.org

NoshWalks and NoshNews
www.noshwalks.com

NY Food Museum
www.nyfoodmuseum.org

Owensboro, Kentucky, Tourist Commission
www.visitowensboro.com

San Antonio Conservation Society
www.saconservation.org

Second Harvest
www.secondharvest.org

Seed Savers Exchange
www.seedsavers.org

Slow Food
www.slowfood.com

Southern Foodways Alliance
www.southernfoodways.com

Southern Poverty Law Center
www.splcenter.org

To Tell the Truth Pictures:
"Mighty Times: The Children's March"
www.tttpictures.com

Traders Point Creamery
www.tpforganics.com

Transom.org
www.transom.org

Weston A. Price Foundation
www.westonaprice.org/index.html

White Earth Land Recovery Project
www.welrp.org/winona.html

ALSO BY THE KITCHEN SISTERS AND JAY ALLISON

Allison, Jay. *The Life Stories Collection*. Atlantic Public Media, 2001.

Nelson, Davia, and Nikki Silva (The Kitchen Sisters). *The Sonic Memorial Project*. Narrated by Paul Auster, 2002.

Nelson, Davia, and Nikki Silva (The Kitchen Sisters) and Jay Allison. *Lost & Found Sound, Vol. 1*. Narrated by Noah Adams. Highbridge Audio, 2000.

Silva, Nikki, and Davia Nelson (The Kitchen Sisters) and Jay Allison. *Hidden Kitchens: Stories, Recipes, and More from NPR's The Kitchen Sisters*. Narrated by Frances McDormand. Audio Renaissance, 2005.

Silva, Nikki, and Davia Nelson (The Kitchen Sisters) and Jay Allison. *Lost & Found Sound and Beyond*. Narrated by Francis Ford Coppola. Highbridge Audio, 2004.

Soundwalk with The Kitchen Sisters. *Ground Zero: A Sonic Memorial Soundwalk*. Narrated by Paul Auster. Oversampling Inc., 2005.

Credits

PHOTOGRAPHS

Nubar Alexanian: page 2

Cheryl Day Anderson: page 60

Laurie Anderson: page 190

Courtesy of Debbie Apple: page 237

Becker County Historical Society and WELRP: page 102, 107

© Bettmann/CORBIS: page 139

Courtesy of Sara Blumenstein: page 29

Celeste F. Bremer: page 10 (judges photo)

Nancy Bundt, courtesy of (WELRP) White Earth Land Recovery Project: page 97

Bob Carrau: pages 173, 180

Chicago Defender: page 200

Chika: pages 14–15

Courtesy of Judith Davis: page 253

Valerie Downer, courtesy of the Southern Poverty Law Center: page 201

Courtesy of Cynthia Ebbert: page 8

John Ehle, courtesy of Southern Historical Collection, Wilson Library, University of North Carolina at Chapel Hill: page 204

Terry Eiler, "Tending the Commons: Folklife and Landscape in Southern West Virginia," American Folklife Center, Library of Congress: page 7

Courtesy of Ken Enck: page 73

Courtesy of Phil Ferrato and *Wired* magazine: page 78

Carl Fleischhauer, "Buckaroos in Paradise: Ranching Culture in Northern Nevada, 1945–1982," American Folklife Center, Library of Congress: page 250

Laura Folger: pages xiii, xvi, 28, 182, 213, 223

Courtesy of Food Not Bombs and Keith McHenry: page 4

Courtesy of George Foreman Sr.: page 19

Courtesy of Angelo Garro: pages 170, 175 (both), 176, 177, 184

Sandra Wong Geroux: pages x (airfield), xiv, 18, 229, 231, 232, 234, 238, 241

Granger, WPA/Arkansas, courtesy of the Library of Congress, Prints and Photographs Division [LOT #13328]: page 154

Ursula Heller: page 179

Courtesy of Sheriff Michael Hennessey: page 219

Jim Hilgendorf, www.jimhilgendorf.com: page 77

Institute of Texan Cultures at UTSA: page 256

Images from the *Green Book 1948* courtesy of the International Civil Rights Center and Museum, Greensboro, NC: pages 195, 210

Courtesy of Stetson Kennedy: page 146

Stetson Kennedy: page 158

Stetson Kennedy, courtesy of the Library of Congress, Prints and Photographs Division [LOT #13328 (F)]: pages 142 (women with pots), 150, 151

The Kitchen Sisters: pages ii, xxvi–1, 53, 54, 56, 88 (lake photo), 92, 98, 99 (both), 101, 105, 114, 117, 118, 120, 122, 123, 124, 125 (both), 126, 127, 128, 133, 134, 137, 144, 203, 208, 215

Roger LeLievre: page 83

Will León: page 42

Library of Congress, Prints and Photographs Division [LOT #13328 (F)]: pages 142 (butchers wrapping), 148, 157

Courtesy of May Broadcasting: page 169 (Jessie Young)

Courtesy of Buz McKim: pages 74, 75

Courtesy of the Lydia Mendoza Family: page 49

Minnesota Historical Society: page 95

MotorSports Images and Archives Photography. Used with permission: pages 58, 62, 65, 68, 70

Courtesy of National Nuclear Security Administration Nevada Site Office: page 111

Anthony V. Ragusin, courtesy of the Library of Congress, Prints and Photographs Division [LOT #13328 (F)]: page 142 (man eating oysters)

John Rottet: page 113

The San Antonio Light Collection, UT Institute of Texan Cultures at San Antonio: pages 30–31, 34, 36, 38, 39, 41, 43, 44 (both photos), 45, 46, 51

Gary Saunders, www.dixiedining.com: page 76

Courtesy of Jennifer Seydel: page 258

Courtesy Solomon S. Seay Sr. Family, *There by the Grace of God: The Autobiography of the Rev. Solomon S. Seay* (Montgomery, AL: NewSouth Books, 2006): pages 193, 197

Calvin Statham: pages 81, 85

Thor Swift: page 174

Courtesy of Marjorie R. Towey: pages 166, 167

Courtesy of Alice Waters, adapted by Sylvan Brackett: page 227

Dorothy West Collection, The Howard Gotlieb Archival Research Center, Boston University: page 152

White Earth Land Recovery Project (WELRP): pages 90, 93

Marion Post Wolcott, Prints and Photographs Div, FSA-OWI Collection, Library of Congress: page xviii

United States Works Projects Administration, America Eats collection, courtesy of the Manuscripts Division, Library of Congress: page 147

ILLUSTRATIONS AND OTHER ARTWORK

Arbuckel Trading Card, The Old Map Gallery: page 10 (Iowa map), 80, 228

Courtesy of Francis Coppola and The North Beach Citizens Association: pages 246–47

Lars Hokason/Francis Cichetti: page 112

"Bird's-Eye View," Augustus Koch, Witte Museum, San Antonio Texas: page 37

"Sunbear and Winona," by Betty LaDuke: page 104

Public Radio Service Cooking School, New Jersey: page 169 (radio lesson ephemera)

"Bay Folk Sketchbook" by Bill Russell, *The San Francisco Chronicle:* page xx

Daniel Ryan, Ralph and Bonnie Kipp, www.Kippfamily.com: page 224

Courtesy of Sandra Sherman: page 9

"Nanabozhoo and Nokomiss Ricing," by Rabbett Strickland, www.rabbettstrickland.com, courtesy of Winona LaDuke: pages 86–87

Ten Thousand Lakes Association/McGill Warner, 1925, courtesy of Craig Solomonson, www.solomonson.net: page 88

Acknowledgments

A big sprawling nationwide collaboration begets a big sprawling list of thank-yous. Bear with us, please. We thank everyone—and that's over a thousand people—who have had a hand in shaping *Hidden Kitchens,* with a story, interview, phone message, image, recipe, or hot tip about a hot kitchen. We could not have done this without you, and besides, it wouldn't have been half as much fun. We have tried to credit all who have contributed. If we left someone out or were unable to find you, please find us, and we will add your name to the roll.

First things first. Though his name is not on the cover, our colleague, friend, coproducer, and inspiration, Jay Allison, is our coauthor of the *Hidden Kitchens* radio project. Jay and The Kitchen Sisters have collaborated on three nationwide public radio series. His heart and mind are so keen and wise, his wit so fierce, and his jokes so good, we keep coming back for more. Many of the words, some of the most compelling and beautiful in the chapters Hidden Kitchens Calling and the Fellowship of Food, flowed from Jay and the stories he created with us for NPR's *Morning Edition.* Deep thanks, Kitchen Brother.

The Kitchen Sisters are more than two friends and a microphone. We are a team, a collaborative unit that has worked together for many years. This book reflects that collaboration and is the work of many, many people who gave their all to capture the wild and beautiful nature of the project and transform the radio series into a book, an endeavor new to all of us. Laura "The Glue" Folger was the driving force behind the book, ceaselessly hunting down visuals, artifacts, recipes, and even better stories to help bring this whole project to life. Her eye and heart are everywhere in these pages. Kate Volkman, Melissa Robbins, Maria Walcutt, and sonic wizard Jim McKee, all brought their big talents, curious minds, and gracious spirits to the project. Leslie Jonath, coordinator, advisor, soul sister, had the *Hidden Kitchen* vision that helped bring this from the air to the page. We could not have done this without her. Thanks also to our "kitchen cabinet" Marc Hand, Valerie Velardi, Duc Nguyen, Mara Brazer, Cindi King, Alan Acosta, Mark Thompson, Wieslaw Pogorzelski, and Paul Zaentz.

A team of collaborators across the nation helped research, record, and gather these stories with us. In Cape Cod, Jay Allison's remarkable team at Atlantic Public Media mined the *Hidden Kitchens* hotline and discovered many of the gems you've read in this book and suggested stories from their side of the divide—Viki Merrick, Chelsea Merz, Helen Woodward, Sydney Lewis, and Ali Berlow. Jamie York traveled to Alabama and Florida collecting interviews for America Eats and Georgia Gilmore's story. Shula Newman in Cleveland plunged into the world of freighter food with us. Heather Dahl went into some NASCAR kitchens and came out with great tape and tales.

Though we have collaborated for some twenty years with NPR, we are independent producers not on staff. And yet, we have had a home on their air since we created our first piece way back when. We thank all those at NPR who have supported The Kitchen Sisters collaborative method. It's not exactly efficient, not exactly deadline oriented, and yet year after year they give us the room to create these unusual, one-of-a-kind cross-country collaboratives. Ellen McDonnell, the executive producer of *Morning Edition* must be thanked for taking the initial risk on *Hidden Kitchens*. She was also the first to say, this has to be a book. The all-night *Morning Edition* staff, hosts Renée Montagne and Steve Inskeep, and our series editors, Neva Grant and Cindy Carpien, also have our gratitude. Jay Kernis, Ellen Weiss, Jeffrey Dvorkin, Robert Siegel, and the hosts of *All Things Considered,* present and past, Barbara Rehm and Kevin Klose have all been in The Kitchen Sisters corner, and we thank you. We also thank our radio community nationally and in particular, Jo Anne Wallace KQED, San Francisco, Stewart Vanderwilt at KUT, Austin, Ruth Seymour and Jennifer Ferro at KCRW, Santa Monica, and Torey Malatia at WBEZ, Chicago who keeps a candle burning.

Sam Freedman from the *New York Times* wrote a story about the NPR *Hidden Kitchens* series that caught the eye of many publishers and agents. There might have been a book without his story, but you never know. Lynn Nesbit—agent, counselor, fellow shoe freak—shepherded this project and offered us her considerable wisdom and experience. She showed us the ropes, gave us a push, and we will always be grateful to her. Bennett Ashley, counsel at Janklow & Nesbit kept us on course and was a friend throughout. Lynn brought us writer Karen Stabiner, who helped these stories find their way from air to paper. We learned much from her experience and craft and thank her for taking the leap.

Rodale Press has gone above and beyond for this book. Rodale is a company of values, organics, and politics, and we are proud to be a small part of their community vision. We thank them and are amazed at the opportunity they have given us to adapt and create. We were all inventing something together, and it took a lot of spirit and patience to let that many people in on the creative process. We thank our editor Leigh Haber, who reeled us in, brought this into being with us, and saw all the possibilities. She carried the torch. Huge thanks to the entire book team, Louise Braverman, Tami Booth Corwin, Caroline Dube, Cathy Gruhn, Chris Krogermeier, Beth Lamb, Karen Neely, John Tintera. Design director Andy Carpenter and designer Trish Field are high on our list for their creative spirit and openness to collaboration. Special thanks to Steve Murphy, we love being on the label.

From what we understand, most books take at least two to three years to write. *Hidden*

Kitchens, our first, was written in six months. You can only imagine how many people helped make that possible. We thank you all. Bharti Mukherjee and Clark Blaise, who led us to Lynn and offered advice along the way. Alice Waters, who just plain inspires, who helped show us the path, and who dances even better than she cooks. Angelo Garro, this whole project is really dedicated to him. Frances McDormand, who was the first person to read these words when she narrated the *Hidden Kitchens* book on tape and our NPR radio specials, and shared her vast and hilarious talents with us, and to Joel Coen who just knows. John Lyons for giving The Kitchen Sisters heart and home in New York for years. Jack Hitt, who listened and helped hatch the plan, and to Don Novello who talked it through and took it to heart. Michael Pollan and Peggy Knickerbocker, our brain trust. Sandra Wong Geroux, whose photography and hula have been part of our kitchen collaboration for years. Martha Ham, who made the journey with us. Ira Glass, because he rocks the boat. Chris Strachwitz and Arhoolie Records, the hidden kitchens of music. Thanks also to designers Marta Salas-Porras, Paula Scher and Hatch Show Print in Nashville and to Chika for the gorgeous photograph of George. More thanks still, to Robb Walsh, John T. Edge, Mark Furstenberg, Susie and Mark Buell, Fritz Streiff, Margaret Engel, Marion Cunningham, Bob Carrau, Niloufer Ichaporia King, Tim Folger, Paul Tough, Myra Alperson and NoshWalks and City Lore in New York, Kim Severson, the Lee Brothers, Bonnie Raitt, and to Misael Reyes who cooks. We also wish to thank Francis Coppola for giving The Kitchen Sisters a home at American Zoetrope, and for the meatballs. And to Eleanor Coppola, who always urges us forward.

Mega thanks to Charles Prentiss, Nikki's wise and funny husband who makes us laugh and keeps us straight; her daughters Molly and Grace for their support, love, and patience through it all; Colette DeDonato, Carlos and Kate Prentiss, Lucia P., and the members of the commune at La Selva—who for twenty-seven years have cooked dinner and gathered round their round table ever ready to contribute their vision and two cents' worth.

The Kitchen Sisters' Graduate School of Journalism Radio Class, Spring 2004 at UC Berkeley were our first collaborators, while this project was still in the incubator. We thank them all for going down the rocky path with us. Justin Beck, Brandi Howell, Carol Hunter, Kathryn Jessup, Rebekah Kouy-Ghadosh, Claudine LoMonaco, Jessica Ravitz, Joseph Rogers and Benjamin Temchine. Also, intern, Alexandra Blair jumped into the process with flair.

Over the last two decades the National Endowment for the Arts, the Corporation for Public Broadcasting, and the National Endowment for the Humanities have helped support our public radio work to document and preserve little known aspects of American history and culture. We thank these remarkable public institutions and the devoted staff that work so hard on behalf of the nation's art and heritage. We also thank the many listeners who contribute so generously to The Kitchen Sisters Productions and make this work possible. Some of the royalties from the sale of this book will support more stories from The Kitchen Sisters on National Public Radio.

Many people helped on many levels with this book. Thanks to all the following who made it happen: **An Unexpected Kitchen:** George Foreman III, the Chicago Coalition for the Homeless, Scott Vogel & Salton Inc. **Chili Queens:** Phylis McKensey and Patrick Lemelle the UT Institute of Texan Cultures at San Antonio, the library staff at the University of Texas at Austin, Marina Rizo-Patron. **NASCAR:** Dawn Gardin, NASCAR Public Relations, Dan Huntley, *Charlotte Observer.* Brian Bell and Paula Smith, Women Auxiliary of Motorsports. **A Floating Kitchen Vision:** Paula McKenna, the Historical Society of Michigan, Inland Seas Maritime Museum, Joe Grimm, *Detroit Free Press.*

Harvest on Big Rice Lake: Sarah Alexander, Betty LaDuke, Candace Fineday, the staff and members of White Earth Land Recovery Project, Native Harvest, Minnesota. **Burgoo:** Moonlite Bar-B-Q Inn, Burgoo Team at St. Pius X, the Burgoo Barn Gang and Dip Makers at St. Lawrence Parish, the Mutton Men at Blessed Mother Catholic Church, Burley Phelan and the Owensboro Chamber of Commerce, Fenton Johnson. **Campaign Cooking:** Karen Schaefer, Gloria Hillard, Janet Heimlich.

America Eats: The Southern Foodways Alliance and the Center for the Study of Southern Culture, Rick Kogan, Kenneth Cobb, Susan Leem, Sandy Oliver, Greg Patent, Charles L. Perdue, Marjorie Wright, David Schoonover, America Eats archive at the University of Iowa Library's Louis Szathmary Collection, Andy Harper, Marvin Kranz and Alice Birney of the Library of Congress Manuscript Division, Maja Kreech and Sara Willett Duke of the Prints and Photographs Division, the Center for the Book researchers Charles Camp, Andrea Kalin, Barbara Kuck, Jerrold Hirsch, and director John Cole. **Radio Homemakers:** Evelyn Birkby.

Georgia Gilmore: Andy Harper, Randall Williams, Mary Terry, David Bundy and the *Montgomery Advertiser,* Penny Weaver and the Southern Poverty Law Center, Rachel Larson and the Nashville Public Library, Joe York, Robert Hudson, Bobby Houston and their Oscar-winning documentary, *Mighty Times: The Children's March,* Crest Harris, Martha Hawkins, Kenneth Hare. **A Prison Kitchen Vision:** Sheriff Hennessey and Susan Fahey. **Milk Cow Blues:** Alan Yegerlehner, Peter Kunz, Traders Point Green Market in Zionsville, Indiana; the Indiana Cow Share Association.

One small note: Remember, we call ourselves The Kitchen Sisters, but up until now, food has never really been our beat. We gather recipes like we gather good stories. Okay, maybe they aren't the most precise and scientifically tested, but they come with a good story you can always tell if something goes a little haywire. We hope you'll cook this book with that in mind.

Index

Underscored page references indicate boxed text. **Boldfaced** page references indicate photographs.